CW00410818

FORMATION FOR KNOWING GOD

Formation for
KNOWING GOD

Imagining God: At-One-ing,
Transforming, for Self-Revealing

F. Gerald Downing

CASCADE *Books* · Eugene, Oregon

FORMATION FOR KNOWING GOD
Imagining God: At-One-ing, Transforming, for Self-Revealing

Copyright © 2015 F. Gerald Downing. All rights reserved. Except for brief quotations in critical publications or reviews, no part of this book may be reproduced in any manner without prior written permission from the publisher. Write: Permissions, Wipf and Stock Publishers, 199 W. 8th Ave., Suite 3, Eugene, OR 97401.

Cascade Books
An Imprint of Wipf and Stock Publishers
199 W. 8th Ave., Suite 3
Eugene, OR 97401

www.wipfandstock.com

ISBN 13: 978-1-62564-457-2

Cataloging-in-Publication data:

Downing, F. Gerald

    Formation for knowing God : imagining God : at-one-ing, transforming, for self-revealing / F. Gerald Downing.

    xxiv + 263 p. ; 23 cm. —Includes bibliographical references and index(es).

    ISBN 13: 978-1-62564-457-2

    1. Revelation. 2. God—Knowableness. I. Title.

BT127.2 D6 2015

Manufactured in the U.S.A.

Contents

Illustrations

Preface

In 1964 SCM Press in London and Westminster Press in Philadelphia published my *Has Christianity a Revelation?* It had received qualified support from a number of my seniors, notably John McIntyre and James Barr. It was then widely and respectfully reviewed, even though my answer to the question was "No, not yet." Its arguments have continued to be taken seriously in a handful of theological discussions since then, but most recently it has been blithely ignored in books claiming "divine (self-)revelation" as a given. This present, somewhat shorter monograph seeks to revisit the issues, but from different angles.

One key starting point remains the same:

> At present we see puzzling reflections in a mirror,
> but one day we shall see face to face.
> My knowledge now is partial;
> then it will be whole, like God's knowledge of me. (1 Cor 13:12, REB)

Anything worth calling divine self-revelation lies ahead; it is a trusted hope, not a present possession, according to Paul and other early Christians. Aspects of God's will may be taken to have been revealed. But any full divine self-revelation lies ahead.

Further, our ongoing Christian failure to agree on God's mind on a wide range of topics we deem important shows how little this divine mind is as yet revealed to us. The arguments of the 1964 book on these scores are just briefly summarized in most of the chapters here. What is new is that the case is now supported by foundational scriptural accounts of divine self-hiddenness. And further elaborated is the first century CE Jewish (Philonic) and ongoing early Christian insistence on divine incomprehensibility: God is immeasurably more than we can hope to get our little minds round.

One very positive starting point is much the same: what we Christians have already is our trust that God has changed our human situation in relation to him/herself. And this strand is now greatly expanded, in terms of:

> God has reconciled us to himself through Christ, and has enlisted us in this ministry of reconciliation. (2 Cor 5:18)

with

> We are being transformed into his likeness with ever increasing glory. (2 Cor 3:18)

These convictions of Paul's are here enlarged in terms of our progress in "deification," becoming like him in response to him becoming one of us. We are being formed, transformed, readied, for a full, or at least, much fuller knowledge of God. We are being stretched to a capacity for deeper—even if never complete—awareness of the one who in love and wisdom so greatly transcends us.

Each chapter is introduced with a design, often trying to recall a well-known picture and meant to raise questions. Here there is a representation of Pablo Picasso's *Guernica*.

SCM Press has kindly allowed me to quote passages from that 1964 book. I am grateful to Cascade Books for accepting this revisitation into one of Wipf and Stock's very accessible lists.

Acknowledgments

THE DIVISION OF CHRISTIAN Education of the National Council of Churches of Christ in the United States of America for the use of the New Revised Standard Version of the Bible.

Loeb Classical Library (Cambridge MA: Harvard University Press).
SCM Press for permission to quote passages from *Has Christianity a Revelation?* (1964).
The Estate of R. S. Thomas, for permission to quote lines from:

R. S. Thomas, *Later Poems, 1972–1982* (London: Macmillan, 1983). Macmillan was unable to trace their copyright; and lines from

———. *Experimenting with an Amen* (London: Macmillan, 1986). Macmillan was unable to trace their copyright. And

Bloodaxe Books, Northumberland, UK, for permission to quote lines from:

———. *Counterpoint*, 1990, now in *Collected Later Poems 1988–2000* (Bloodaxe Books, 2004).

And my son, Christopher Downing, for illustrations by him, and improvements to three of mine.

Abbreviations

AB	Anchor Bible
ANF	Ante Nicene Fathers
ANTC	Abingdon New Testament Commentary
ATR	*Anglican Theological Review*
BCE	Before the Common Era
BIS	Biblical Interpretation Series
BiTS	Biblical Tools and Studies
BNTC	Black's New Testament Commentaries
BZNW	Beihaft zur Zeitschift für neutestamentliche Wissenschaft
CB.NTS	Coniectanea Biblica. New Testament Series
CE	Common Era
CBQ	*Catholic Biblical Quarterly*
CNT	Commentaire du Nouveau Testament
CSIR	Cambridge Studies in Ideology and Religion
CWS	Classics of Western Spirituality
EKKNT	Evangelisch-katholischer Kommentar zum Neuen Testament
FAT	Forschung zum Alten Testament
FP	*Faith and Philosophy*
ICC	International Critical Commentary
JSNT	*Journal for the Study of the New Testament*
JSNTS	Journal for the Study of the New Testament Supplement

JSOTS	Journal for the Study of the New Testament Supplement
JTS	*Journal of Theological Studies*
LCL	Loeb Classical Library
LNTS	Library of New Testament Studies
LPT	Library of Philosophy and Theology
LXX	Septuagint, Greek Translation(s) of Jewish Scriptures
NCB	New Century Bible
NIGTC	New International Greek Testament Commentary
NovT	*Novum Testamentum*
NovTSup	Novum Testamentum Supplement Series
NPNF	Nicene and Post-Nicene Fathers
NTS	*New Testament Studies*
PC	*Philosophia Christi*
PQ	*Philosophical Quarterly*
RPT	Religion in Philosophy and Theology
RS	*Religious Studies*
SBS	Stuttgarter Bibelstudien
SBT	Studies in Biblical Theology
SC	Sources Chrétiennes
SWBA	The Social World of Biblical Antiquity
WBC	Word Biblical Commentary
WUNT	Wissentschaftliche Untersuchungen zum Neuen Testament

Silly old granny!
The whole thing is
great-grandad's
self portrait.
And very
revealing it is.
We know!

Granny says,
it's a present
from
great-grandad.
With suggestions
for using it.

Just as he was . . .
Austere.
No, engaging.
But rigorous!
No, easy going!
Impressive . . .
Sympathetic, I'd say.
Unchanging!
Very adaptable.
Always obliging.
Extremely self-willed . . .

BUT WE ALL
AGREE,
A VERY REVEALING
SELF PORTRAIT.
YOU MUST
KNOW THAT!

Introduction[1]

The Argument

At present we see puzzling reflections in a mirror,
but one day we shall see face to face.
My knowledge now is partial;
then it will be whole, like God's knowledge of me. (1 Cor 13:12, REB)

Tap "divine self-revelation" into a computer search engine, and you receive links to a plethora of sites assuring you their authors are already recipients of God's revealing, often, God's self-revealing (with or without further qualification). Usually they will claim support in their particular understanding of Jesus Christ as revelatory divine emissary. They will mostly base all this on their respective readings of "the Bible" (whether the longer Catholic or Orthodox versions, or the somewhat shorter Protestant collection). Some may specify that their God has revealed truths about himself, and his designs and demands; but many will insist that these are adjuncts to the main issue, God's self-revelation, specifying the kind and quality of awareness of God thus already possible, and (one way or another) available.

Rather than going online look back into the history of the Christian church(es). There you find, perhaps to your surprise, that making such claims about God "revealed" in and through Christ and the Bible are relatively recent. A major focus on the term "revelation" starts to emerge in the controversies of the Reformation, fueled by humanist intellectualism with its stress on communication, especially in Calvin. But it really gathers weight as a defensive response to the European Enlightenment and then Deism in the seventeenth and eighteenth centuries, typified by a contrast

---

1. Here, and for chapters 1 to 8 following, there is an opening illustration, hoping to encourage preliminary reflection on what it points to (rather than its draughting). Here there is a reminder of the varieties of biblical and then subsequent Christian characterizations of God.

between "revealed" and "natural" religion.' Then it was only in the late nineteenth and the twentieth centuries that divine *self*-revelation in very deep, interpersonal terms was widely affirmed as a present possibility and presented as the central achievement of God's gracious love in Christ.

Prior to all this (and more in keeping with the surface at least of the shared Scriptures), God was certainly trusted to have conveyed some truths "about" himself (always "himself," of course), and some commands and plans for humankind; and all this was important. It is most likely taken as definitively stated, and on occasion "revealed" is used. But God's main purpose in Christ was taken as other. It was (in some sense or senses) to change the human situation: to make humans more acceptable to himself, and also (perhaps at the same time) to change them so they (at least the compliant, perhaps if also pre-chosen) would (ultimately) "enjoy him for ever." What God had affected in the life, death, and resurrection of Jesus was expressed in terms other than "revelation": it was reconciliation, justification, salvation, atonement, redemption, new creation (or, as the Church of England's *Book of Common Prayer* puts it, "a full, perfect and sufficient sacrifice, oblation and satisfaction for the sins of the whole world"). Believers were expected and encouraged to respond in faith by accepting ongoing strengthening, transformation, sanctification, enlightening. It was the inauguration of all this that had been made possible and was already to be found effective in individuals-in-community. "Revelation" in any full sense, a full and clear shared enjoyment of the "beatific vision," would, however, only be possible after our own death and resurrection (along with those of us still physically alive at Doomsday).

Of course what God was held to have done in and through a very visible Christ was in keeping with his character, and so was indicative of it and afforded in his physical absence some inklings (Paul's "now . . . puzzling reflections in a mirror"). But the details, the implications, the understanding and appreciation (let alone explanation of it all), any full responsive enjoyment of our inaugurated "at-one-ing", our reconciliation, justification, salvation, redemption, must wait till the completion of our transformative formation: our full sanctification, our total re-creation. Then we would not just be "accounted right" but "made righteous," fully enlightened, fully capable of receiving, comprehending, responding, "seeing and knowing," and enjoying.

Meanwhile there were debates and arguments, even bitter and physically violent disputes, in the sad and often cruel history of the Christian

2. See McDonald, *Ideas of Revelation* and his *Theories of Revlation*; Downing, *Has Christianity a Revelation?*, 9–17.

movement over what quite obviously had not been made clear, revealed, as to the purposes and the nature of the God and Father of Jesus. Even whether we would *ever* fully comprehend this God was open for discussion (as will be illustrated later). How is it possible to make coherent sense of these contradictory assertions?[3]

In the late 1950s and early 1960s questions about this recent emphasis on "divine (self-)revelation" were in fact being raised by a handful of English language theologians. John McIntyre wrote,

> Not only did the Church for many centuries find it possible to describe what happened "when the Word was made flesh and dwelt among us," without using this term, but further, because of the history of theology in the last hundred years or so, the term "Revelation" has acquired a significance for us which it has never had in the whole history of the Church.[4]

John Knox also noted, "There is no evidence whatever that the Early Church entertained the view that the purpose of Christ's death was to disclose the love of God." And James Barr reached a similar conclusion: "it is doubtful whether the common theological use of 'revelation' for the divine self-communication is appropriate in the light of the biblical usage."[5]

With some support from McIntyre and Barr I published *Has Christianity a Revelation?* in 1964 (It was not my chosen title; I would have preferred *Christianity Without Revelation*.)[6] This present study attempts to bring that earlier one, including both its positive and its negative conclusion, up to date, in response to criticisms (and misunderstandings) over the intervening fifty years. For there still seems to persist an apparent and widespread lack of awareness of the disadvantages of any uncritical deployment of the term.

Of course, revelation as a fuzzy idea has advantages, as some of its users have insisted, and as *Has Christianity a Revelation?* acknowledged. Someone revealing something, and even more, someone revealing his/her self is usually taken as having the initiative. It is an act of grace, not a discovery, not an uncovering, a knowledge, that you, the other, have to achieve for

---

3. One study available at the time that seemed to display some awareness of the problems of Christians' inability to discern an agreed clarity, was Niebuhr, *The Meaning of Revelation*.

4. McIntyre, "Frontiers of Meaning," 133; and in his *Christian Doctrine of History*, 2.

5. Knox, *Death of Christ*, 146–47; Barr, "Revelation," 849.

6. However, I was allowed to keep "Christianity without Revelation" as the heading for the final chapter. In 1999 Barr reaffirmed his agreement in *The Concept of Biblical Theology*, 485.

yourself. There is a further (often only implicit) advantage (or risk). If God is revealed to me or us, then I/we must be right about him/her; and if you disagree with me/us about God and his character, his will, his demands on us, you must be wrong.

Yet there is little evidence, in our very mixed and divergent Christian responses to God, that any one extensive group among us has received, been given, an agreed divine revelation. Still less has any such gained an effective, transforming, and agreed divine self-revelation. We all differ and bicker (and still even come to blows) not just between but within our groupings: Catholic, Orthodox, Anglican, Lutheran, Presbyterian, Pentecostalist, Baptist, Methodist. . . . We might well *like* to have a graciously granted and assured clarity and certainty, but it is surely graceless—and, frankly, dishonest—to arrogate it to ourselves before it has graciously and effectively happened.

I argued this in that first book, and here reinforce the argument in a fresh chapter outlined a little later. Of course, as I allowed fifty years ago and reaffirm, it is possible to use any word impressionistically, including "revelation." But the uses I cite critically are the ones that claim with it a distinctive clarity—and only that accords the supposed advantages.

Issues of making sense of talk of divine revelation/self-revelation in the light of disagreements and schisms, from the earliest days right up to the present, were broached in the previous book. They are re-examined here in the light of others' responses and my own ongoing critical reflections. But further, the logic of "at-one-ment" talk, reconciliation already, in advance of any fuller or final culminating revelation of God, is now subjected to a similar critical questioning (only implicit in the earlier book's discussion of "salvation" already procured).[7]

The concentration on explicit verbal usage in Scripture that I deployed, with support from Knox, Barr, McIntyre, has itself been criticized. "Absence of a particular word from the biblical writings does not mean that the concept is not to be found in them," quite fairly objected Timothy Gorringe, with explicit reference to Downing and Barr (and echoing some earlier reviewers).[8] I thought that I had anticipated the point; however, it will be more forcefully addressed in what follows, in chapter 1, on the semantics of religious language. Although the "analytical" philosophy I attempted to deploy in that previous study is now no longer the dominant Anglo-American fashion, the issue of clarity in usage remains important, especially when

---

7. It was reassuring to find "at-one-ment" picked up recently by Kathryn Tanner: Tanner, *Christ the Key*, 256.

8. Gorringe, *Discerning Spirit*, 8.

clarity is claimed. However, initial reviews and ongoing discussion have made me recall that in 1963–64, while I had absorbed something of John L. Austin, I had at that time not encountered LudwigWittgenstein, with his important insistence on the "use" of words, use in context, rather than insistence on "the meaning." So, in chapter 1, I survey more recent discussions of language in use, noting where these bear on the issues in hand. "Revelation" in much if not all use—for metaphorical "unveiling"—involves claims to "knowledge". Chapter 1 also takes more account of contemporary epistemology, theory of knowledge, than did the previous study.

Then, in more detail, in chapter 2 I try to explore less sharply defined uses of "reveal," "self-revelation," but also, newly, uses of "self-identification" and "self." Also I then freshly explore the logic of recent talk of being reconciled, "at one" with someone or some others, often person or persons not yet fully known, in fact possibly still badly misunderstood.

My analysis of usage (similar to Barr's) in canonical Jewish writings is only summarized here, in chapter 3. More space is now given to assertions of and complaints against divine hiddenness, especially in the Psalter. Freshly minted are also considerations in these documents of "self" and "(self-)identification."

First Cor 13:12 and arguably similar passages, along with "reconciliation already" (2 Cor 5:17–19) and divine (self-)identification, are then considered in some detail, in conversation with recent commentors (chapter 4). John's gospel, however, may seem the canonical source most resistant to my negative case, and is therefore also discussed afresh.

In chapter 5 examples of patristic usage are now taken from additional sources, especially in relation to "negative theology" and divine "incomprehensibility," and our (inaugurated) transformation to "share the divine nature" to be "deified."

We are assured in the Qur'an that nothing from God's side conceals God: the only veiling is ours, our ignorance, intransigence, refusal to learn, to comply with God's will. "Whithersoever ye turn, there is the face of God."[9] The Qur'an on divine self-disclosure came to my attention some while after writing and publishing my 1964 monograph. It next returned to my attention on discovering John L. Schellenberg's 1993 argument on divine hiddenness (an issue that has occasioned a cluster of journal articles, especially in the quite recent past).[10] Both he and I agree that adherents' disagreements, and much else beside, "reveal" that God remains unrevealed. However, for Schellenberg, that forms a base for an "atheistic" argument—no truly loving

---

9. Arberry, *Sufism*, 17, citing Qur'an 2.109.
10. Schellenberg, *Divine Hiddenness*.

deity would be so coy—while I take it as innate *and coherent* in Christian, as in other "Abrahamic" theistic, traditions. My attempt to join in this recent debate forms chapter 6 in the present book.

The concluding chapters—chapter 7, "Faith While Awaiting Revelation" and chapter 8, "A Very Brief Agnostic (Unknowing) Systematic Theology for Awaiting God's Self-Revelation"—echo some of the concluding arguments of the previous study, but develop them further in reflections on living a prayerful, imaginative, and agnostic Christian faith in the light of reliance on a lovingly reticent God whom we trustingly imagine to intend to transform us in the power of the Spirit into a full Christlikeness, Godlikeness. This God whom we "imagine as real" will, we may trust, change us so as to be able to enjoy being drawn deeper together into the life of the divine Trinity, "face-to-face."

These reflections are enriched, I hope, by engagement with Sarah Coakley, George Herbert, Grace Jantzen, Kathryn Tanner, Rowan Williams, and a number of others.

Footnotes are for the most part purely bibliographical, with only very occasional explanatory comments.

A Continuing if Occasional Debate

Looking back at my original file of reviews, I am amazed at the number (two dozen) that reached me (in addition to private letters from friends and acquaintances). By no means were all persuaded, but all seemed to take the argument seriously, some writing at considerable length, such as Diogenes Allen in *Theology Today* (largely in approval), Richard E. Koenig in *The Christian Century*, K. Runia in *The Reformed Theological Review*, F. C. Copplestone in *Heythrop Journal*, N. Clark in *Baptist Times*, Eric Routley in *British Weekly*, H. E. W. Turner in *Theology*. It was discussed in some detail by Gerald O'Collins in *Foundations of Theology*, and, rather more cursorily, by Avery Dulles and by Paul Helm.[11] In response to these and others I contributed an article, "Revelation, Disagreement and Obscurity," to which the latter two responded personally—still unconvinced.[12] Some of this latter article's further arguments and clarifications appear in the forementioned chapters.

Since then I have noted occasional further references to my study: Timothy Gorringe, referred to earlier, accepted my critique of "crying

---

11. O'Collins, *Foundations of Theology*, 142–49; Helm, *The Divine Revelation*; Dulles, *Models of Revelation*.

12. Downing, "Revelation, Disagreement and Obscurity."

'Clarity! Clarity!' where there is no clarity," but no more than that.[13] John F. Haught in 1993, admitted that "the church" had managed without any such theology, and allowed the need to be "sensitive" to the attention I drew to the lack of clear unanimity, and to others' objections, insisting nonetheless on its appropriateness, emphasizing "the prevenience of God" (without observing that "prevenience" had previously been effectively stressed without this factitious aid).[14] In 1995 Colin Gunton, in his Warfield Lectures, *A Brief Theology of Revelation*, allowed that I raised some very interesting questions (without, however, himself seeming to deal with them), while accepting my case that a concentration on this theme unbalances faith. The implications of diversity among believers, in response to what is claimed to be revealed, are not considered.[15] In the same year Stephen W. Williams, from Belfast, published *Revelation and Reconciliation: A Window on Modernity*, where his contrast between "epistemology" and "reconciliation in history" has some superficial (and independent) resemblances to my preference for "salvation" talk over against "communication" talk, but ignores the factor of communal divergence (despite his date and place).[16] Kathryn Tanner, in "Jesus Christ" in the 1997 *Cambridge Companion to Christian Doctrine*, cited my book with approval, especially my critique of "self-communication" as the focal purpose discerned for God in Christ. In her more recent (2010) and much fuller *Christ the Key*, her stress on incarnation as commonality with us, enabling our gradual healing for life with God to be "fully manifest in us only at a time in some unknown future" is much as I urged earlier and here argue afresh.[17] Noel Leo Erskine, with his "How do We Know What to Believe? Revelation and Authority" seems to be struggling to allow divine salvation as our ongoing present hope, and divine self-revelation as its aim, ending as he does with 1 Cor 13:12; compare Joseph Augustine DiNoia, in his "What About *Them*?" in the same collection.[18] In his *A Modern Introduction to Theology* (2006) Philip Kennedy only uses the word "revelation" three times, and in passing; "knowledge" ("of God") is touched on, also three times and also only incidentally, under "epistemology."[19]

13. Gorringe, *Discerning Spirit*, 7–8.

14. Haught, *Mystery and Promise*, 107–8.

15. Gunton, *Brief Theology*, 8 and 18.

16. Williams, *Revelation and Reconciliation*.

17. Tanner, "Jesus Christ," 270n8 and 271n25; and in *Christ the Key*, 98–99, 170, and quoting 198.

18. Erskine, "How Do We Know What to Believe?" citing 48; DiNoia, "What About Them?"

19. Kennedy, *Introduction*; but few of the other chapter and section headings in this present text receive much, if any, attention either.

Ben Quash, "Revelation," in the 2007 *Oxford Handbook of Systematic Theology*, overlooks the issue of divergence among supposed recipients of divine revelation, despite his reliance on Rowan Williams on the centrality of "participation and formation." Richard Topping, *Revelation, Scripture, and Church* (2007), also ignores the kinds of issues I tried and would now hope again to bring to attention.[20] Mike Higton—significantly qualifying "revelation"—prefers to speak of God believed to "identify himself," offering his "self-identification" in loving address, a phraseology that will be taken up, but critically, later on.[21] Alister McGrath, *Christian Theology: An Introduction*, while noting James Barr's reservations, insists on "the self-disclosure" of God, which, albeit partial "is nevertheless reliable and adequate."[22] On the other hand, Catholic author Anthony Towey, in his very recent *Introduction to Christian Theology*, can avoid any main heading under "revelation," touching on the theme only in passing (and without reference, so far as I can see, to *Dei Verbum*), and also without any talk of divine "self-revelation."[23]

It was, then, with some surprise, that this year (2014) I found very recently the English translation of Michael Welker's *God the Revealed: Christology*, and I then obtained Ingolf U. Dalferth and Michael Rodgers' collection, *Revelation*. Welker boldly opens with "'God has revealed himself in Jesus Christ!' Christian faith has proclaimed this for nearly 2000 years."[24] In the unqualified terms deployed that is simply untrue, as was, for instance, shown by McDonald, even though he approved of this innovation. Welker surveys something of the range of recent German and wider theological disagreements, but without, it seems, even considering that this might raise the question: If God is revealed, how come this unclarity? (I note also that Welker completely ignores 1 Cor 13:12.)

Dalferth and Rodgers' collection again has much of interest in itself (some to be noted later, but mostly, while thought-provoking, are tangential to the discussion here). However, the contributors fail to consider any of the critical questions that were raised in *Has Christianity a Revelation?* and are repeated in what follows. Dalferth, in his "Introduction" mentions but then

---

20. Quash, "Revelation," 325–44, citing 337; Williams, *Christian Theology*; Topping, *Revelation, Scripture, and Church*.

21. Higton, *Christian Doctrine*, see ch. 2, "Knowing and Loving," 31–52.

22. McGrath, *Christian Theology*, 153, relying on Martin Luther; cf. "a rigorous correlation between God's self-disclosure in history and God's eternal being," 244.

23. Towey, *Christian Theology*.

24. Welker, *God the Revealed*, 11; for McDonald, see n. 1. My surprise is compounded by finding that otherwise I have much in common with Welker, with his attention to Bonhoeffer, and his Trinitarian, incarnational, and sacramental theology, a lot of which I found both reassuring and enriching.

ignores Barr on the relative lack of talk of revelation in the Scriptures, while others, apart from Claudia Welz, either offer passing references or largely ignore biblical tradition.[25] Welz also draws helpfully on Jewish mysticism and its take on divine incomprehensibility. Apart from Kirsten Gerdes' apposite attention to Hadewijch of Antwerp, Christian mysticism and apophaticism (God beyond speech) are bypassed.[26] The Jewish reflections adduced are particularly illuminating, so it is regrettable that no Islamic theologians were included. Further, in the collection as a whole, far too often abstractions are reified, foremost when we are told what revelation "is," without attention to the variety of stipulative definitions then affirmed. What is disclosed if the disclosing itself is clearly seen as so diverse? It is simply assumed that using the same word ensures they are all concerned with the same topic, without checking. Although Michael Rodgers allows that pluralism creates a problem, he does not discuss it.[27] Of course, the contributors might well still say in response that my critical questions are misconceived, off-beam, and irrelevant. The reader is left to decide.

I am not aware of any other recent discussions with "revelation" in the title or subtitle.

25. Dalferth, "Introduction," 8; Welz, "Resonating and Reflecting."
26. Gerdes, "Materiality of Metaphor."
27. Rodgers, "Finding Meaning in God's Actions," 49.

"My name is Alice, but—"

"It's a stupid name enough!" Humpty Dumpty interrupted, impatiently. "What does it mean?"

"Must a name mean something?" Alice asked doubtfully.

"Of course it must," Humpty Dumpty said with a short laugh. . . [later he gives an example:]

". . . There are three hundred and sixty-four days when you might get unbirthday presents."

"Certainly," said Alice.

"And only one for birthday presents, you know. 'There's glory for you!"

"I don't know what you mean by 'glory.'" Alice said.

Humpty Dumpty smiled contemptuously. "Of course you don't—till I tell you. I meant, 'there's a nice knock-down argument for you!'"

"But 'glory' doesn't mean 'a nice knock-down argument,'" Alice objected.

"When I use a word," Humpty Dumpty said, in rather a scornful tone, "it means just what I choose it to mean—neither more nor less."

"The question is, said Alice, "whether you can make words mean so many different things."

"The question is," said Humpty Dumpty, "which is to be master, that's all."

". . . however, I can manage the whole lot of them! Impenetrability, that's what I say!"

"Would you tell me, please," said Alice, "what that means?"

". . . I mean by 'impenetrability' that we've had enough of that subject . . ."

1

Seeking and Securing Clarity and Unity in Talk and God-Talk[1]

(a) Words and Other Communication

IT IS CLEARLY POSSIBLE to represent reconciliation and revelation in pictures (Rembrant's "The Prodigal's Return," Caravaggio's "The Conversion of St. Paul"). We may accept this while still allowing that interpreting classical European iconography is an acquired skill, a skill itself extensively formed by verbal communication.[2] Or we could enact silent charades, even a sequence illustrating diverse takes on a theme. Yet we should be aware that gestures are also often culturally specific: a nod of the head may not denote agreement, a shake may not indicate dissent. But to discuss divergent responses at all thoroughly, will most likely require words, asking "What did you mean by that?" or "Could you not have expressed it better another way?" or "Was that last sketch not really the same as the first?"; or, importantly, "Where have we any record of it ever really having happened like that, where have we or may we expect to find any evidence of it actually, here and now, happening the way you suggest it does?" Or one can compose and play music, which may be powerfully expressive, formative, yet it still seems for most of

---

1. John Tenniel's Humpty Dumpty and Lewis Carroll (Charles L. Dodgson)'s dialogue, opposite, on our un-selfcritical ways of doing things with words, should still prompt reflection.

2. Since drafting this, I've been delighted to read Jane Heath's *Paul's Visual Piety* (2013); it cogently takes issue with scholarship that ignores the importance in the ancient world, and in our own, of seeing (and emphatically not just art works). She includes Caravaggio's "Conversion of St. Paul" as one of her examples. In support of "visuality," cf. Kurek-Chomycz, "The Scent of (Mediated) Revelation."

us to demand verbal interpretation if not accompaniment: it is "so abstract, so semantically fluid."[3]

Striking in relation to this, however, is Kirsten Gerdes on "the materiality of metaphor," along with Claudia Welz on "linguistic synaesthesia," that is, spoken words engaging other senses. These insights have brought me to make clear a basic presupposition of this study, that all our thought, whether articulated or not in speech or writing or in other ways, is material from start to finish, in inception in our brains as well as in expression. There is no "ghost in the machine" stirring the brain cells.[4]

Questions of "what" and "where" meaning and reference arise in words. Does or must "revelation" indicate clarity—and, if so, how much and how extensive? Does or must "atonement" imply "atoning for," and does or must that imply punishment, pain, payment? Might the old sense, "at-one-ment" be better and/or more fruitful for translating Paul's Greek? Does or must the "re-" of "reconciliation" betoken returning to a previous harmony that has been broken? And is just anything said about or ascribed to God (or Christ, or Krishna, or Zeus or Mr. Pickwick) to be taken as referring to one and the same person as named, whether real or imaginary, or possibly to another or others sharing that name? How precise ought our usage be: is there a spectrum beween unusable rigidity and "don't get it right, get it written" (well, it sounds impressive)? All such issues need to be discussed, and the terms of the discussion assessed, even if they are unlikely to be settled. And all that before examining and appraising in more detail recent theological reflections centering on our themes of revelation and reconcilation.[5]

This chapter attempts to pull together, briefly, the present author's aided general and specifically theological reflections on language, reflections accruing over the last half century. These reflections have fairly recently been reorganized with the help of William C. Lycan's *Philosophy of Language*, supplemented by a number of other recent studies.[6] Be it realized that the aim here is not just to list but coordinate work that seems to fit

3. See the essays in Begbie and Guthrie, *Resonant Witness*; here citing Begbie and Guthrie, "Introduction," 3.

4. Gerdes, "Materiality of Metaphor"; Welz, "Resonating and Reflecting the Divine," 156; Carruthers, *The Architecture of the Mind*.

5. On clarifying usage, avoiding (tendentious) obfuscation, cf. Coakley, "Sacrifice Regained," lecture 2.

6. Lycan, *Philosophy of Language*, 1–71. Lycan notes only minor revisions in the 2nd edition. On what follows see also Downing, "On Doubting Dichotomies." The best recent alternative account of language that I have met is in Rowan Williams *The Edge of Words*. It often overlaps with mine, but diverges in insisting that "meaning" can only properly be verbal. See (l) below; and in being much readier to trust traditional metaphysics see (g) below.

together, which usually appears with little or no reference to other studies touched on in what follows.

(b) Reference and Identification

Lycan begins with Bertrand Russell on reference, trying to sort out such sentences as "The present King of France is bald," with Russell arguing for a complicated analysis of such grammatically well-formed but puzzling sequences. Russell's analysis was later countered by William Strawson, arguing, cogently, that rather than words or sets of words referring, referring is something that speakers or writers do in context. This (so Lycan himself, and others, have since added) limits the range of reference, either in quantity or by quality. "Nobody believes that" is implicitly restricted in description and in range to "no adult passing for sane and of whom I am aware" (though instances of sane adult strangers believing what I don't might shake even my confidence in the critical acumen of my closer acquaintances).

I hope the following examples will suffice to show that this sort of discussion is relevant to the themes of this study. In Robert Louis Stephenson's *Dr. Jekyll and Mr. Hyde*, the narrator finally discovers that these two very different named characters—visually so distinctive, the gentle physician and the raging killer—occupy the same physical space. In a more recently set version of the story, fingerprint or iris recognition, or, still better, DNA, would be taken to identify them definitively as, in a conventional sense, "the same person." If a police officer in an updated version were to ask who to apprehend, one in the know could say "that man," with ostensive reference to Dr. Jekyll. If brought to court, Dr. Jekyll would probably not be held responsible for "his" actions under the influence of drugs, but remanded to a secure unit for the public's and "his own" safety.

What does it mean to be identified as "the same person"? Ludwig Wittgenstein advised anyone willing to notice to appreciate that "same" (like other words) can be used in varying, context-dependent ways.[7] A relative newcomer to a workplace recognizes a colleague who has taken on a fresh name and appearance as "the same person" whose occasional eccentric behavior cost the first a serious injury. But is the latter still "that same person"—or is she "the same but different," cured?

An acquaintance says, unashamedly, "I'm one person at home with my wife and family, a different person at work, and different again at the golf

---

7. Wittgenstein, *Philosophical Investigations*, 34, 208, 214, 254, 378, and 606. On potential ambiguities in reference, see also Trexler, *Introduction to Psycholinguistics*, 241–65.

club." In a chance conversation you might not bother, but take him as you found him currently. Yet if you were thinking of entering into a business partnership, you might want to know just how different, and whether one behavior-set, one character, were dominant. Could you trust him, if you did not really know which "person" you were engaging with? If his club had a reputation for not so subtle racism and sexism, could you trust him to work with a black woman as a senior partner? Would he take her to lunch at his club, or if that seemed unfair to her, relinquish his membership? (Anyway, these multiple roles might end the man with an identity crisis.)

It is no use pretending that there is a clear answer. I guess we are likely to find it easier to trust somene who is consistent, not subject to wild mood-swings. But perhaps we also value a measure of adaptibility: consistency but not rigidity. Thus, in our pluralist western culture, and as suggested at the start of this section, we may have to decide—by all means, with ongoing debate, but decide—whether all, some, or very little other talk of "God" (Dios, *elohim*, Allah) refers to the same being, person, existent (whether the one we trust or the one we refuse to believe in). You perhaps claim that your God, "the one and only God," is the revealed one; then how do you respond if I claim the one and only true God has revealed him/herself to me as clearly very different, with different attitudes to war, women, property, the wider "natural" world? If this comes as revelation to her, why does it not to you? Especially if you both claim to follow the same Scriptures. (But we return, in chapter 6, to attempts to respond to this conundrum.)

So to of Jesus: are some, most, all sketches by historians, novelists, song-writers, or comedians, of a character they name "Jesus (of Nazareth)," to be taken as refering to "our" or "my" Jesus, even if very mistakenly? Or perhaps we prefer to say, no: if they differ at all widely from mine or ours, they refer to one or more quite other, fictional characters, figments of their own creation. Theirs are characters that share only the same name, even if they are also accorded a larger or smaller range of similar settings, opinions, and deeds. The scope and range of reference and identification, and so of Jesus as supposed mediator of revelation, warrant a measure of clarification.

In my Introduction I noted Mike Higton's recent proposal of "self-identication" as a significant gloss for self-revelation.[8] It has seemed to me worth pursuing, though to deploy it rather more critically than Higton himself does. "Self-identification," "identity," "self-definition," and "identifying with or as," as aspects of "reference," are thus relevant to this present study, and will be topics in their respective literary settings in the following chapters. But imagine yourself given a valued membership to an association. You

8. Higton, *Christian Doctrine*, 31–52 and 57.

guess it stems from someone you know well, but a hitherto quite unknown benefactor identifies herself, with convincing detail, as the actual donor. The membership would still be yours for the taking, without the motive, let alone the overall character of the donor being known or explained.

Another example: "Who's there?" you ask, startled, in a cave you thought empty. "Don't worry, it's only I/me." "Sorry, but who? Could you identify yourself, please." "I'm the woman you met in the newsagent's. I told you about this cave." "But why are you here today, now, when you only said you'd known about it but never thought it worth visiting?" It might take a little while and a little more detail for the self-identification to reassure you. Might this not be the woman who's been pestering you on Facebook?

My dictionaries offer "personality" or "character" as a meaning (a possible use) for "identity"; but it is by no means necessary—and likely impossible—to give a full account, a consistent revelation of your character or personality, in order to identify yourself.

Some thirty-five years ago a series of studies was published, titled *Jewish and Christian Self-definition*, with "self-identity" a convenient alternative in the texts.[9] Individuals and social groups define their identities by distinguishing between themselves and others. However, what is distinctive is not necessarily what is in practice most determinant: day-to-day the distinctive may actually be marginal, however emphatically brandished as badge or flag. It may be most important in relations with those actually closest: perhaps those with whom you share the same sacred writings but disagree over their detailed interpretation. "You outsiders may identify us with them—us Christians with those Jews, us true 'Gnostics' with those 'mere Psychics'—but we don't." Making manifest who you agree or refuse, tacitly or explicitly, to identify with, or who identifies or refuses to with you, as kin or friend or ally, may, then, be interpersonally and/or socio-politically very significant. Yet it may leave an outsider quite mystified: the distinctive reveals very little of the real you.[10] Perhaps, even, you two do actually share the same God, but have for now different cerebral articulations to puzzle one another and the observer with—until some effectively definitive self-revelation is granted in some future, which is still in your deity's hands?

9. Sanders et al., *Jewish and Christian Self-Definition*; cf. Sterling, *Historiography and Self-Definition*.

10. On "social identity theory" see e.g., Esler, *Galatians*, 40–57, with reference to H. Taefel.

(c) Meaning or Use?

In this study I have already been following Wittgenstein in preferring to talk of "use" rather than "meaning." This is especially so when "meaning" is treated as a "thing" that a word contains, or at least denotes, points to, a thing that can be denoted by or transferred into another word, in translation, like a beetle taken from one box to another, to a fresh receptacle for meaning as contents. Yet we can never encounter the meaning-beetle or, for that matter, an empty word-receptacle ready for this meaning. If we ask after either, we are given more words, albeit words supplemented by gestures, pictures, objects. Ask what "hammer" means, we could be given a ball-peen hammer, one with a head rounded at one end, flat at the other, and be shown what "hammer" as a verb means. Picking up a claw hammer, we could be told, yes, in our society, that is another kind, and you can use it in some of "the same" ("similar") ways, but also for different purposes. Then, in words, without being shown, we'd probably be told that there are lots of other kinds, with other different uses. We might be shown a tool-maker's catalog, but then told we could use all sort of things to hammer with: we'd still never be shown the naked meaning of "hammer."[11] Words in sentences (one-word or many-word sentences) are meaningful in experienced social use.

No one I have encountered offers to show us what "self-revelation" or "make known" invariably means.

Actually, I have to say, I think Wittgenstein was unfair in picking on Augustine of Hippo as an example of one who thought words named meanings as objects. Rather it was that people in the world of Jesus and Paul (and Augustine) take it that words-as-names are used to "label" and "evoke" ideas, ideas that might be supposed precise or vague, but were in no way contained in or defined by words or sentences, though one could always look for a more effectively evocative word or sequence of words.[12]

I argued a few years ago that this posited, loose fit between word and thoughts-in-the-mind was interestingly akin to the modular model of the mind/brain increasingly deployed if variously elaborated by linguists with an informed awareness of clinical research, practice, and findings.[13] One pleasant surprise in reading a very recent *Introduction to Psycholinguistics* was to find the author quoting the idea of words as "labels" for ideas—a

11. Wittgenstein, *Philosophical Investigations*, 1–133 (and throughout); Lycan, *Philosophy of Language*, 73–99.

12. Wittgenstein, *Philosophical Investigations*, 1; Downing, "Ambiguity"; see also Downing, "Words and Meanings."

13. Cf. Carruthers, *The Architecture of the Mind*, arguing his own case, but in conversation with many others.

usage I thought I had risked coining. Various kinds of brain damage can leave people able to think and understand others' words, spoken or written, able to produce well-formed words in response, but not the ones they want, while readily aware that they are not what they intend. Some part of the thought module has had its link with word production and articulation, the label-finding module disrupted. Or someone can manipulate tools effectively, but not respond to verbal suggestions, requests, orders, written or spoken.[14] The "translation" from within a customary range of sequences of auditory/visual stimulation proceeding into thought and thoughtful action has been disrupted. (We return to words as labels for ideas in a discussion of metaphor, below, but then drawing Paul specifically into the picture.) Looking for what divine self-revelation means for every speaker of some form of English is futile—quite apart from trying to distill it from or impose it on a whole range of theologies and theological systems of ethics.

Language only works by being imprecise, a set of almost endlessly adjustable tools, by being deployed imaginatively: not a ready vehicle for communicating a given and supposedly definitive revelation.

Nonetheless, as noted in the introduction, Timothy Gorringe made the valid observation that the absence of a precise term for divine (self-)revelation in the Jewish canon of Scripture does not entail the absence of any such idea.[15] Something very like it might well be implied, even without any word or phrase demanding that English one in translation. In fact, I have recently argued at some length that ideas of self-control, control of the passions can be found composed in Hebrew in some ancient Jewish texts without any similar vocabulary, and not solely in those Jewish writings in Greek clearly adopting the regular Greek terminology.[16] Without one language's special vocabulary—say, some calcified metaphor such as "reveal" ("unveil")—talk about divine (self-)communication may well be more difficult, but that does not entail impossiblity. So, in chapter 3, I reconsider the evidence, and look wider for what is being said, not just at the choice of key words. Yet, while such absence of a precise terminology ("reveal," "revelation") is not decisive, it may well be held significant. A particular vocabulary can be shown not to be necessary, but it "may make some cognitive tasks easier."[17] Tools clearly apt and available for a particular kind of use left unused suggest there is no such use perceived.

14. Ibid., 18, 63–64, 187–88, 240.

15. Gorringe, *Discerning Spirit*, 8.

16. Downing, "Order Within."

17. Traxler, *Introduction to Psycholinguistics*, 23–27.

I must also concede that asking for "the meaning" still remains a useful short hand way of asking for the semantic range, other words with more or less widely overlapping uses: though an example or two of use may be the most helpful response. So, in chapter 2 there are surveys of uses of "reveal," "identify," and "self" from a range of secular and theological authors.

Along with a dismissal of "meanings" as supposedly intangible "things" contained in words, also dismissed are "propositions" and "concepts" as more complex intangible things, contained in or conveyed by sets of words in sentences. Again this may be helpful shorthand, encouraging a speaker/writer/hearer/reader to be aware there may well be other distinct sequences of words that are, for the purpose at hand, nonetheless as or similarly effective. There may well be patterns of thinking with important features in common, deployed sufficiently often to warrant a term like "concept." A test of understanding is often whether you are able to "say it" in other words, in a fresh sequence that may be validated by eliciting an appropriate reponse, even a quite complex practical response, intended or hoped for: near enough "the same" to warrant labeling both sets of words "that author's concept" of reconciliation or self-revelation, or whatever.

The worst danger lies in talk of "*the* biblical concept of *x*," or "*the* Hebrew" as contrasted with "*the* Greek" concept of, say, being human. That would be to imagine that all Hebrew speakers over a millennium thought of, say, fellow humans in a uniform and precise homogenized way; or that ordinary Greek speakers, and philosophers of all schools, and poets, from 500 BCE to 500 CE, conceptualized a uniform and standardized but quite distinctive one. This is not to say that there may not be significant common features, "family resemblances" (Wittgenstein, again), shared variously where *anthrōpos* (possibly *phōs*), or *ish, adam, enōsh* are discursively focal among many Greek or many Hebrew or Judaean Aramaic speakers, respectively. But how variously numerous the resemblances, and how clustered, may well differ not only from community to community and from person to person, but from product to product of "the same" author.

Christian or other faith is quite regularly said to afford believers "the meaning" of life (and everything). Different translations of the Judaeo-Christian Scriptures may be accepted as each representing a fair shot at "the sense" of a given passage. But the question must arise, how divergent can an attempt be and still be accepted as conveying anything like "the same sense"? And then, presented, say, with a plurality of divergent Christian interpretations of "the meaning of life," even if many claim to be based on the same Scriptures, how does one decide which if any represents "*the* meaning"? Rather than asking for the elusive meaning, we may do better to use the resources of Christian or other traditions to suggest purposes, aims, visions to draw us with others, into attempting to realize them together. A conviction of being divinely and costingly loved may lure us on together.

The puzzle of evil challenges any sense of meaningfulness, and the demand for meaning entices us into attempting to make sense of it. Then we can leave it as it is. But our religious traditions do not emerge as philosophical explanations for explanation's sake, but primarily as techniques for attempting to ensure well-being and avert ill, even if that includes at the time accepting some ills as apparently unavoidable. Ill is a practical problem at the heart of each religious practice, not an intrusive surd disrupting a prior coherence. Taking Gen 3:16 (labor pains) as applicable to women for ever, as telling how many things are meant to be, postponed pain relief in childbirth for millions of women in the West and elsewhere. Yet a pragmatic response would have been much more in keeping with the underlying pragmatism of the source culture.[18]

(d) Use

So to "use": Wittgenstein offered a fairly random and not exclusive list of "language games," ways in which words can be used:

Giving orders and obeying them—
Describing the appearance of an object, or giving its measurements—
Constructing an object from a description (a drawing)—
Reporting an event—
Speculating about an event—
Forming and testing a hypothesis—
Presenting the results of an experiment in tables and diagrams—
Making up a story; and reading it—
Play-acting—
Singing catches—
Guessing riddles—
Making a joke; telling it—
Solving a problem in practical arithmetic—
Translating from one language to another—
Asking, thanking, cursing, greeting, praying.

---

18. See Downing, "Problems of Evils"; and cf. Surin, *Theology and the Problem;* Williams, *Dostoevsky,* 232–33.

> It is interesting to compare the multiplicity of tools in lan-
> guage and of the ways they are used, the multiplicity of kinds
> of word and sentence, with what logicians have said about the
> structure of language. (Including the author of the *Tractatus
> Logico-Philosophicus*.)[19]

It is not just the final line of the list, but all that precedes it, that can be
found in kinds of God-talk (and in books in the religions section of any
large library—and even in the present author's small private theological collection). Such flexible use, seeing one thing in terms of another, involves
imagination, which is discussed again, below (g).[20]

I prefer to bring in John L. Austin at this point, though Lycan leaves
him to a little later in his survey. At much the same time as Wittgenstein
in Cambridge, Austin in Oxford was assessing word-use, in speech and in
writing, as purposive and (often effective) action. His analysis was published after his death as *How to Do Things with Words*.[21] We do things *in*
the act of speaking, writing, signing; we affect things *by* the act of saying,
inscribing. Thus when Paul has his amanuensis write, and that person or
another in Corinth read (perform) the sequence, *katallagēte tō, theō,* he is
urging his hearers to "be reconciled to God," to become, to become afresh,
to become increasingly at one with God. Or is it, to accept, accept afresh,
accept increasingly, unity with God? But further, *by* urging this, Paul may in
effect persuade. The implication is not that it was God taking unitive action
instead of human response, but to engage human response. *In* telling of God
uttering a promise (say, to Abraham), God is taken to have made a promise,
irrespective of Abraham's interest or even awareness. But here it is only *by*
God (through Paul or others) effectively persuading people to accept atonement that, for them, at-onement happens.

The majority of Austin's "performatives" are not statements, "they do
not describe or report . . . they are not true or false," they make no factual
claims.[22] Austin's insights have been widely taken up by Christian (and perhaps other) theologians. One of the first was Donald D. Evans, in his *The
Logic of Self-Involvement*. When the fourth evangelist has Thomas say to
the risen Jesus, "My Lord and my God," it is not on the same level as an

19. Wittgenstein, *Philosophical Investigations*, 11–1. The author of the *Tractatus
Logico-Philosophicus* was, of course, Wittgensein himself. Well, a differently minded
Wittgenstein.

20. Ibid., 197–215 (English); he uses a larger range of German words.

21. Austin, *How to Do Things*.

22. On "neither true nor false," see ibid., 148, on the way that in practice, "truth"
and "falsehood" can variously merge. Despite the distinctions he analyses, Austin was
averse to dogmatic dichotomies.

actor saying of the drama she is rehearsing, "Jean Smith is my Queen." In saying these words Thomas acknowledges Jesus' status; by saying them he involves himself, commits himself afresh to Jesus. "No one can say 'Jesus is Lord' except by the Holy Spirit," Paul assures us (1 Cor 12:3). Well, in a sense they might. "Not everyone who says to me 'Lord, Lord,' will enter the kingdom of heaven, but only the one who does the will of my Father in heaven" (Matt 7:21). But Paul's "Jesus is Lord," like that of Thomas, is an act of self-involvement.

In *Has Christianity a Revelation?* (hereafter, *Has Christianity?*) it was argued, with the help of many contemporaries, "Christian language about 'God' is intended to express and elicit commitment (and so, but very incidentally), describe ['allude to' would have been better], commitment to him." Sometimes it was further proposed that commitment is the primary function (or force) of the words, and I risked quoting R. B. Braithwaite. Braithwaite had argued, with others, that this was the entire force of God-talk. I insisted that Braithwaite is wrong in taking the commitment to live "agapeistically" as representing the whole force of the words as used by most Christians, and I offer instead: "I intend to live in love, in as complete as I may *humble* love, loving *dependence* on God-who-acted-first-in-love-towards-us-in-Christ."[23] Not all reviewers registered that (repeated) insistence (thirteen pages), which is reaffirmed here.

In his penultimate chapter Austin gets round to allowing that specific "performative" actions, such as "stating" or "affirming" do include a factual element, making them liable to a challenge, along the lines of, "I know you've asserted it, but it's only partially true," or "It's not true at all," in the way that "I promise," "I remit" cannot be untrue (though it my be misleading). On "factuality" I do need to add further reflections, some occurring not long after *Has Christianity?* was published; see the next section, (e).

Whether *by* the New Testament writings, alone or with supplement, God does effectively persuade people to accept these as a definitive revelation of himself must surely affect our decision as to whether that was his intention *in* (one way or another) giving them to us.

(e) "Facts"

God talk is not "factual" in the sense that talk about making computer chips is factual: people from diverse cultures can learn how the latter is done, and do it succesfully. They can do so without worrying about eccentric ultra

---

23. Downing, *Has Christianity a Revelation?* 179–92; citing here, 179 and 185, original emphases; see also Downing, "Revelation," 229–30.

postmodernists. And they can agree on tests for its working, and can perform them succesfully. "That little piece is a 'diode' and it fits in this way. See, it allows the current to flow only along this route." God talk does not, in practice, work interculturally like that.

Often, of course, "fact" and "factual" are themselves less than clear-cut. In a contested legal case, it is agreed, that there are "facts" at stake, there are "done things" (*facta*, from Latin *facio*, "I do"). Statements about them are "statements of fact." The statements of fact are not themselves the events, the happenings, but assertions about them that implicitly claim to be true. Yet what those events were still remains in question, even if their factuality is agreed upon. Were they "done" in the sense of done deliberately, and, if that, deliberately on the spur of the moment, or with pre-meditated forethought. These are issues that jurors or magistrates or judges have to decide, and reach—if possible—a common mind. Those then become "the agreed facts": that is, what it is agreed, happened. People of differing faiths do not seem enabled to reach such agreements.

Often, and much less formally, "the facts" are what is "in fact" currrently commonly agreed (e.g., "this earth is flat") and that was used as a basis for shared activity, even if later it is "common knowledge" that this planet is "in fact" ("in true statement of fact") roughly spherical.[24] The tally of undisputed facts can change over time. Job's friends insist (in line with Deuteronomy and many psalms, and more) that the facts show that human life is ordered justly by a divine moral agent. Job insists that the facts belie any such conclusion, and, as most of us see human society and the non-human world around us, Job is clearly right.[25] Job in the poems still accepts the reality of a truly amazing creator, though one who leaves us humans to our own devices.

Job is far from denying that God could intervene, and justly, for he wishes he would. But the facts, Job insists, show that God does not. There are, these days, philosophically minded theologians who insist that it is possible to envisage God able to adjust the complex physical system we discern without disturbing its appearance of being rule-bound.[26] There is no

---

24. Cf. Austin, "Unfair to Facts"; Downing, *Church and Jesus*, 141–47; Downing, "Dissident Jesus," 294.

25. For a recent defense of the distinctive voice of the poetic Job, see Kang-Kul Cho, "The Integrity of Job."

26. Best on my list are Peacocke's *Theology for a Scientific Age*, and especially, *Paths from Science*, 91–115, where God is imagined immanently shaping the direction of the whole system from within it, thus undetectably, with no tests available, and with all the tragedy and injustice allowed for. This is perhaps a good way to imagine God sustaining all there is; but not if so immersed as to preclude our imaginative trust in his empathetic awareness of each of us in our individual relationships.

attempt here to dispute such theories, only to point out that if it happens it does not happen in a way that looks consistently just, let alone loving. (The implications of faith in a God who resolutely refuses to intervene in his/her creation are discussed in more detail is chapters 6, 7, and 8.)

Christian faith invites us, rather, to trust, imaginatively, that in Jesus God identified closely with one entire human life. And such faith may then (also) encourage us to trust that the creator God is lovingly and attentively and sustainingly present in and with all that happens, letting it evolve freely, while sharing its joy and its pain. We may even trust that we are being drawn into sharing in the interpersonal life of the triune God.[27] Living in imaginative faith, we see ourselves as being drawn into an interpersonal life which soon came to be thought of as triune: Creator, Redeemer, Hallower. Such is the argument of this volume and its predecessor. But that is faithful imagining, not a demonstrable fact.

Theologies that deny an interventionist God are regularly dismissed as rationalistic and "deist." What is offered here is very different from classical deism's detached deity (with antecedents in Aristotle or Epicurus or both). The God I am faithfully encouraging us to imagine as real is emotionally involved with us (see chapters 7 and 8), and much more engaged than the very traditional passionless deity taken as metaphysically "proven" by some theologians claiming Thomas Aquinas with roots in Aristotle. Such theologies themselves rely just as much on imagination as anything suggested here, but style it as metaphysics. And they often demand some very difficult imagining, like William Cooper's smiling face behind a frowning providence. (On imagination, see section (g) below ; on Trinity, chapters 4, 5, 7, and 8.)

Theologies that make no shared or at least sharable factual claims are also dismissed with the term "fideist." They are accused of demanding a leap into blind faith. What is presented here invites, rather, an open-eyed appraisal, finding multiple points of contact, varied paths in from where the reader or hearer may stand in her or his current context, not a leap into something wholly other.

Talk about Jesus, as claimed to be a real person in the past, probably aims to be—but cannot yet make good any claim to be—factual even in this common sense. It cannot make good on the claim to be a commonly agreed fact, while committed Christians and other scholars have long offered competing interpretations of the supposed witnesses to the life and character of Jesus. There is no "common mind" on "what actually happened" even though there is widespread agreement that there are facts at stake. (That "Jesus" is a figure entirely invented by the evangelists has itself been proposed

27. For a succinct and lucid exposition, see Tanner, "Is God in Charge?"

as "factual, but is also very hard to substantiate.") And not a few have also asked, and very seriously, whether Paul's Jesus has enough in common with the Jesus of any one or all four of the gospels to warrant asserting that all five "in fact" refer to, identify, "the same person" (see above). Matthew's and/or Mark's and/or Luke's (let alone John's) accounts, represent teaching ascribed to Jesus as central to what he is about, rather than occasional and even then ignorable—as it seems to be in Paul (e.g., 1 Cor 7:10–11; 9:14–15).[28]

For what it is worth, my own answer is, yes, they do all five refer to the same Jesus, but it needs arguing in detail. But the "fact" is, we only have competing reconstructed stories of the early years of the Christian movement, and there is no *proof* that any is more than a story.[29] Quite a number are "complausible." Just so there is no proof that our varying and competing stories of God and Jesus and Holy Spirit are other than stories—perhaps elaborate self-images. Nonetheless, some of us, many of us Christians, take them as stories to affirm and live by, more or less imaginatively (and do so with varying success rates). We trust this God we variously imagine is real in a way responding to but correcting the best we can imagine and attempt to emulate, offering the hope that we may become "perfect as our Father in heaven is perfect."

(f) Fact, Science, and Value

I have preferred to focus on general "factuality" rather than claimed and/ or disputed "scientific facts." There is no room here for any thorough discussion of "fact and value," "is and ought," or the possibility of value-free "scientific" facts. I would agree with John L. Austin, "the familiar contrast of 'normative or evaluative' as opposed to the factual is in need, like so many dichotomies, of elimination"; and would point the reader to a recent and very helpful discussion by Sarah Coakley in her 2012 Gifford Lectures.[30]

28. For a very recent discussion of the diverse emphases of the early supposed sources see Tucket, "What is New Testament Study," but also my comment, chapter 7 n. 57. There are other significant common features in the our sources that are retained by the majority of subsequent Christians, despite the genuine discrepancies on the issues Tuckett notes.

29. On this and the preceding paragraph, cf. Downing, *Church and Jesus*, and esp. 171–92.

30. Austin, *How to Do Things*, 148; Coakley, "Sacrifice Regained," lecture 1. On the "is-ought" dichotomy, see Coakley, ibid., lecture 2; and, from long ago, Downing, "Ways of Deriving."

(g) Metaphysics

There is an ancient tradition of inventing "facts" out of the logic of the meanings taken to be contained in words. One's deity "must" be infinite, so "incarnation" seems, in fact, precluded. Or one may ask, what is "being" in itself? And wonder how to answer one's question. Are we limited by what we perceive, so that we discern only what our senses tell us, not what things in fact "really" are in themselves (Immanuel Kant)? Can we ever be sure we know even what we mean, let alone what others mean?

One particular dichotomy that has had a stranglehold on Christian theology is perfect and imperfect. You seem "bound to" to say your God is perfect. But that seems to mean he (she?) cannot change. You cannot become more perfect than perfect, and any other change would be to imperfection. So God is changeless, immoveable, timeless, apathēs.[31] It seems to oblige us to try to make sense of an unaffected affection, a passionless compassion, as well as the infinite becoming finite. Ah, well, we have been told these are unavoidable paradoxes. In Has Christianity? it still seemed necessary to attempt to make sense of them, rather than abandon them, and Ian Ramsey's device of a "cone of meaning" was deployed. With that we may try, for instance, to shave away various kinds of imperfection that we do not want to ascribe to God, and then stop before we reach vanishing point, hoping we are seeing ways of improving our understanding of divine reality.[32] It now seems to me obviously more helpful to use experientially based metaphors and admit their likely inadequacy, than abstractions with no experiential basis, and claim these are better just because experientially void.

However, in the meantime there has been a considerable willingness to query perfection metaphysics, a much greater willingness to follow an occasional aspect of Martin Luther's theology taken up by a few nineteenth-century German Lutherans, and then by English Anglicans, but also in other ways by North American and other philosophical theologians, and to talk of a God open to suffering, God in process.[33] Do we not now do better simply to use adverbial forms, and think of God as perfectly adaptive, perfectly responsive, infinitely loving, changelessly faithful?

---

31. I was encouraged to find that discussions of apathy and passionlessness in the early Christian centuries were much more critically sensitive than the version rigified in the west; Downing, "Passions A" and "Passions B."

32. Ramsey, Religious Language, 49–89.

33. Sarot, God, Passibility and Corporeality; Pinnock, Most Moved Mover; also, Downing, "Passions: A," 83–84; "Passions: B," 103–5.

I see the above discussion as an instance of deploying a useful distinction (yes, another dichotomy) between "prescriptive" and "descriptive" metaphysics.[34] "Perfection" metaphysics prescribes: this is what "perfection" (abstract noun) means, and so, precribes an unavoidable concept. Descriptive metaphysics on the other hand tries to describe the underlying logic of what we actually say, or want to say. So we still have to ask, can we really envisage unwavering integrity in someone endlessly responsive to a very great number of others? Must integrity mean total attention to one thing or person at a time? It would be odd to ascribe that to God. But we might think of a teacher we know, whose integrity impresses us, who heads a school of a thousand, and seems to know each one, not just by name but by character and family. So, what constitutes her integrity? Perhaps it is that she takes the same critical encompassing interest in each, those we'd see as high-flyers and those we'd think of as dullards. Is that what we want to say of God? And how might that fit with other things we also want to affirm? (This is relevant to any talk of being at one with, reconciled to God.) So even descriptive metaphysics may rule some ideas out; but the distinction can be a useful rule of thumb. ("Descriptive metaphysics" in fact covers Kant's "transcendentals" with their prescriptive exclusion of the social pressures on us all, our scientists included, to "see" the observable world in terms of current pardigms.)

Avoiding prescriptive metaphysics at least reduces the number of paradoxes we propose, maybe even obviates them entirely. With these out of the way, perhaps we'll have the courage to not let anyone get away with "hidden revelation." At least we may be emboldened to ask if they can describe what they mean by it.

I suppose one could see past metaphysic as a sort of poetry, a play with words. But it is better done by such "metaphysicals" as Donne and Herbert, who encourage the words to dance to their tune, not remain left standing, frozen.

In this essay the reader is invited to take note of what has been argued metaphysically by past theologians, to assess the worthwhileness of the conclusion, and decide whether it can stand on other grounds, or even in its own right.

---

34. I take the distinction from Strawson, *Individuals*, 9, though he contrasts "descriptive . . . content to describe the actual structure of our thought" with "revisionary." Historically, "perfection metaphysics" induced Christian thinkers to revise the God-talk they found in their Scriptures. See Downing, previous note; and see further, below, chapter 7. Though I have gained a lot and here cite quite often, from Sarah Coakley, I have to confess, I part company with her on her acceptance of what I can only see as her prescriptive (Thomistic) metaphysics.

(h) Imagination

But must God and Jesus and Holy Spirit then be held, even by believers, as *merely* imaginary? Imagination seems always to be malign in the older English translations of the canonical texts (AV, RV, RSV), not welcome in any way. I cannot find it used at all in more recent versions (REB, NRSV). Yet when Jesus in the Synoptic Gospels tells parables, he is inviting hearers to imagine the rule of God; perhaps first asking them for what they themselves imagine, before suggesting a lead. And what is rcounted then prompts the evangelists, their predecessors, and their successors, to further imagination. Yet that is still to imagine what is clearly taken to refer to what is real, as well as to prompt appropriate practical responses in real life.

The Hebrew prophets and psalmists imaginatively deployed multiple metaphors to indicate the elusive deity they certainly treated as real. Ezekiel actually writes of being challenged on the issue (Ezek 20:40).[35]

"You must consider [*logizesthai*] yourself dead to sin and alive to God in Christ Jesus," insists Paul (Rom 6:11), leaving his hearers to imagine what it might mean to do that, perhaps hoping he's dropped enough hints, with more explanation to follow. But even trying to consider myself dead and newly alive takes a lot of imagining.[36] Yet Paul, too, using his own picture language (much less vivid "parables" than those ascribed to Jesus), does so to evoke enacted real-life responses to imagination of divine reality.[37] Earlier, we have noted, God is taken to have "considered" us (same verb), "imagined" us as set right with himself, and actually treating us in the light of that imagining (Rom 4).

The question of imagining what is taken to be real was raised in the earlier book; here I propose a fresh way to deal with it. In many stories characters in the narrative imagine things—dangerous tigers, a burglar downstairs, an act of unfaithfulness—we know or find out are, in the narrative, purely imaginary. Other things, beings, happenings, places, of which the characters imagine and wonder as to their reality, turn out to be real—real, in the story—and the characters involved may end convinced of this, never disillusioned. Christian believers, I trust, can and may live their versions of the story, imagining the triune God as real, while expecting to be enlightened, finding the truth, the reality, ultimately "revealed" to them. Perhaps they will be disillusioned about themselves and fellow believers, while never

35. Cf. Middlemas, "Divine Presence," and here, 200.

36. Cf. Robert Browning's "An Epistle" imagines Lazarus trying to recount his experience to the skeptical "Karshish the arab physician."

37. See Kalas, *The Parables of Paul*. Other individual studies discuss Paul's various figures in Paul as parables.

expecting ultimate disillusion, only a resolution better than the best imaginable hope, corrected, enlightened, but far from disappointed. That is the gist of my entire argument: believing as real a variant of a shared story, they expect to be validated if also splendidly corrected.

Happily, there is an onceasing willingness to allow for the place of imagination in many fields, not least, that of scientific hypothesizing. In English language theology it was pioneered by Samuel Taylor Coleridge in the early nineteenth century, and then toward the end, carefully weighed and argued by John Henry Newman. To paraphrase, I hope fairly: you have the credal propositions of the church, and you may be convinced intellectually, but they only come alive for "theological assent" with the help of imagination. John Coulson more recently restated Newman's case, in the light of the reflections of Ludwig Feuerbach and T. S. Eliot.[38] Mary Warnock produced a very helpful survey, starting with Coleridge, ignoring Newman, taking in Husserl and phenomenology, but culminating with Ludwig Wittgenstein.[39] David Tracy mentions these predecessors, if at all, only in passing. His "imagination" (unelaborated) seems to focus on a very literary creativity, just amounting to substituting fresh metaphors, despite his emphasis elsewhere on "experience."[40] There is also a helpful survey of yet other proposals, older and more recent (ignoring Coulson, but also Newman), by Garrett Green in his 1989 *Imagining God*, in a discussion vitiated, however, by an uncritical "positivism of revelation" of "*the* Bible" (Protestant canon assumed) as "*the* Word of God."[41] Green, nonetheless, actually comes quite close to my proposal here. When viewed from outside, our Christian imagining may, he allows, seem to be "seeing as if" what we imagine is true, but "we" insiders "see as true" what we faithfully imagine: and he further insists that this "seeing as true" makes full allowance for 1 Cor 13:12 and 1 Jn 3:2.[42] I prefer, however, to retain "imagine" and not paraphrase it with "see," as that seems to risk appearing to betoken a still unwarranted objectivity. Rather do we imagine as real our various imaginings of God, aware that diverse if often overlapping imaginings (not "seeings") are all we have.

38. Newman, *Grammar of Assent*; Coulson, *Religion and Imagination*; cf. Brown, *Tradition and Imagination* and *Discipleship and Imagination,* though he uses "revelation" far too easily; I note also, Micklem, *A Religion for Agnostics*, 56–57.

39. Warnock, *The Analogical Imagination*; here referring to 184–95; Wittgenstein, *Philosophical Investigations*, 197–215, again.

40. Tracy, *Analogical Imagination.*

41. Green, *Imagining God*. He seeks to escape the charge of "a positivism of revelation" (Dietrich Bonhoeffer and others against Barth), by allowing for pervasive imagination: but nowhere does he offer warrants for his own Biblicism.

42. Ibid., 134–45.

It is not only that I find predecessors in my reliance on imagination. Many much more traditional believers invite me to share their imaginings: for instance, that a just and compassionate deity, omnipotently in control of everything, secures my present comfortable wellbeing while ignoring the present and pressing misery of millions no more wicked than I, and, maybe, much more generous, selfless, self-giving. I do not suggest that we should feel obliged to imagine just anything.

Some people, in my experience, place great store on "pictures in the mind"; some will pick and choose whether to spin them or allow their arousal; others again prefer abstraction. It is important to discern how important actual seeing is for all of us sighted people, as it was in the culture of the early Christians, with speakers trained in conjuring up visual imagery (*ekphraseis*).[43] However, imagination in our ordinary use is not pinned to "mental imaging," but it is there in all use of language. We rely on our imaginative use of language in situations new to us, in articulating fresh responses to existing relationships. Imaginatively, most of us, and not just the recognized poets among us, explore, propose, and deploy family resemblances, common features of things to be talked about, identified, shared.[44]

Of course, there may be revelatory moments when a poem or an analogy seems to throw a convincing light on some aspect of things. Whether the imaginative construct is valid, whether it really works, fits, is "true," may still have to wait for a possible demonstration. That is as much the case in astrophysics as in theology. (One may note the increased use of "we think" and "imagine" and the offer of alternative theories in Caleb Scharf's recent account of the possible and likely implications of black holes.)[45] Or one can note how much in astrophysics is mathematical imagining, playing with an internal logic, without clear checks on whether objective realities are being enumerated.

On this topic, see further, below, (j), on metaphor.

(i) Implying and Inferring

Austin pointed out, as noted in passing above, that in the vast range of performative utterances much is implicit. The one saying in a Christian

43. Cf., especially, Heath, *Paul's Visual Piety*; Kurek-Chomycz, "The Scent of (Mediated) Revelation?"; Downing, "God with Everything: Dio," 26–27.

44. See also, Williams, *Dostoevsky*, x–xi; and *Faith in the Public Square*, 13–14, on "imaginative construction," trying to see things through others' eyes.

45. Scharf, *Gravity's Engines*, 171 onwards, with alternative theories (hypotheses?): "we think," 172, "we don't know," 173, "imagine," 210, 212.

ceremony "I take you to be my wife/husband," implies, for instance, that he or she is in a single state, is serious, and realizes that this is quite other than a film set. And people present may legitimately infer as much. For "implying" Lycan instances using a demonstrative, "this is a fine red one" where we who only hear or read the utterance have no idea what "this" implies, refers to. Sarcasm is another example: "Oh, well done!" on seeing a pile of plates dropped. Lycan discusses inference (R. V. Sellars) and implication (H. Paul Grice) before his account of Austin; I continue to take it that both, and especially Grice on "implicature," derive from Austin, historically as well as logically.[46] Grice argued that there is an implied contract between speaker/ writer and auditor(s)/reader(s), to inform and not mislead, allowing also that silence, what is deliberately left unsaid on matters the hearer might expect to be mentioned, itself may be significant and informative.

With "implicature" we come to what Lycan terms "psychological" theories, where others talk much more widely of "psycholinguistics."[47] As I explained earlier, I prefer to use the term more inclusively still, to include what others separate out as "cognitive science," and have already touched on this.[48] Lycan allows that "most of our intentions in utterance are only tacit" (which seems very close to "implicit"), and then outlines four objections, concluding rather dismissively with: "it is generally agreed that speaker meaning must in *some* way be a matter of speaker's intentions and other mental states."[49] Grice and implicature is taken forward very thoroughly and much more perceptively, I judge, by Robyn Carston, in her *Thoughts and Utterances,* and, much more briefly by Traxler, and in a wider setting by Yan Huang (though with only a passing note on psycholinguistics).[50]

Sometimes we do need to ask, "What are you implying?" Just what inter-subjective objectivity do you claim when you say you have God-given knowledge of God? What depth and extent of "self" have you in mind when you talk of God's self-revelation?

"Discourse analysis" is essayed by quite a few New Testament scholars these days, attempting to discern how sequences fit together and interlink. Thus they will try to imagine what Paul or others imply and seem to be attempting to achieve. Often this will these days be with the obvious help of

46. Grice, *Studies in the Way of Words.*

47. E.g., Traxler, *Introduction to Psycholinguistics,* ranging much wider than implicature, and subtitled "*Understanding Language Science,*" includes a chapter, 8, on Grice etc.; cf. also Crystal, *How Language Works;* Dietrich, *Psycholinguistik.*

48. Traxler, *Introduction to Psycholinguistics,* 27–28.

49. Lycan, *Philosophy of Language,* 102–8, original emphasis.

50. Carston, *Thoughts and Utterances;* Traxler, *Psycholinguistics,* 306–10; Huang, *Pragmatics,* 198–201.

the ancient rhetoricians' discussions of *inventio* (what to say) and *dispositio* (arrangement), as well as current rhetorical theory (so long as neither is taken too woodenly).[51] In chapter 4 we have to consider what, if anything, we can discern of Paul's inter-linkages and intentions, especially in 2 Cor 5:17–21, with its repetitions and changes of tense and mood, and the very condensed final phrase.

This unpacking of what our use of terms may imply, and may legitimately be taken to imply, clearly has considerable theological ramifications. I mention one in terms of focal belief. Classical reflections, "pagan," Jewish, and Christian, on the unity of deity clearly took this as not just indicative of a desire for human unity, harmony, concord, but as an urgent inducement to just such "at-one-ment."[52] Another relates to what has long been in practice: the risky but unavoidable procedure of those deploying and expounding authoritative texts. No text attempts to articulate everything its intended readers or those who might hear it read already know or believe or are likely to. Thus even original hearers or readers are likely to have been left wondering, "does he know/suspect that we already do what he condemns, or does he think us likely to, or that we just might be tempted to?" Much elaborate scholarship is devoted to arguing over what we ascertain may have been relevantly taken for granted, implied by an author such as Paul. Allowing that he is presenting his side of the argument, how well-informed of the others does he seem to assume he is; how much allowance is he having to make for his hearers being independently informed on Paul's own views? So also, as a matter of interest, scholars attempt to discern a reader or his/her hearers' likely responses.[53] But, of course, reaching even a fair approximation is much more difficult at this distance in time, and in our other and varying cultures. Paul is often writing for audiences containing people he has met, or has news of, or has a letter from; and there may have been occasions in the past when he has found he misjudged things at least to some extent (see 2 Cor 7:8, 12: "For even if I did . . . it was not"). We lack those interactive advantages.

Varieties of use, and of saying "it" in other words, and of implication and inference, each demands a consideration of metaphor, which now follows, though Lycan leaves it last of all.

---

51. Cf. Quintilian, *Institutes*, 3.3.1–10; Porter, *Handbook of Classical Rhetoric*; Porter and Carson, *Discourse Analysis*; Porter and Olbricht, *The Rhetorical Analysis*; Traxler, *Psycholinguistics*, ch. 5, "Discourse Processing," 187–229.

52. Downing, "Order."

53. Oakes, *Reading Romans in Pompeii*.

(j) Metaphor

Janet M. Soskice has argued, in discussion with many others, and has persuaded many of us, that "metaphor is that figure of speech whereby we speak of one thing in terms suggestive of another," and, as such it is open and "irreducible."[54] No simple account is satisfactory, least of all the suggestion that metaphor is a time-wasting puzzle. "It is pervasive in everyday life, not just in language but in thought and action."[55] Lively metaphors can stimulate the imagination, even prompt mental imaging.

I found modern discussions especially intriguing in the light of usage in Paul's world. For educated Greeks and Romans, *metaphora* and *translatio* were their respective words for what we call metaphor but also for what we call translation, and meant, not the transfer of "meaning" from one term to another, but the "transfer" (same complex as *translatio*, of course) of name ("label") from one idea to another. This way of seeing it is there in Aristotle, and reappears in Cicero and in the *Ad Herrenium*.[56] Significantly, the rhetorician and grammarian Quintilian could judge that even in the same language, this could be "necessary," because the new label is more significant, or simply better (more effective). Much the same is said by a contemporary, Demetrius, "some things are . . . expressed with greater clarity and precision by means of metaphor."[57]

It is worth showing how Paul displays awareness of the ancient discussions of language that underlie this understanding of metaphor. I was struck some while ago by a passage from Dio of Prusa, where metaphor can be as effective as literal seeing :

> The human race has left unuttered and undesignated no single
> item that reaches our sense perception, but straightway puts

54. Soskice, *Metaphor and Religious Language*, 15 and 93; cf. Lakoff and Johnson, *Metaphors We Live By*; Kohl, *Metapher*, 119–20; Middlemas, "Divine Presence in Absence," 197–200; Lycan, *Philosophy of Language*, 207–26; Carruthers, *The Architecture of the Mind*, 324–26; Traxler, *Psycholinguistics*, 267–98. Lively, but without explicit interaction with these or their interlocutors, see Brown, *Tradition and Imagination* and *Discipleship and Imagination*. Green, *Imagining God*, 130–33, wants a definition closer to analogy, to curb the freedom for which Soskice argues. On this openness, a remaining unfinished, see also Welz, "Resonating," and Gerdes, "Materiality of Metaphor."

55. Lakoff and Johnson, as cited in Trexler's discussion, *Psycholinguistics*, 285.

56. Aristotle, *Poetics*, 21–22, and *Rhetoric*, 3.2.6–7; Cicero, *Orator*, 24.80–92; anonymous, *Ad Herrenium* 4.34. It is a shame that Gerdes, in her interesting "Materiality of Metaphor," 187–91, perpetuates the thought of transfer of meaning when the ancient authors insist it is a transfer of name, *onoma*, *nomen*, for an idea. It makes a difference.

57. Downing, "Ambiguity"; Quintilian, *Institutes of Oratory*, 8.6.4–6 ("institutes" meaning principles); Demetrius, *On Style*, 2.82.

upon it what the mind perceives, the unmistakable seal [my "label"] of a name, and often several utterances [*phōnas*] for one item, so that when anyone gives utterance to any of them, they convey an impression not much less distinct than does the actual matter in question. Very great indeed is the ability and power [*dunamin*] of humans to indicate with words whatever occurs.[58]

This may usefully compare with:

There happens to be any number of utterance systems [*phōnas*] in our world, and nowhere are such lacking. If I do not perceive the force [*dunamin*] of the utterance I shall be a barbarian babbler to the speaker and the speaker to me. (1 Cor 14:10–11)

I have argued the particular and the overall relevance of these insights at greater length elsewhere. But I repeat (with additions in brackets) here the conclusion drawn:

What all this does mean is that we can never justifiably assume that an author in this Greek and Roman culture has intended his or her individual words themselves to *contain* a precise "meaning," let alone a clear and readily shareable distinct meaning. "Names" are just not expected to function like that. They *contain* nothing; rather may they summon up, evoke ideas. Ideas of such topics as "faith" or "virtue" or "justice" or "freedom" or "law" [or "at-one-ment" or "revelation"], it is hoped, are coherent and shared or shareable to some worthwhile degree, but can only be named and more or less elaborately evoked, not in any other way conveyed. And then no author can be claimed to have used a disambiguated connotation of a lexeme unless or until she or he has made that disambiguation fully explicit. And such disambiguation seems very unlikely in terms of what the ancients said about words and metaphor and translation. If you could trust that a common idea was already "out there" to be evoked by one among perhaps many common names or sequences of names for it, there was no need to define further the names themselves; indeed, their rich ability in common usage to evoke varied impressions might well be part of, even integral to their power to evoke the particular idea assumed to be on call.

Words, phrases, sentences, paragraphs, spoken and heard, written and read worked then (as they work now), but only by being free to flex and adapt, in shared use in life lived together,

58. Dio, *Olympicos, Discourse*, 12.65 (LCL, lightly adapted).

free to adapt, and not ossified, hardened, made brittle. Sequences of words in our Christian scriptures where we in English (by μεταφορά, *translatio*) use "faith," "believing," "trust" words, as with many other such clusters ("love," "justify," "kingdom," "knowledge" ["at-one-ment," "revelation"]), should be allowed much the same free semantic wealth and varying emphasis as their Greek counterparts enjoyed in the passages we study.[59]

This is, again, not to suggest that the ancients' brains worked differently. It is very unlikely that any major genetic change has occurred over just two millennia. The human language function then was surely just as complex as it is today, as complex as is taken for granted in current debates over psycholinguistics.[60] There is no justification for expecting the definitive precision in language that many claimants of revelation (of/by God) presuppose.

(k) Intercultural Comprehension

In just the lifetime of the present author there have been repeated fashions of doubting the ability of people in one culture to understand another, with obvious ramifications for our interpretations of our inherited sacred texts, "the Bible," and, very likely, most or all of our post-biblical heritage.

There has been the powerful influence of Karl Barth, reacting, it would seem, against the ease with which Christian Europe accommodated itself to, even justified, internecine war. Though one gathers Barth softened a little later, for a long while he refused outright any suggestion that there could be a meeting point of any kind between asserted divine revelation and the wider world, secular or religious. Many who read him were persuaded, though many more, of course, were not: among them Catholics with a reliance on traditions of "natural theology," and missionaries from many Western churches working in Africa and Asia. Barth's stance implies that it is possible to use a fairly standard German vocabulary and syntax without its secular or liberal-religious use impinging on his *Church Dogmatics* or its expositors. I have failed to find any attempt to justify such an assumption, not even any awareness of it among devotees. Such a stance lingers on, I think, (in largely Anglo-Saxon) "radical orthodoxy."[61]

59. Downing, "Ambiguity," 167–68.

60. Taken from ibid., 160–61. Kind permission from *NTS* 56.1 (2009) 139–62. In a footnote there: "This is to allow that 'language' includes more than words and sequences of words spoken/heard, written/read."

61. See the careful discussion in Tanner, *Theories of Culture;* and cf. Millbank, *Word*

Contemporary with Barth, and contrasting, was Rudolph Bultmann's insistence that "modern man" who switches on electric light cannot make sense of the mythic world of the Bible, including the New Testament. The only way over this cultural gap is to engender a fresh language, specifically that of existentialism, as expounded by Martin Heidegger, and urged in Britain by, among others, Dennis Nineham. For sure, we could find it very difficult, for instance, to live in a culture whose language had no past tense; but, as Traxler shows, Daniel L. Everett among the South American Pirahã was able to cope, in practice.[62] Cultures are not Nineham's self-contained "totalities," "encapsulated." Others, as well as I, have shown this for our own as for the first-century Mediterranean world. The latter was as mixed, diverse, disparate as our own, with very similar ranges of skepticism and credulity.[63] Nineham was fond of quoting from Leslie P. Hartley's *The Go-Between*, "The past is a foreign country. They do things differently there," where "the past" in question is in fact within the narrator's lifetime. In practice we can always, with care, feel our way into life as it is or was lived by others, checking on our assumptions, our ideas of consistency and entailment.

Yet another variant was proposed by self-styled Wittgensteinians such as Peter Winch and Dewi Z. Philips, insisting that "language games" are self-contained, only engageable from within. Christianity has its own rules, its own distinct "grammar," untransposable. From such a stance Alasdair MacIntyre wrote in 1963:

> The most perceptive theologians wish to translate what they have said to an atheistic world. But they are doomed to one of two failures. Either they succeed [*sic*] in their translation: in which case what they find themselves saying has been transformed into the atheism of their hearers. Or they fail in their translation: in which case no one hears what they have to say but themselves.[64]

In fact, in later writing MacIntyre has relinquished this dichotomy, and is sure, for instance, that it is possible for us to assimilate the ethos of St. Benedict. But those who claim Wittgenstein for such a take on "language games" ignore the force of what he said about them and about "boundaries" in general: they appear as our creation, not innate in how things are.[65]

Made Strange; Ward, *Christ and Culture*.

62. Traxler, *Psycholinguistics*, 1–6.

63. Chester, *Unreached*; Downing, "Access," *Strangely Familiar*, and "Magic."

64. MacIntyre, "God and the Theologians," 7.

65. Downing, "Games."

Yet another challenge comes in the form of "postmodernism," with its insistence that there is nothing outside or behind or beneath the text: nothing is accessible but the text itself; or, perhaps, nothing but what you the reader bring to the text from other texts that have been encountered. It means what you make of it.[66] That does not work with a whole range of technical manuals. It might seem plausible with novels, poems, metaphysical treatises. On the surface it may well look very similar to an important ramification of the ancient view of words as transferable name-tags: in classical allegory, a whole sequence of words-in-phrases can represent and be expected to evoke various distinct sets of ideas. There is, however, an important difference even here, in that for the ancients the ideas evokable were expected to be inter-subjective, shared or shareable, not private. Further, this postmodernist program can only be demonstrated if it is only partially, only occasionally the case. Usually diverse, even conflicting readings can be discussed and argued over: you can see why she read "it" her way. If you cannot tell how and why you disagree, you cannot know that you do. Perhaps you actually mean "the same" by readings that only seem very different from one another? A similar argument cuts against William V. O. Quine's conclusion that you could have two systematically and completely different translations of "the same" discursive, non-technical text. You could only tell that they were different translations if you could show how and why they were achieved. (I have not been able to find an actual example, offered by Quine or anyone else.)[67]

Both Quine and then Derrida seem to have been fazed by the imprecision of at least non-technical language. Yet surely its openness, the imaginative adaptability of individual words but also phrases, even whole sentences, to fresh, and marginally, and even very different situations (circumstances exhibiting but a few discernible resemblances), is what allows linguistic communication to work. A nominalist "fresh word for every feeling, hope, judgment, as well as every size of tomato from the same plant," would be useless; a fresh phrase to express every one of, say, a thousand degrees of liking, would clearly be unworkable. What seems to have disturbed Quine and Derrida is what delights the later Wittgenstein (and the present writer).

Yet being persistently made aware of the possibility of carefully argued variant readings, being alerted to what one's own cultural formation leads one to take for granted, is salutary. Not least, it raises questions about the

---

66. See, e.g., Derrida, L'écriture and Of Grammatology; and for my argument, Bannet, Structuralism, 210–11.

67. Quine, Logical and Word; cf. Dancy, Epistemology, 97–109.

Scriptures as supposedly revelatory texts for most or even for all readers/
hearers, but also about being "made one" with God, united in diversity.

(l) But Can't We Just Think?

It seems widely agreed that words, or words-in-sentences, are, at least, a
great help. They allow us to communicate with one another, exchange information, plans, desires, problems and problem-solving, and much more
(see Wittgenstein's list, above). But do we need them, can we have (and even
share) wordless thoughts? Some say yea, some nay. Either way there are issues for God-talk. If words are essential, then we seem at least likely to exclude anyone completely inarticulate, and maybe many merely with limited
oracy or literacy. If words are not held necessary for communication with
or about God, do we know whether verbal prolixity (even this short work)
hinders rather than helps comunication? (St. Francis is often accorded the
saying, "Preach the gospel, in season and out of season. If necessary, use
words.")

Among the nay-sayers are many recent philosophers. Peter Carruthers
instances Wittgenstein, Worf, Davidson, Dennett (I would here add Lycan)
who insist there can be no thought without words. Among the yeas insisting we (most adding, along with other animals) can think wordlessly, Carruthers lists Russell, Grice, Fodor, Pinker.[68] Among authors cited here who
see themselves primarily as linguists, and who say no, I note Jean Aitchison.
Among those who insist yes, there is pre- and non-verbal shared cognition,
I place Traxler and Carruthers himself.[69]

Babies show attentive awareness to some spoken sounds, including
those to which they have been habituated in the womb, long before they are
able to distinguish them, let alone use them as words. Newly born they can
protest (at) "something," and protest again if the practical response received
fails to deal with whatever "it" was. Even if sometimes it happens that the
response given provides some distracting satisfaction, distraction will not
always work, and the protest will be repeated, even reinforced. Someone
so anesthetized as to be incapable for a period even of "inner speech" can
later report his or her thinking engaged during that time; so could someone after an epileptic coma (even acting "thoughtfully" while also totally

68. Carruthers, "Conscious Thinking," 115, and *Architecture of the Mind,* passim,
but cf. 372-73; Lycan, *Philosophy of Language,* 78, citing Joseph Locke, but none of the
latters' classical antecedents.

69. Aitchison, *The Articulate Mammal,* xix; Traxler, *Psycholinguistics,* 326-55; Carruthers, "Conscious Thinking"; Pinker, *The Blank Slate.*

inarticulate). Deaf children in Nicaragua, once brought together, initiated and then elaborated their own sign language without exposure to any adult sign system, producing what we would intepret as common nouns, collectives, verbs, and the ability to communicate reflections on what was being exchanged.[70]

(m) Master or Servant?

> "When *I* use a word," Humpty Dumpty said, in a rather scornful tone, "it means what I choose it to mean—neither more nor less." . . . "The question is," said Humpty Dumpty, "which is to be master. That is all."[71]

Perhaps it is agreed, words are there for us to use, we can think without them, but can call on them as and when we want, to serve us. So we are the masters? If we want to communicate, receive and give information, of course we cannot tyrannize, we have to cooperate with other word users. We have grammars and dictionaries to help us conform to common usage, though we may welcome or tolerate or resist neologisms ("googling," "texting"; "mitigate against" for "militate against;" "split infinitives" and loose prepositions to happily seek out).

But there is still a danger that words will themselves master our thinking; especially as they have done in years gone by, dividing and ruling; and by encouraging metaphysical speculations (see [g]). For instance, binary oppositions can afford a convenient short-hand, rule of thumb; but they have in the past taken and still can take control. Hot and cold, black and white, in and out, us and them, up and down, time and eternity, finite and infinite, perfect and imperfect, permanent and evanescent, is and ought, right and wrong, either one or the other, male and female, being and doing: these and many other dichotomies can prompt us to "see" boundaries where there are none, impose boundaries where none is justifiable. A hot tap and a cold tap can be useful, but a mixer tap is often a great improvement. Anyway, how hot is hot, how cold is cold? Most if not all our common dichotomies resolve into a spectrum.

70. Traxler, *Psycholinguistics*, 325-60, and 17-19; cf. Carruthers, *The Architecture of the Mind*, 324.

71. Carroll, *Through the Looking Glass*, 269.

(n) Well, What Do You Know?

"I know that my redeemer liveth," proclaims Job (Job 19:25, AV), splendily set to music by Georg Friedrich Händel (though modern translators construe the Hebrew differently). How we use the words "know" and "knowledge," and then how we warrant, justify claims to "know" affects, of course, all talk of our knowledge of God, or of the validity or force of various translations of sacred texts, or of our own or others' general or sometimes distinctive "religious" experience.

I have before me four volumes, dating from mid-1960s to 2011, discussing these sorts of issues interestingly but unsatisfyingly. For instance, only one, Robert Audi, includes religious knowledge.[72] All of them talk of knowledge as justified true belief, and discuss ways of justifying assertions of belief so as to warrant using the terms in a full, intersubjectively shared way. Of course, we can insist we "know" in the sense of strongly believing, having great confidence: "On the basis of the polls we knew we would win, but electoral fraud has robbed us of victory."[73] There was some justification for the belief; but public opinion polls have sufficiently often proved misleading (participants lied, changed their minds, did vote after all, but for somone else . . .), warning against any claim to know in advance the result even of a fair ballot.

Audi, the most recent of the four, is more thorough on the majority of the issues commonly adduced: perception, memory, reason, testimony (including a chapter on "social testimony") as justifying belief as true: but with the one exception of the issue of agreed as opposed to disputed testimony. On the latter only David Hamlyn among these four argues, with Wittgenstein in support, that agreement in judgement is necessary if not sufficient to warrant (not prove) claims to knowledge. Thus there are those who claim to know the laws of economics and those of us who dismiss this as ideology. A few scientists seem to "know" that humans cannot cause climate change, where many more say they are 90 percent sure they have been doing and continue to do so. The majority, it is accepted, may be wrong (as majorities have proved in the past: the "flat-earthers"), but failing agreement, some claimants to knowledge about some topic must be wrong. That is so even if opponents' better substantiated conclusions still lack definitive proof. Where theoretical research is at issue, most will remain tentative. And of course, the claim to a clear knowledge afforded to and openly shared by all

---

72. Audi, *Epistemology*, 319–28; the others are Dancy, *Epistemology*; Griffiths, *Knowledge and Belief*; and Hamlyn, *The Theory of Knowledge*.

73. Cf. Audi, *Epistemology*, 246.

of a specific group, the more vulnerable is the claim to divergent accounts by members of what their group says and can show it knows.[74]

Audi examines theories of sensory perception in general, then later, in relation to religious knowledge. Neither in general nor in religious contexts does he rule in or out some "mystical" or more ordinary awareness, say, of God speaking, or just being present. All he asks is how one might discriminate between genuine awareness and hallucination. He confesses that discussions in epistemology tend to focus on individual claimants, and, as noted, he has devoted a chapter to social testimony, judging it to be indispensable, and repeats this again in relation to scientific claims and then to claimed experiences of God. Yet that still, and regrettably, fails to discuss the relevance of socially disputed testimony even among scientists, let alone among believers.[75] It is this believers' disagreement among themselves, which remains at the heart of the difficulty argued in the previous book, and again here, of warranting belief in past or current divine (self-) revelation as affording knowledge, propositional or personal, of God.

In line with the confessed individualism shared with fellow epistemologists, Audi's and the others' discussions of "the past" concentrate on a living person's memory, even while Audi allows, it would seem, if only in passing, that testimony to earlier events can count as "knowledge of the past."[76] He is also happy to talk of "introspection," ignoring Gilbert Ryle's argued preference for "retrospection," knowledge of our own past. Retrospection does not claim multiple overlapping layers of conscious attention to mental processes, processes that more recent psycholinguistic research indicates are pre-conscious.[77] Audi argues, cogently, I think, that I have better access to my own thoughts (I would insist, my own past if very recently past thoughts) than anyone else has. But he insists that such privilged access does not itself validate any conclusions I may have reached about events external to me, or even happening to me. I can be right in knowing I believed that I was listening to God, while this does not mean that I was.

Other issues are also discussed by these authors, under these headings of "knowledge" or "epistemology," such as reason, inference, and skepticism: all relevant to God-talk, but not obviously pertinent to the main themes of this present study.

74. Hamlyn, *The Theory of Knowledge*, 177–78; Audi, *Epistemology*, 303–8.

75. Audi, *Epistemology*, 150–72, 305, 323.

76. Ibid., 63.

77. Ibid., 96–101; Ryle, *The Concept of Mind*, 156–60; cf. Carruthers, "Conscious Thinking."

In our Scriptures there are contradictory stances on the propriety of testing God. A test is sanctioned at Jdg 6:36–40; Ahaz is rebuked for piously refusing to "put the Lord to the test" (Isa 7:10–17); and Paul claims to have displayed the validating "signs of an apostle" (2 Cor 12:12).[78] The Synoptic Gospels, however, have Jesus pick up and emphasize the prohibition in Deut 6:16, and elsewhere sternly rebuke those seeing probabative signs (Matt 4:7; 12:39; 15:4 and parallels); compare Paul at 1 Cor 1:22. In practice, a test for the presence or absence of a God claimed to be omnipresent would seem harder to envisage even than a test for theoretically ubiquitous "dark matter" seems to be. Still more importantly, in personal relationships we unavoidably rely on implicit trust. My trying to prove a friend's good faith would constitute a relationship already broken from my side (an argument elaborated further, in chapter 6).

(o) Sociolinguistics

Most of us are able to communicate well with one another, even if we find on many occasions that someone else misunderstood what we meant (and it may be more our fault than hers). All of us convey a lot by body language—posture, touch, movements of lips, eyes, limbs, head; and intonation and stress in such words as we utter. Even people who are autistic bodily convey their failure to "read" others' facial expressions. Some of us, however, may rely much more on a varied choice of words and phrases to convey, discriminate, nuances of feeling, which others entertain but communicate in different ways. For such, utterances are expected to be clear and precise: statements of fact, of set opinions, of preferences, of command, without lots of ifs and buts and qualifications and anticipations of disagreement or doubt or confusion. Basil Bernstein and associates argued this in the sixties and seventies (and their studies have continued to be reprinted), discerning it as a British "class" issue: the more open and adaptable linguistic code was "middle class," the linguistically restricted code was working class. The adaptability and restriction applied only to the use of language, and did not correlate significantly at all with intelligence or the subtlety of affective social interaction as a whole.[79] As one might expect, Bernstein and associates did not meet with universal acceptance.[80] However, their findings certainly

78. The Fourth Gospel attributes signs to Jesus, but these seem to be symbolic rather than probative.

79. Bernstein, *Class, Codes, and Control.*

80. Rosen, *Language and Class,* 10–12; Hudson, *Sociolinguistics,* 222 (but both are unfair in ignoring the evidence supplied). Aitchison, *The Articulate Mammal,* 61–62,

(for what it is worth) tallied with my own experience as an Anglican parish priest in mixed working class (unskilled and skilled) and middle class areas, at a time when "the vicar" was still likely to find friendly entry into a variety of homes. I was able to appreciate the perceptiveness of people who spoke in different styles. These included narrative nuances in some linguistically simple storytelling. But I also discovered people's ability to adjust closer to my linguistic register while still reproducing (quoting verbatim) other conversations that deployed their more usual and quite distinctive registers. And, yes, there were exceptions.

Some major issues of "sociolinguistics" were touched on in previous sections of this chapter: performatives, implicature, the surmountable difficulties of not having a precise word or phrase for something you want to say. "Restrictive codes" may hamper; they do not have to imprison. But the fact remains, I suggest, that even people with a normal range of hearing and speaking, and not only those with congenital or later disruptions in or to the brain, may differ considerably in the ways they use and enjoy language, spoken and written. Put at its crudest, are God's supposed self-revelation, or God's supposed at-one-ment with the world, only to be enjoyed with those who have acquired an elaborate ability to accept and use words—if not happy to engage with Barth's *Church Dogmatics*, or even this volume, then at least with C. S. Lewis's Narnia series? Is Christianity, are some forms, pathologically verbose?

And individual words do matter, for all of us, and especially for those of us who expect words to mean (be used for) for what we are accoustomed to them meaning (being used for). I was warned at theological college that "sin," "sex," and "love" were (in late fifties UK) largely co-extensive. I doubt whether "sin" is now (though one intelligent adult confirmation candidate confirmed it for me: "I have no sins to confess. I never made love before marriage, and after that, only with my husband"). With "sin" as extra-marital sex no longer common newspaper parlance, I doubt (unscientifically) whether it is part of common UK parlance at all, except possibly perhaps in matters of diet: the cream cake is a sin, but it's nice.

Using an alien register can be alienating; using strange individual words, or, as bad, familiar ones in strange ways, can be estranging even when inviting reconciliation, obfuscating when offering revelation. In the next chapter the reader is invited to reflect on ways in which "revelation," "self-revelation," "(self-)identification," and "reconciliation" are used in at least some evidenced practice, as well as to imagine other likely instances.

---

refers only to one article, failing even then to specify of just which language a working class child may be said to be deprived

In the final chapter of the book, the possibilities of an at-one-ment with God that can be even wordlessly enjoyed will be explored.

2

"Reconciliation," "At-one-ment," "Self," and "Revelation" Today [1]

(a) Introductory: "At-one-ment"

> If anyone is in Christ, there is a new creation: everything old has passed away; see, everything has become new! All this is from God, who reconciled us to himself through Christ, and has given us the ministry of reconciliation; that is, in Christ God was reconciling the world to himself. . . . So we are ambassadors for Christ, since God is making his appeal through us; we entreat you on behalf of Christ, be reconciled to God. (2 Cor 5:17–20; NRSV)

This passage on reconciliation, along with Rom 5:10–11, 11:15, is taken by a number of expositors as the heart of Paul's theology, despite the infrequency of his use of the terms. The texts themselves will be discussed in a little detail in chapter 4. Here it suffices to note the agreement of a number of recent commentators that despite the "re" of English "reconciliation," Paul makes it clear that he's talking about God making endemic gentile enemies into friends, not restoring old friendships. Thus, I shall urge, we would do well to adopt William Tyndale's sixteenth-century English translation. Tyndale offered the words "atone," "atonement," an older term signifying making one, "at-one-ment," which might well seem closer to general Greek usage and to what Paul says here.[2] Paul emphatically insists that something very

---

1. The sketch opposite is intended to recall the Joseph story, and especially Gen 44:18, as interpreted, I gather, by later rabbis in terms of Ezek 37:18: Joseph representing Ephraim as the northern kingom made one with Judah, the southern kingdom. The story is explored further in the next chapter.

2. The Greek is *katallassō* not *anallassō*, which is not found.

important and quite new has happened, the beginning of the process of (re)conciling the world to himself, the basis of the appeal "be (re)conciled" to those who obviously still are not, even though others (Paul and his associates), it seems, have already come in.[3]

Later Christian reflection decided that in the instance of Adam and Eve humankind as a unity had indeed, though briefly, been at one with God, a relationship now being renewed. To this the Latin translations seem to witness, always using *reconciliare*, with the "re-" seeming to convey the restoration of an earlier, now broken harmony (even though *conciliare* would have been closer to the openness of the Greek). While Paul *could* have supposed a restoration of Eden, or of one or more of the covenants, he in fact says differently.

However, Eastern and Western theological reflection and dogma have until recently mostly if not invariably maintained the once-good-relationship-broken-but-now-restored interpretation. Integral to this has been a conviction that the break was blameworthy, and the disruptive offense had to be "atoned for" by the offenders or an agent on their behalf. Yet "atoning for" and "at-one-ing" seem distinct from one another, even if sometimes happening to be related—or so it will be argued.

(b) Reconciliation as At-one-ment

(i) Reconciliation as At-one-ment: Common Usage.

As noted in the Introduction, my examples of various uses of "revelation" in *Has Christianity?* were criticized by some for being "too secular," even though many instances of (similar) theological use were in fact also included in (unread?) footnotes. With "reconciliation" there is appreciably less room for a similar complaint, as those I have come across discussing general interpersonal, civic, and national reconciliation often acknowledge and respond to its source in theological, and mostly Christian theological reflections and practice.

In what follows there are (usually brief) reminders of discussions of language in the previous chapter.

A fairly random selection of primarily "secular" and then some primarily Christian theological discussions have been consulted, and a number of issues these bring to our attention are listed. From the former group I use as a basis two collections of essays. One by academic lawyers, I found

---

3. Compare the discussion in Thrall, *A Critical and Exegetical Commentary*, 420–38; Martin, *2 Corinthians*, 138–58.

particularly helpful: *Law and the Politics of Reconciliation* (2006), edited by Scott Veitch. Another, by German academic ethicists, some of them theologians, afforded a useful supplement: *Versöhnung, Strafe and Gerechtigkeit*, edited by Michael Bongardt and Ralf K. Würstenberg. In what follows these are further supplemented by Erin Daly and Jeremy Sarkin's *Reconciliation in Divided Societes* (2007), and an earlier collection, *Reconciliation in Northern Ireland* (1993) edited by Dermot Keogh and Michael H. Haltzel. Similar issues, and some others, were raised by Gerry Johnstone, *Restorative Justice* (2001/2011).[4]

Andrew Schaap insists on *not* presupposing an original harmony: the "re-" of "reconciliation" does not determine the meaning-in-use. Schaap (I think significantly) also argues that "reconciliation is what makes the revelation of truth possible," for the parties may initially have very different understandings of themselves and of each other (again, "the facts"). It is (or at least may be) "revolution, not restoration"; but that demands a revolutionary moment of reconciliation that participants can look back to.[5] Roy Foster also deprecates taking any fantasized golden past as a starting point.[6] Such "facts" matter.

Daly and Sarkin insist that reconcilation is a process, and others would seem to agree.[7] As Zenon Bankowski (deploying Girard, Arendt, Weil, Williams) says, both sides have to go on creating new identities out of an absence of common ground, changing attitudes not only to the other, but to oneself.[8] (Simply identifying the other by her past is to be avoided.) It should then at least ensure, argues Kerby A. Miller, that past injustice is not replicated.[9] But Daly and Sarkin also urge that truth must be known before the process can be said to have worked, though achieving clarity is not easy. Fernando Atria adds, "reconciliation may reveal us to ourselves."[10] It may, however, need a long interval before more of the truth can be faced by op-

---

4. Veitch, *Law and the Politics*; Bongardt and Würstenberg, *Versöhnung*; Daly and Sarkin, *Reconciliation in Divided Societies*; Keogh and Haltzel, *Northern Ireland*; Johnstone, *Restorative Justice*, and only recently coming to my attention, a very thorough discussion in Philpott, *Just and Unjust Peace*. For a brief critical appraisal of Philpott, see Downing, "Reconciliation, Politics and Theology."

5. Schaap, "The Time of Reconciliation," 9, 15; cf. Daly and Sarkin, *Reconciliation in Divided Societies*, 1–15.

6. Foster, "Anglo-Irish Relations," 22.

7. Daly and Sarkin, *Reconciliation in Divided Societies*, 49.

8. Bankowski, "Cost," 51; cf. Bhandhar, "Spatialising History," 94–95.

9. Miller, "Revising Revisionism," 60.

10. Daly and Sarkin, *Reconciliation in Divided Societies*, 52–56, 69–70, 142–52; Atria, "Reconciliation and Reconstitution," 40; Tutu, *No Future Without Forgiveness*, 92–52.

pressors and their heirs: Stefan Rinke on post-Pinochet Chile and, Walther Bernecker, on post-Franco Spain.[11]

But this then prompts me to ask, if we accept, as Paul says, that those "outside" come with hostility needing dispelling, how might they/we state their/our cause against God, articulating our hostility? Paul does not elaborate. The nearest classical antecedents I can find to this issue lie in complaints in some of the Psalms (e.g., 44), or in Job (e.g., 9, 13). In the ninth century "The Good Friday Reproaches" appear: "My people, what have I done to offend you?"[12] And this might seem to suggest God offering us atonement, a thought I shall touch on briefly in the final chapter. I would guess, however, that for Paul the cause was human failure to appreciate God, and he would not blame God for that (cf. Rom 9:14).

Claire Moon (citing Tutu) insists on reparation for harm done, with individul therapy-by-truth necessary but not sufficient. Atria also urges that full reconciliation involves at least some reversal of harm suffered.[13] Reports on life in South Africa, May 2014, suggest that restorative justice is still barely noticeable for many. Yet it is readily arguably that the punitive "reparations" demanded of Germany in 1919 constituted an important factor in the rise of Adolf Hitler. Victors' vindictiveness may well have helped to make life worse than it arguably might have been for the entire next European and wider generations, pre-eminently European Jews and Roma, but millions more as well. It was by not asking too much from the beneficiaries of oppression that some of the worst excesses of apartheid were ended. And perhaps postponing even truth-finding, in Spain and then in Chile, had even better results.[14] "Peace trumps justice" Jonathan Friedland argued very recently. This might sound too counter-intuitive to many.[15] But eschewing a strict justice today that might ensure, or, at least, risk worse suffering for generations to come, might be a better statement of the aim. There seems to be no risk-free option. In seeking to halt the "spiral of violence" one may indeed leave quite unreformed oppressors with power to reinstate it.[16] At

11. Rinke, "Die Gegenwart"; Bernecker, "Vergangenheitsaufarbeitung."

12. In the Orthodox liturgy, thence in the Catholic west; retained, I gather, by Lutherans, only last century by Anglicans.

13. Tutu, *No Future Without Forgiveness*, 55; Moon, "Reconciliation as Therapy," 180–82; Atria, "Reconciliation and Reconstitution" 42; cf. Daly and Sarkin, *Reconciliation in Divided Societies*, 123–49; Johnstone, *Restorative Justice*, 11, 33.

14. It was disappointing that Gerhard Werle ("Völkerstrafrecht," 130–31) discussed the 1919 Versailles Treaty only for its significance in the development of justice between nations. On Spain and Chile, see n. 10.

15. Friedland, "Whatever Gerry Adams' Past."

16. Cf. Gauck, "Gerechtigeit"; on the spiral, Bongardt, "Endstation Strafe?" On

best, it is a matter, one might say, of making some concessions to what was tantamount to blackmail in all three cases, but in the hope of gaining some worthwhile concessions for the oppressed and their descendents.

Paul, of course, insisted that the holy, just, and good aims of the Sinai law, the at-one-ment of God and humans, could only be fulfilled by God justifying, not by punishing, the ungodly. Yet, while Paul assumes punishment would have been warranted, Jesus in the Synoptic Gospels relieves sufferers of illness seen as punitive, without troubling to evaluate the diagnosis.

Be it noted, Ralf Wüstenberg makes a cogent contextual distinction between the dismantling of the DDR (East German communist regime), and the retention of sullied police, judiciary, and army in South Africa. In the former case, West German structures were on hand to be introduced; in the latter, there were no alternatives available.

In the light of discussions of reparation for harm done, to what harm from our enmity might we actually imagine God to be susceptible, and actually to have suffered? Could raising this issue still prompt "satisfaction" understandings of atonement? For Paul God overcomes our enmity; but does that still imply that he might want more from our side than our friendship henceforth? Paul does not say so; but perhaps some still might: see further, just below.

And then, if reconciliation is a process, is it only meaningfully termed "reconciliation" when it is an at-one-ment as full as hoped for? Thomas Hoppe persuasively insists not just on socio-enomic integration, but the healing of ancient psychological traumas.[17]

It would seem, from these essays, that to consider reconciliation as a possible project already betokens a self-committing movement towards it, so that, in effect, it is already on the way (with no success guaranteed). Is that what we are we to make of Paul saying "God was, in Christ, reconciling the world to, at-oneing the world with himself." Did Paul really mean God was in some sense achieving it even before humans responded, and with no guarantee that many or even any would accept?

Donald L. Horowitz introduces "zero-sum" isues of relative status, and Stewart Motha asks what the program may imply without saying it: how reconciliation can avoid (sometimes renewed) domination, "victor's justice": so I ask, if the initiative is with God, do we simply surrender, or may we expect

---

making things worse, leaving the US supported army in charge, one might cite Egypt after Hosni Mubarack, on the cost of instantly purging the old, the murderous chaos of Iraq.

17. Cf. Beeman and Mohoney, "Churches and the Process," 150–59; Hoppe, "Erinnerung."

God to treat us as partners (even if not equals)?[18] Gerry Johnstone asks how productive in social experience is deeply shaming, humiliating the offender, so that no sense of self-worth remains.[19] Paul (and others) talk of God inviting a bold Godward approach, not imposed terms of humiliating surrender, even if much Christian teaching has seemed to encourage grovelling penitence.[20] Intriguingly, Lorna McGregor notes that reconciliation may well bypass law and necessitate its transformation—with which compare Karin van Marle. Peer Zumbansen proposes that reconciliation demands the creating of a whole new language, and Festo Mkenda and Louise den Toit would agree, in light of past convention where women engaging in public politics were seen as making themselves common property, rather than "reconciling" themselves to their domestic subordination.[21]

None of these, I note, suggests "revelation" of either party to the other as the start or means of reconciliation, and some explicitly or at least effectively reject it. It is the argument of this book that divine self-revelation, or considerable progress towards it, may nonetheless be seen as the goal.

Before moving on to theologians' use of such terminology, it is necessary to clarify a term so far unmentioned, but related in English translations of the German *Versöhnung*. *Versöhnung* in theological talk is rendered, sometimes indifferently, either as "reconciliation" or as "atonement." In common English usage, the latter means "atoning for," "to give satisfaction or make reparation (*for*)."[22] Atonement as "making one, reconciling, are obsolete" aver the lexicographers. In Ian McEwan's novel, *Atonement*, later a film, "atonement for" is attempted, perhaps to the offender, Briony's own satisfaction, but there is no reconcilation with those offended—only, and just possibly, of Briony with herself.[23] It was then encouraging to find Wüstenberg paraphrasing *Versöhnung* with *Einigung, Vereinigung*, "uniting, unification."[24]

18. Horowitz, "Conflict and Incentives," 175; Motha, "Reconciliation as Domination."

19. Johnstone, *Restorative Justice*, 97–108.

20. So, e.g., Williams, *Revelation and Reconciliation*, 155–56: "seeking restoration, penitence, admission of guilt."

21. McGregor, "Reconciliation;" van Marle, "Constitution as Archive"; Zumbansen, "Transnational Law"; Mkenda, "Language, Politics"; du Toit, "Feminism"; Okure, "Church-Family." Against these authors, Philpott, *Just and Unjust Peace*, gives a strong, secular argument for retribution.

22. *Chambers Dictionary*, 2003; cf. OED, 1956.

23. McEwan, *Atonement*. Myra Hindley, convicted of cruel murder, after thirty years in prison, pleaded publicly, "I have paid my debt to society, I have atoned for my crime"; quoted, by Gorringe, *God's Just Vengeance*, 33.

24. Wüstenberg, "Gibt es eine Politik?" 101, 103.

Although there are debates for and against punitive justice in the discussions touched on above, there is no suggestion there that awareness of penal punishment suffered itself "atones" for it in the minds of the victims; but neither does "having paid the penalty," on its own, reconcile the parties involved, even though penitent confession may help. When Paul uses language that is clearly metaphorical ("redeeming," "liberating," "expiating," or "propitiating," "adopting," "cancelling an account," "sacrifice,") does he seem to intend a suggestive metaphor? Or is it rather, as some have argued, a precise explanatory analogy, one he can take for granted will be understood by all (Jew and Gentile, learned and unschooled), in just one and the same detailed way? It might be possible that this is what he meant by assuring his Corinthian hearers that "we [unlimited] have the mind of Christ" (1 Cor 2:16). Or, perhaps, Paul's Greek words "mean" whatever we choose to make them mean. Our "secular" authors seem rather more determined to echo shared common open usage, avoiding any precise, stipulative definitions of the terminology. However, we now turn explicitly to current instances of theological usage.

(ii) Reconciliation as Atonement: Theological Usage

As already emphasized, I am reading Paul on "reconciliation" as a matter of being made by God at one with God. If (which I doubt) there is in Paul any thought of Christ "atoning for" our hostility, it is incidental to "at-one-ing." Being made at one with God by God is the point of what he is saying here, and is what he elaborates in other positive terms elsewhere. He talks, for instance, of being put right with God in a trusting and faithful receptivity, of peace with God, of accepting God's acceptance of us—and that without even waiting for our repentance, let alone penitence. (This understanding of Paul will be elaborated in chapter 4, and will be taken up again in chapter 7, but has already been addressed in some detail by me elsewhere.)[25]

So, then to general theological usage: for sure, to repeat, there is no *a priori* reason why Christian or other theologians should be bound by wider, common, "secular" usage. But if they/we wish to be understood, and to understand one another, they/we do well to diverge only intentionally, with warning, and for good reason, and into a use that is coherent, and whose

25. See Downing, "Justification," esp. 317–18; similarly, Tanner, *Christ the Key*, 86. Paul notably makes little if any use of such other "backward-looking" terms as "forgiveness." On all this, see the clear distinction between "atonement for" and "reconciliation" in Gorringe, *God's Just Vengeance*, and "judicial punishment"; and in Atherton, *Public Theology*, 66–90; but without considering that "at-oneing" might be a better term in translations of Paul than is "reconciliation."

distinctiveness is throughout made clear to readers and hearers (and the author, her- or himself). In practice, of course, there is a range of usage among theologians, as in the "secular" examples, but with rather less sensitivity.

There is no room here for a history of theological usage, though further examples from post New Testament times will be presented in chapter 5. Here, as a preliminary, we may note that in his *Adversus Haereses*, Ireneus (late second/early third century CE), while not, I think, talking of reconcilation as such, speaks of the "recapitulation" of "man's" original relationship with God (with Genesis 1–3 taken as factual), and so sets (or confirms) the basis on which any future Christian talk of reconciliation would see it, as restoration, re-creation, not new creation.[26]

Coming abruptly then, to today by way of late-ninetenth-century Europe: Albrecht Ritschl, an influential instance, rejected talk of "original sin," and therefore reconciliation as restoration to a once positive relationship. His German word *Versöhnung* with its background in *Sünde*, "offense," involving guilt, is, as just noted, nonetheless taken by him and other German language theologians to cover both "atoning for" and "at-one-ing." The latter, (re-)creating unity, it would seem is there under the influence of the Reformers', and later continuing use of the Vulgate *reconciliare*, even though Ritschl bases his own exposition on Johannine talk of unity with God, rather than on Paul's use of *katallassō, katallagē*.[27] Ritschl also often emphasizes the importance for his theology of "the dispensation of revelation," for instance in the same context as discussing "life in fellowship with God, at peace with God," but only once does he seem to connect them as interdependent. This is in talk of Christ as our representative "displaying, as the Revealer of God, the grace and truth—the love of God to sinners—which purposes their reconciliation without first having to be evoked by the human merit of the Mediator." Here Christ at the same time acts as our representative for our reception of the forgiveness "which God first guarantees by Christ's grace and truth."[28] The connection asserted, of revelation with at-one-ing, seems neither elaborated nor further explained.

A fairly similar (re-)interpretation was proposed in 1966 by John Macquarrie, arguing that "reconciliation is [timelessly, it seems] the highest providential activity of God . . . the activity by which the disorders of existence are healed, its imbalances redressed, its alienations bridged over. . . . It is not that at a given time God adds the activity of reconciliation. . . . Rather

---

26. Ireneus, *Adv. Haer.* 3.23.

27. Ritschl, *The Christian Doctrine*, 328–29, with 71–75 (from ET of *Die christliche Lehre von der Rechtfertigen und Versöhnung*).

28. Ibid., 501, 551.

it is the case that at a given time there was, in Jesus Christ's life and ministry, a new and decisive revelation of the activity that had always been going on." However, it is only that revelation that makes us aware and so allows us to believe it (and take advantage of it, "realize it"?).[29] (Again, his own version of the Christian story, myth, is taken as objective, factual, without evidence adduced.)

Karl Barth, in his massive *Church Dogmatics*, agrees with Ritschl on some things, for instance, that only with revelation in Christ was the reality of human sin revealed. But he emphatically insists that reconciliation in Christ restores a covenant, a harmony that once obtained, but was broken:

> "Reconciliation" is the restitution, the resumption of a fellowship that once existed . . . the maintaining, restoring and upholding of that fellowship in the face of an element which disturbs and disrupts and breaks it. . . . Jesus Christ is the atonement [reconciliation, *Versöhnung*]. But that means he is the maintaining and accomplishing and fulfilling of the divine covenant . . . as such he is also the revelation of the divine will and therefore of the covenant. . . . In his own person he is the eschatological sovereign act of God who renews men and summons them to obedience by forgiving their sins.[30]

Only by this revelation "can it be known to be true that peace is given to man and he can have it."[31] (How we can be held to have broken a covenant of which we are only made aware when it has been patched up—and that only, if vitally, restored in the person of Jesus remains unexplained. Words are there, it seems, to do what the user wants.)

For more recent modern exploration I shall again rely for the following sequence on a collection of essays: *The Theology of Reconciliation*, edited by Colin Gunton. These pieces are also supplemented in what follows from a fair number of other authors.[32]

Christoph Schwöbel speaks of reconciliation as "the re-establishment of the originally intended relationship between God and his creation," without telling how and where it ever actually obtained, and that is despite his insistence earlier, and again here, on "new creation." For sure, it is insisted, God in Christ does more than reveal his loving and forgiving attitude towards his creation; but God's reconciling the world to himself "is dependent

29. Macquarrie, *Principles*, 246–47; 251.

30. Barth, *Church Dogmatics* 4.1, 22, 35.

31. Ibid., 83.

32. Gunton, *The Theology of Reconciliation*. As noted above, in Bongardt and Würstenberg, *Versöhnung*, the theologians take better note of secular usage.

on God's disclosure of Christ as the one in whom God has reconciled the world to himself." Other believers may well agree that "appropriation" is essential, but it is not explained how making something happen can depend on showing-for-appropriation that it has happened already. Gunton firmly approves both "re-establishment" and "revelation," though none of the other contributors make this link.[33] Interestingly, only Stephen Williams, among those consulted, insists on penitent admission of guilt as a precondition for reconciliation.[34]

The "objectivity" of God's reconciliation of the world, making human/humankind at one with the divine self in Christ, is widely agreed by Roman Catholic and Protestant theologians alike.[35] How such very different accounts refer to, identify the same activity of the same deity, is not made clear—nor, really, how these theological language games relate to one another, and to wider usage, other than that they evince and invite a high level of commitment to their deployment. Were you to imagine that talk of God reconciling the world to himself expressed commitment to reconciliation with all who accepted God's invitation, becoming at one together, you would probably be told not to be silly. It means be reconciled to God in our way if you want to be at one with us to be at one with him.

Douglas Campbell cogently advises readers to be aware of the all-or-nothing quality of Paul's rhetoric in Gal 3:26–28, on being made "one in Christ," without reference to how and how quickly. That is left unexplained, even though this appropriation (my term) can be found in and balanced by other thinking in Paul, especially Rom 5–8, and previously outlined at Gal 5:5, 16–18; 6:1–10.[36] Having praised Barth on reconciliation, Douglas Farrow critically supplements that account, emphasizing "at-one-ing" as the work of the incarnate ascended Christ, in a Levitical, priestly way, "to bring man and God 'to friendship and concord', presenting man to God and revealing God to man," but without, on my reading, explaining how we become any part of what is taken as done for us.[37] (And, if all this is "revealed," how could it be so unclear to an admired fellow Christian such as Barth?)

33. Schwöbel, "Reconciliation," 21–22, 31–32, 35; Gunton, "Introduction," 2, and "Towards," 172.

34. Williams, *Revelation and Reconciliation*, 155–56, again, "seeking restoration, penitence, admission of guilt."

35. Stewart, "Reconciliation," 129; Sauter, "Reconciliation," Fiddes, "Salvation," 178; McGrath, *Christian Theology*, 317–18; Towey, "Introduction."

36. Campbell, "Reconciliation in Paul," 52, 57–58. On appropriation and God's continuing activity, cf. Fiddes, "Salvation."

37. Farrow, "Ascension and Atonement," 85–86.

Murray Rae raises the issue of appropriation: the finality of God's accomplishment in Christ (as insisted on by Barth) notwithstanding, "it is also the case that the reconciliation of the world in Christ involves—through the continuing event of divine grace—the Spirit inspired but very human event of response and new life." For sure, our response is admitted to be far from perfect, but Christ our high priest (as in Farrow) intercedes with the Father for us. Yet that still leaves the puzzle: how does our imperfect and disunited response tell the world that it is reconciled to, at one with God, as Rae focally proposes?[38] One might have hoped that John Webster, on "The Ethics of Reconciliation" might have enlightened us here, taking up as he does Rae's theme of the church as (effective) witness. Instead he simply criticizes Miroslav Volf on learning how to live at peace "in the absence of final reconciliation." For Webster it seems more important that the theology affirms "reconciliation done" than attend to the discordances in actual Christian response—appropriation—let alone in the adversarial, even hostile varieties among our affirmations

Teresa Okure's pastorally minded critique of her large Roman Catholic part of God's church's performance seems much more relevant than Webster's defense of formal theological propriety.[39] Her discussion is aptly rooted in shared and recorded social happenings, in a culturally varied continent. Meeting the same criteria, Sue Patterson (happy with Volf) is perhaps more helpful than others in Gunton's collection in accepting the need for and urging the use of imagination, and so of appropriate action. In particular she argues that we should act in the light of the "cultural constructs of 'man' and 'woman'," "as if" our oneness in Christ were real in our own practice: a sort of pragmatic "virtue ethic," perhaps.[40] A process of reconciliation, making one with God, is usefully elaborated by Robert Schreiter (picked up by John Atherton).[41]

Robert Jenson offers a Trinitarian trust in God as affording a model of unity in distinctiveness, and a unity into which we are drawn in Christ. The "re-" would, however, seem otiose: there is no suggestion here of "reconciliation" entailing a prior breach in God: the secular usage is taken for granted.[42] In the final chapter Gunton allows that full reconciliation is to come, eschatological; a proviso and reserve missing in much of the forego-

---

38. Rae, "A Remnant People," 94–95, 104–8.

39. Webster, "The Ethics of Reconciliation," 114; Okure, "Church-Family."

40. Patterson, "Between Women and Men," 126, 138.

41. Schreiter, *The Ministry of Reconciliation*, 14–19; Atherton, *Public Theology*, 18–19.

42. Jenson, "Reconciliation in God."

ing, save perhaps implicit in Patterson (certainly not warranting a mention in the collection's index).[43]

It is borne in on me that the theologians' emphasis on the "objectivity" of reconciliation in Christ distracts them disappointingly from the complexities of human responses to, appropriation of, offers or suggestions of reconciliation. Issues in inter-human reconciliation (with or without an acceptance of the Spirit's part in that), are analyzed far more sensitively, it would seem, by the "secular" lawyers and others instanced. It has also been much harder to find anything meeting the criteria outlined in the previous chapter—much harder than with the "secular" authors (and that, despite the latters' reliance on an explicitly theological theme). Stephen Williams does attempt to offer an imaginary secular case study of inter-human reconciliation, but he seems to have felt bound to forge one with anguished pain as the cost of atonement, ignoring alternative pain-free scenarios.[44] (In some Western Christian dogmatic apologetics, it is not the whole "Christ event" that is the base for reconciliation. Rather it is the heart and center of reconciliation in the final hours, the most painful of part of Jesus' life as narrated. Pain is taken to be needed to "atone for" sin, and only so, achieve reconciliation of God and humans.)

Let us take it that we do accept with Paul that God indeed was reconciling the world to God's self in and/or through Christ, in some meaningful sense. Then how is it that those who claim to be Christians are so poorly reconciled to each other, that they may rarely if ever meet together and talk amicably with those from whom they diverge theologically, and will not even share the eucharistic meal together? How is it possible to be at one *with God* and not in practice with one another (1 Jn 4:20)?

Here I take up again a familiar motif: Does not the insistence on having received divine revelation itself encourage each group to imply if not say out loud, "We have been given revelation, revealed truth of how to be one with God. So any who disagree with what we insist has been given to us must be wrong. They remain outside, still at odds with God. We mustn't tamper with the revealed truth received, we can't compromise." The plausible conclusion is that "revelation" as something already received may itself constitute a major barrier to unity, to being in practice "one in Christ." A conviction of divine self-revelation already seems in practice to stand in the way of reconciliation enjoyed in common exploration, open to mutual transformation, moving towards being prepared for a fuller and richer awareness of the God who draws us.

43. Gunton, "Towards a Theology," 172–74.

44. Williams, *Revelation and Reconciliation*, 155–56, again.

(b) "Self"

(i) "Self": Common Usage

The term "self" received no explicit treatment in *Has Christianity?*, nor, for that matter, did "soul." The focus was on persons, and persons in relationships. John Macmurray's *The Self as Agent* had been published in 1957, but was not referred, to even though the main topic was an appraisal of the "self-revelation" of God. Macmurray in fact concentrates mostly on "the ego," and on the persistent emphasis on the "I" as thinker, as "thinking substance" in early modern reflection (Descartes and then Kant, with enrichment from Kierkegaard). Charles Taylor, in his *Sources of the Self*, proposes Augustine as the effective forefather of modern elaboration of "the self" as a distinct topic for reflection, distinct enough to demand a term like modern English "self" (and not just "soul"), if with a late acknowledgement of such as Epictetus as Augustine's forebear. Others and I, however, have since argued for a much wider and richer ancient argument for there being *"in some effective sense a self, an 'I,' that is at least potentially other than its feelings and capable of being in control of them rather than controlled by them (or by any other externality."*[45]

As with the other main topics discussed in this chapter, I have consulted a fairly recent set of half-a-dozen varied essays on the theme in today's world: Galen Strawson's collection *The Self?* (2005). From there I quote:

> It is very natural for us to think that there is such a thing as the "self"—an inner subject of experience, a mental presence or locus of consciousness that is not the same thing as the human being considered as a whole. The sense of the self arises almost irresistibly from fundamental features of human experience, and is [in] no sense a product of "Western" culture, still less a recent product of it, as some have foolishly supposed.
>
> This does not settle the question of whether there is such a thing; or, if there is, the question of its nature . . . all six [contributors] allow there is or could be such a thing as the self.[46]

That there is this agreement, among the contributors and more widely is factual: both claims can be and are justified. But I confess that I do not

---

45. Macmurray, *The Self as Agent*; Taylor, *Sources of the Self*; Downing, "Persons," and "Order within," citing the latter, 83, original italics; on ancient thought see also the essays in Crabbe, *From Soul to Self*, especially Sorabji, "Soul and Self."

46. Strawson, *The Self?*, vi. On "self" as not culturally specific, see also Crabbe, *From Soul to Self*. Neither Dainton, "The Self and the Phenomenal," nor Perrson, "Self-Doubt," nor van Inwagen, "The Self," in Strawson, *The Self?* cites common usage.

see much point in discussing various possible "factual" "thingynesses" of "self" when clearly "it" or "the meaning of the term" is so ill-defined. There is certainly no place for a distinct "self" module in current modular brain theory; even "self-monitoring" may be seen as a function of the general "mind-" (intention) reading module; and that in turn is only one aspect of the subject matter of self-talk.[47] Rather than trying to identify a reference to some "thing" we might be talking about, much more interesting, I suggest, is accepting that we do use the word and seem able to take our varied distinctive usages, and their common and their distinctive features, as topics for discussion and a basis for action, including shared action. (There might even here be a place for "descriptive metaphysics.")[48] I've not found any suggestion that "self" can be used as a metaphor for something else; but, in effect, it is deployed as "suggestively" as metaphors can be, as able in use to evoke wide-ranging reflections. So, in line with the previous chapter, I move straight to "use," picking up some of discussions of (self-)identity, identifying oneself, identifying as, identifying with.[49]

"At the sound of an unexpected footfall, the intruder conceals himself behind a curtain, but, losing his balance ever so slightly, disturbs the drapery. He hears a swift intake of breath from the newcomer, warning him that he may well have revealed himself." His "self" each time is his physical presence, not yet even his specific identity (as hidden friend or as hidden foe), let alone his particular purpose. That is hardly appropriate for any post-Enlightenment talk of divine self-revelation.

However, someone reading a local UK newspaper's account of a man in a macintosh "revealing himself" will probably take it that he displayed his genitals. That is all, the only fact at issue. One might be tempted to speculate, infer, that at the time the culprit thought his genitals the only possible source of attentive recognition by a fellow human being. So the act might seem to suggest a little more about him, his sense of self, but that speculation would demand more investigation, and, even if validated, would factually tell one still very little about the man as a person, how important his genitals were in his entire self-identity. Again, not a likely model for God-talk.

"Who made that silly noise?" barks the unpopular school teacher. The culprit refuses to identify herself. Her friends characteristically identify with

47. Carruthers, *The Architecture of the Mind*, 178–83.

48. As, of course, do all those cited here. Fraassen, "Transcendence of the Ego," 110, considers "thing," "substance," but rejects it.

49. I think all the disscussions of divine self-revelation in Dalferth and Rodgers, *Revelation*, would usually have been better served by talk of a deity identifying his otherwise undisclosed self as the agent in particular events, including the giving of a name by which he may be addressed, as at Exod 3:13–15. See further, chapter 3.

her rather than with their baffled teacher, and offer no suggestion; but a pair of downcast eyes and a crimson blush can be very revealing. She inadvertently identifies herself as the source of the noise, while still revealing nothing more than that of her complex self as such. Still little help.

A young woman, A. K. Summers, "always had a butch identity, but could not express it in the 1980's [US mid-west]. 'I didn't know any gay people at all,' she says. 'At the time, it seemed I would never be able to reveal myself—that deeply closeted adolescence makes you really fearful.'" In the newspaper piece the "self" is her identity as a (butch) lesbian, and just (though importantly) that. It is only in the rest of th article that she goes on to disclose in some detail much more of herself to the interviewer.[50] One always has to look carefully for the extent of "self" intended.

We hear, in a somewhat fraught conversation, "The trouble with you is, you're always thinking about yourself." We are, I imagine, more likely to take it as a complaint against a failure to take note of others' needs and wishes, always insisting on her own. We are probably not worried about her persistent meditative "introspection," or at her puzzling over the phenomenology of selves, when she might be attending to her designated study of astrophysics.

In her "Self Expression and Self Control" Marya Schechtman observes,

> It is a commonplace that people are sometimes "not themselves." Frequently this is said to happen when the usual control mechanisms of self-control are compromised—when someone is drunk, for instance, or under a great deal of stress. Strangely enough, these are precisely the circumstances under which it is also often said that people are "most fully themselves" or "reveal their true natures."[51]

As her title indicates, she sees both expression and control as "aspects of what it means to be a self." They inter-link, for you may control your self-expression to fit the person you want to be (or to be thought to be), or you may let yourself go. Is one of these your "true self"? How is one to tell? Vestiges of her or his "old self," aspects pleasing and/or unpleasing, may be discerned in someone suffering from dementia. It can be difficult to quantify their respective significances. And, of course, someone may express a great deal of himself, deliberately or accidentally—and yet be misunderstood, mis-interpreted. What is expressed may not in fact reveal him to others: may not reveal him very far, or not at all, even if he intends it to (and he may

50. Cochrane, "Pregnancy."

51. Schechtman, "Self-Expression," citing 45. Her themes touch on those of Downing, "Order within," noted and cited above.

not). Regarding someone's self-revelation, how much of that person do we take to have been made knowable or known?

"How much of God has God revealed?" does not seem a very fruitful question.

In his recently published Gifford Lectures, *The Face of God*, philosopher Roger Scruton in effect links self, self-revelation, and self-concealment, with passing reference to the often-cited reflections of Emmanuel Levinas together with Paul Grice: "I lie *behind* my face, and yet I am present in it, speaking and looking through it at a world of others who are in turn both revealed and concealed like me."[52] But when he comes to talk of "seeking God's face," it seems to consist in searching for a sense of God's affirming presence to be given, "revealed": not a deep self-exposure.[53]

Urge someone, "Tell me about yourself," and (I find), I hear a story, usually quite brief, and selective, a C.V.: age, marital status in an adult, birth family in a younger person, education (perhaps), current paid occupation, depending on the setting, perhaps special interests. When I asked two elderly women friends, they related things they had recently done that they had probably not mentioned in other recent conversations: snippets of stories of the self as agent. A skilled psychoanalyst might, over many interviews, tease out a long and even evidenced story, amounting to full and penetrating "self-disclosure," and colleagues might offer very similar analyses. On the other hand, Galen Strawson argues determinedly against narrativity. While fully aware of its popularity in much discourse about "self," and allowing that he too might in that context mention things he had done, yet he insists that life and self are episodic. No agreed common narrative would be forthcoming.[54]

I accept that there may be divided selves: people with a clinically diagnosed "bi-personality disorder," say; or people who adopt multiple persona in different settings: home, work, club, solo behind a steering wheel (these were illustrated and discussed in the first chapter, section (b) on "reference" and identity). But usually we don't expect to have to ask, "Which self is it today?" or "just now?" Of anyone, and certainly of God, we would expect to find the sort of continuity that could afford a coherent narrative. A comprehensively revealing narrative history of a timeless God or even of the post Big Bang episode of God would seem implausible.

---

52. Scruton, *The Face of God*, 78.

53. Scruton, ibid., urges us to "regard the experience of community as a *preparation* for the experience of God, and the experience of God as a *revelation* granted in response to it." But different communities, including different Christian communities, differ in characterizing the ethos of the affirmation sought or itself affirmed.

54. Strawson, "Narrativity," 65, 83–84.

Discussing Hannah Arendt and Carol Gilligan among others, Seyla Benhabib, in her *Situating the Self*, argues against any notion of the "ideal" independent (male) ego, in favor of our varied formation in inescapably social interaction with one another: with those who, significantly, are in all probability, not transparent to one another.[55] But, clearly, this only works if we can, on the whole, depend on one another's at least general consistency, and mostly we continue to, despite occasional disillusionment. We may, if we are Trinitarian believers, imagine the divine persons as transparent to one another, and even in some sense formative of one another (though not all would allow that). But just that disagreement shows they are not transparent to us.

To my mind a telling illustration, bringing together much of the above, is afforded by Charles Dickens in his *Great Expectations*. As a little boy Pip has helped an escaped convict, Magwitch. Magwitch has rapidly built himself a new and prosperous life in Australia and becomes Pip's anonymous and distant benefactor, identifying himself with Pip as his gentlemanly alter-ego, in allowing him to grow up appropriately, someone with "great expectations." Pip meanwhile imagines the benefaction comes from the wealthy and respectable if eccentric Miss Haversham, whose ward, Estelle, he hopes he was becoming suited to woo and wed. Only three quarters' way through the book, when Pip is twenty-three, does Magwitch identify himself to Pip as his real benefactor—to Pip's initial but complete consternation, dashing all those great expectations. Thus they are united again, brought together—well, in the same room, in touch. But it takes much longer for Magwitch to tell his story, and much longer still for Pip to be become aware of and appreciate positively even something of his benefactor's real self. Only then is Pip reconciled to Magwitch as he is, as well as reconciled to the impact this disclosure of identity has on his own view of his propects—and of his own social self. Self-identification can be very significant, but may not constitute effective self-revelation: even though such self-revelation may come to pass, it need not.

Perhaps that helps us make sense of being at-oned by God's self with God, with God's self still far from revealed to us, while we on our side continue to grow into that conciliation, at-one-ment.

---

55. E.g., Benhabib, *Situating the Self*, 124–29, with reference to Arendt, *The Human Condition*; and Gilligan, *In a Different Voice*, 148–77.

(ii) "Self": Theological Usage

I have been unable to find any analysis of the use of "self" among those who assert the self-revelation of God, nor is clarity afforded me by the context. Is it one or more of the above uses, or something different again? Of course, the more elaborate and penetrating the disclosure claimed, the more vulnerable it is to discrepant accounts by others.

I confess I am not aware of much theological discussion in book form under the heading of "the self." John Macmurray's *The Self as Agent* (mentioned above) is written by a self-designated philosopher. His Gifford Lecture is, strictly speaking, an essay in natural theology. However, it is the first part of Macmurray's *The Form of the Personal*, whose second part is *Persons in Relation*. It is this latter terminology that mostly appears in recent theological discussions.[56]

The issue of justifying talk of "knowing" other people, including being in "deeply personal" relationships with others, was critically discussed and at length in *Has Christianity?*[57] Mostly we hope and trust that we are relating to the other as she or he is, the real probably quite fluid self, not some fiction he or she or we project on them, or attempt to mold them to.[58] We are confirmed in our sense of awareness of them as they are, rather than of some fiction, by being in physical contact with them, hearing what others around can hear, aware of facial expressions, a whole body-language.[59] We become, if willing, able to anticipate many of their initiatives and responses, and are not put out even by actions or reactions we might not have been able to forecast in detail, but that seem to us to fit, to cohere. Though unforeseen they are not "out of character." Animals form valued relationships with one another, displaying signs of mourning (wimpering, refusing food) or bereavement. Yet before that they are obviously accurately aware of each other's individuality, not surprising one another into alarm, anger, or cringing. This is what constitutes a "person-to-person," "I-Thou/Thou-I,"

---

56. For example, BCC, *The Forgotten Trinity*; Thatcher, *Truly a Person*; LaCugna, *God for Us*; Torrance, *Persons in Communion*; Coakley, *Rethinking Gregory*; Downing, "Patristic," and chapter 7, below.

57. Downing, *Has Christianity a Revelation?*, 195–200.

58. Welker, *God the Revealed*, 249, has a brief passage on holding together different impressions as of "the same" person much changed over time, as an analogy for trusting the Galilaean, risen, returning Jesus as the same Christ.

59. Cf. Fraassen: "I express and reveal myself through bodily features and movements: my posture, my physical comportment, my way of walking, my 'body language,' my interaction with my natural and social environment"; in his "Transcendence of the Ego," 98.

relationship. We humans can also be thoughtfully aware of, responsive to, others (and this sense at least, we can certainly "think" without words).

There are other tests for whether my relationship really is with her, or just with my ideal other. There I offered my own examples of projecting an image on another. Only in a footnote was I able to refer to a much stronger illustration provided by C. S. Lewis (under the pseudonym, as only later revealed, of N. W. Clerk):

> Already, less than a month after her death, I can feel the slow, insidious beginning of a process that will make the H. I think of into a more and more imaginary woman. Founded on fact, no doubt. I shall put in nothing fictitious (or I hope I shan't). But won't the composition inevitably become more and more my own? The reality is no longer there to check me, pull me up short, as the real H. so often did, so unexpectedly, by being so thoroughly herself and not me.

He added, a little later,

> Today I had to meet a man I hadn't seen for ten years. All that time I thought I was remembering him well—how he looked and spoke and the sort of things he said. The first five minutes of the real man shattered the image completely. Not that he had changed . . . But . . . they had all faded out into my mental image of him.[60]

As I wrote fifty years ago, of course, we simply do not have with God

> the sort of relationship that is objectively shaped by physical contact with the Other, and empirically verifiable from moment to moment by the accuracy of conscious and unconscious forecasts of moods and wishes. He does not, at present, offer himself to us in this way, the richest form of "knowing" a person. *We do not yet have an "I-Thou, Thou-I" relationship with God.*

We have to ask, still, do those who affirm God's self-revelation seem nonetheless to be responding to the same person known in penetrating detail? Or are they just affirming a trust in an indeterminate divine presence, individuality still undisclosed or only guessable?[61]

I also considered claiming to know a celebrity well, on the basis of news media reports, but argued that for that to be at all reliably intimate, some reports would still need to come from one or more in close physical contact.

---

60. Lewis, *A Grief Observed*, 18–19.
61. Downing, *Has Christianity a Revelation?*, 198.

And it would still not be I-Thou-Thou-I. Another possibility canvassed at some length, but with which I am now even less happy, was a relationship with a pen-friend, taking Scripture and tradition as the "letters" from the other, as letters interacting with you their reader through the Holy Spirit. But there is so much room in any such literary relationship for reading what you want to read into it: witness disillusionment with Facebook friendships. And, as was argued in 1964,

> The greater the diversity of the groups to which [a Christian] allows the name Christian, the less his justification for saying they "know God," in any meaningful sense of the word; the less his justification for saying "God has made himself known." Then, the only way to justify a claim to "know God," a claim that "God had made himself known," is to restrict the list of the enlightened to a group that agrees together about "God" on as many major and minor issues as possible.

(I would now say, on all issues accepted as major.)[62]

Concluding the discussion of "self" in talk of "self-revelation" and "making oneself known," we can allow that the lack of definitive divine self-revelation leaves us free to imagine God's selfhood—and to argue about it, as in fact we do. Do we choose to imagine God as "a person," or, at least, as "personal"; or do we prefer to talk of God as "beyond personality"? And, preparing for the final chapter of this book, if we are happy to talk of God as "person" do we also talk of God as essentially "persons-in-relationship," Father, Son, and Holy Spirit (or Source of all being, Eternal Word, and Spirit of Life; or some other)? These may seem to be too anthropomorphic, human-shaped, for some, and insufficiently aware of more formal inherited alternatives. Yet one may as readily dismiss all the alternatives as also, indeed and inevitably, anthropomorphic in their own way: we only have human talk (including abstractions) in which to share thoughts, and behind that, culturally schooled thought modules. "Beyond personality" may betoken a caution against defining God too readily in simply human terms, but it may as readily betoken a retreat into infancy, or into autism, or into the independent male ego: all inescapably human.

62. Downing, *Has Christianity a Revelation?*, 203.

(c) "Revelation"

(i) "Revelation": Common Usage

The section on "revelation" in the 1964 study took thirty-two pages. There is no attempt to devote even that proportion (10 percent of the whole) to that again.[63]

"Reveal," "revelation" are used in secular talk and writing, and particularly as a fictional or autobiographical trope. But no secular monographs on such a topic have come my way, not even individual essays. I rely mostly on incidental instances in recent newspaper reports, articles, and reviews.

Colin Tudge, reflecting on his exposure to evolution as an explanatory model, recently wrote, "There was a sense of revelation . . . total understanding."[64] The model afforded, granted a life-shaping clear insight into how living things on our planet have come to be as they are. "Total understanding" of whatever is denoted, referred to, constitutes what one would expect to be intended when the term "revealed" is used. That is so, unless careful qualification is added, explicitly or by context, as to scope and quality of clarity conveyed. A revelation is not a hunch, "anyone's guess," but something claimed to be objectively given: here, an agreed basis for experimental checking. Such claims to givenness, objectivity, cannot be self-validating. Why should anyone accept them? Evolution as affording "total understanding" may have come as a revelation to Tudge, but it has not to many others of his and our fellow humans. Tudge knows that, and knows he has to provide evidence and arguments to support his claim to the model as "revelation," grant total understanding (as he does in this book and has done in others). Here usage seems common, there is no explicit or even implicit qualification, nothing asking for a separate dictionary definition of its "meaning." It is, in effect, a "dead" metaphor: no one feels the need to explain the covering, the curtain that did the concealing (though we may take it that the experience of something hidden becoming seeable and seen

---

63. As a guide, to any wondering whether to seek a stored copy, the sub-headings in *Has Christianity a Revelation?* (206–38) were: "Etymology"; "Literal and Metaphorical"; "Finality"; "Finality and ἐφάπαξ in the New Testament"; "The Initiative of the Agent"; "The Ambiguity of 'Revelation'" (in non-literal use, "the revealing" of "the matter made known"); "The 'Revealing' of Facts"; "'Propositional Revelation' and the Bible"; "(a) The Literal Content"; "(b) The Meaning"; "(c) 'Revelation' 'in' the Bible"; "(d) 'Revelation to 'Me'"; "(e) 'Self-Authenticating' 'Revelation'"; "'Revealing' 'Partially', 'Gradually', or 'of a Mystery'"; "Can Talk of 'God' be barely Propositional?"; "'The 'Revelation' of 'God' as 'Person'"; "What is Left to Say of Communication between God and Man?" SCM, I was told, *might* reprint (by scanning) on demand.

64. Tudge, *Genes are Not Selfish*, 56.

is universal.) It is/was with some reluctance, then, that it seemed/seems still necessary to look at a whole range of actual and possible twists and turns in attempts to make the term serve in theological discourse.

The next five examples are from *The Guardian*, a London newspaper.

> The first official government admission that Iain Duncan Smith's flagship plans . . . has [*sic*] hit trouble emerged when the Cabinet Office's review of all major Whitehall projects branded the universal credit programme as having fallen into "amber-red" status. . . . This revelation came when the government for the first time published the performance of its 170 most expensive projects. . . . Data has [*sic*] been exempted from only 21.

The Major Projects Authority had in 170 cases published, revealed, all the data relevant to and substantiating its assessment.

In another example, "Angela Merkel has expressed contempt for the disgraced Anglo-Irish Bank executives caught on tape mocking Germany's involvement. . . . The Irish taoiseach . . . admitted after hearing Merkel's comments that this revelation had damaged Ireland's standing." The full release of the tape—available for anyone to hear or report to others to understand and assess its insight into the attitudes of some Irish bankers—is a revelation of a conversation and of its potential import.

More recently, the chair of the British parliamentary intelligence and security committee, in relation to disclosures by Edward Snowden concerning US and UK surveillance, spoke of them as "revelations," their truth widely uncontested. Their truth is supported by their being generally taken, by his committee and others, as "factual," at least in the sense of inter-subjectively agreed; factual, not imaginative fiction. To dispute their authenticity would be to cast doubts on any claim that they "revealed" anything relating to those surveillance practices.

In a quite different context Paul Ilett wrote, "And I must say, the quality of customer service you get when you are newly bereaved is something of a revelation." It came as a new insight, a surprise, but as something for which he then recounted supporting evidence. Here, obviously, the revelation is verbally articulated; but it may originally have occurred wordlessly.

"Heaney's last poem revealed," ran a front page headline: not just made seeable somewhere, but actually seen by some and there to be seen in that issue of the paper.

In another instance, an anonymous reader posted a comment on the novelist Ruth Rendall's website: "hers is often a slow reveal, by a narrator who knows the whole story and only releases the facts trickle by trickle." The whole story will be known when the last of the facts is revealed. "She is keeping us (each and every reader) guessing"—not misinformed, as such, but ill-informed. As a result, we meanwhile may guess differently, or simply rest puzzled. The whole story, the plot including salient aspects of the main characters, can for now only be conjectured—even if correctly conjectured. "I knew it!" perhaps says one reader, after the final disclosure. "I told you I did, well before the last chapter." In one usage of "know," perhaps. But suppose another reader responds, "You 'knew' it before the end of her last novel, but you were wrong." "Well, I was sure." You could not in any full sense validly claim to *know* the novelist's whole story until you had her version, and could clearly show others your guess was right.[65]

There is in strictest usage (see ch. 1) a distinction between being sure but not proving it, nor able to, and knowing-and-proving it (or, at least, able to show the reasons for your confidence). It is a fair question to ask in which sense "know" is being used. I can be confident and wrong, confident that that I really do know, and still be wrong. Confidence may be persuasive, it is not proof.

In one of his collection of essays on the poet John Clare, and here appraising him as a naturalist, Ronald Blythe observes, "We pour over Clare's scrappy autobiography finding every sentence a revelation not to be missed . . . 'This is who I am.'" Blythe then elaborates at the end of the essay: "Prose reveals his unusual intellect. it [sic] is strong, eloquent and candid." Aspects of character and ability, but specified, can be said to be individually revealed; it does not have to be the whole picture, but the elements in question are clear and indisputable. Thus, elsewhere, "Clare draws his own tombstone in his Journal, and reveals how depressed he is" at finding three men laying out the line for a railway through his countryside. To a visitor reflecting on that landscape, judged that "its unbroken tracts strained and tortured the sight," Blythe responds, "But not the poet's sight, of course. This it nourished and extended, its modest images proving to be, when properly seen, a full revelation of the human spirit and of nature."[66] What is potentially revelatory must remain so until there is a seer who, like Clare, has come to exercise a proper, an appropriate seeing.

Some of the above examples also remind us that "revealing" can be in someone else's gift, afforded by someone who does know. The decision of the current British government to allow disclosure of the progress of major projects was, at least at the time, an "act of grace," in contrast with previous

---

65. *The Guardian*, May 25th 2013, 8; June 29th, 2013, 38; Sept 21st, 2013, 8; Oct 26th, 1; and "Guardian Money," also Sept 21st, 1; "Review," March 3rd, 2013, 16; respectively.

66. Blythe, *John Clare*, 97, 101, 122, and 117.

governmental secrecy (however much this administration subsequently would resist the conclusions drawn from such revelations.)

I have still not found in ordinary usage any talk of fuzzy revelation, something still open to multiple interpretations becoming seeable let alone seen.[67] Nor have I noticed suggestions of a "progressive" revelation, nor yet of a paradoxical "veiled" revelation; nor, in fact, have I encountered assurances of "self-revelation." Doubtless, if there were such in secular talk, we could try to discern in context whether and if so how the speaker or writer clarified her or his intention, we would not assume it was nonsense. At least we might imagine what sense(s) might have been meant. Of "partial" we could ask which part or distinguishable parts; of progressive, can the progress be in any way quantified or assessed, and is it steady, is it without backsliding; can we gauge when, if ever, it will be complete? Of "self-revealing," how full, how detailed a revealing of "self," and then, how consistent a "self" does or will appear?

Suppose a group of neighbors meet in a bar. Each says he or she has been visited by someone who identified herself as an independent candidate in a forthcoming local election. One describes her, others chip in, and all agree, it was the same person. "She revealed her whole approach to life before touching on details." They all concur. "She is unreservedly in favor of immigrants." "No, only if fluent in English." "No, only to fulfill long-term job vacancies." "No, only from a short list of countries." "No, she's totally opposed to any." And so on, through a great list. How long before they agree only that "She's a typical politician, say anything for a vote, not to be trusted, doesn't even seem to know her own mind, if she has one. Or she refuses to reveal it?"

To reveal is to make seen, make known. "Spending three months working every day alongside her was a revelation." "Do specify," you urge. "Well, she was much more approachable than her reputation indicated. I felt I'd got to know her well." "I heard she was very prickly on environmental issues—quite unapproachable." "To be honest, we covered lots of ground, but not that. I touched on it, but got the impression, she couldn't care less." "On education?" "Oh, wide open, knowledgable." "I broached the baccalaureate, and she snapped my head off." How far would such discordant impressions have to go before the claim, "I felt I'd got to know her well!" would be withdrawn—or dismissed as opinionated obstinacy? As argued in the previous chapter, words can be—need to be—very flexible in communicative use, but to enable clarity not circumvent it.

67. As imagined in *Has Christianity a Revelation?*, 225–29.

In some instances it might be better to use "display," or even the rather archaic "manifest." "The Council's intention to close the footpath was revealed in a tiny handwritten notice pinned round the back of the sign post. Nobody saw it." It could surely be better put, "The Council's intention was poorly displayed in a tiny hidden notice. It was only revealed when the wind blew the signpost down, exposing the notice to a curious passer-by. It was badly displayed."

(ii) "Revelation": Theological Usage

Twentieth-century usage among Christian theologians up to around the 1960s was illustrated in the previous study, beginning with an instance from Karl Barth: "we are transposed into the greatest clarity: such clarity, that we make for ourselves very definite thoughts, clear in themselves, about what is being told us, that we can react to it with our whole inner and outer attitude in life."[68] William Nicholls was even more emphatic:

> Revelation means, then, that God of his own free will and because he loves us has drawn aside the veil that hides him from us, and has shown himself to us as he is. Just as we must not in any degree minimize the truth that revelation is God's act and not man's achievement, so we must not in any degree minimize the completeness of the act of revelation when it comes, for both errors minimize the love of God for men. God reveals *himself*.[69]

Not all would agree that what is revealed is itself clear. "What is mysterious cannot lose its mysteriousness even when it is revealed," asserted Paul Tillich (and a number of other near contemporaries' similar cautions were cited).[70] What benefit accrued was not discussesed. Thus, in setting his riddle, Samson revealed an enigma, a problem. It got no one anywhere till Delilah revealed its solution. Then and then only did the companions "know" (Jdg 14:10–18). Compare 1 Cor 13:12, again.

But there was a further problem. For some what God reveals is truths about himself; others insisted that "revelation" could not be "propositional." For such as Rudolph Bultmann and Paul Tillich the revelation is "really," "existentially," about ourselves, our self-understanding, the ground of our being.[71] For others it was person-to-person, "I-Thou." I argued then and

---

68. Barth, *Church Dogmatics* 1.1, 198.

69. Nicholls, *Revelation in the Christ*, 44; original emphasis.

70. Tillich, *Systematic Theology* 1, 121.

71. References in Downing, *Has Christianity a Revelation?*, 12–13.

still hold that in many human cases this is a false dichotomy: most of us use words-in-propositional-sentences about ourselves and one another as part and parcel of our personal relationships. The ability to articulate a relationship in words could in fact be integral to it, even if it need not be. But in our case, as Christians we expect to check with what others have expressed in words passed down in scriptural texts and in traditions of interpreting them, and in what others say and do about the relationship they claim. If we disagree in what we say *and do* in response to the God we claim has vouchsafed to us knowledge of himself, has revealed himself to us, there is surely something amiss. Either God is as inconsistent, incoherent as we are, or some of us are wrong. Or we all are mistaken, perhaps, to differing and mutually undecidable extents.

Nonetheless, I was able to cite a wide range (Catholic, Orthodox, Anglican, Protestant; Anglo-American, and European continental Christian) who agreed that divine revelation (whether about God or of God, and with many individual tweaks) was God's purpose in Jesus, as witnessed in the Christian canon of Scriptures (the New Testament, along with various versions of "the Old").

"Revelation" talk as encountered then, be it noted, was never about visual (or tactile, gustatory, or olfactory) experience. It was a matter of ideas and relationships that could be and were (massively) verbalized, shared, and evoked in words in print and sometimes spoken in sermons and lectures. It was—or, at least, risked being—intellectualist, cerebral, even in its most existentialist versions. For sure, "revelation" could be "witnessed to" in music and painting, as increasingly insisted by Barth, I gather, but still only as assessed verbally.[72] No more than the natural world around could the arts be in themselves revelatory. Yet we might well consider that, in many human situations, being reconciled, being at one with someone else, can be experienced, welcomed, cultivated without involving words at all. (Perhaps "poor little talkative Christianity," as dismissed by E. M. Forster's Mrs. Moore, need not be quite so garrulous.)[73]

Has much actually changed in Christian theological reflection on revelation (or reconciliation) over the recent half century? The most significant development was, it would seem, the Second Vatican Council, which was taking place while I was working on the book. The dogmatic constitution,

---

72. Begbie, many contributions in *Resonant Witness*, esp. Moseley, "Parables"; Bridge, *The Image of God*; MacGregor and Langmuir, *Seeing Salvation*; Pattison, *Art, Modernity, and Faith*; Brown, *Tradition and Imagination* and *Discipleship and Imagination*; Coakley, "Seeing God," chapter 5 of *God, Sexuality*, 190–265; and chapter 7 in this volume.

73. Forster, *Passage to India*, 148.

Dei Verbum, was promulgated by Pope Paul VI in November 1965. As Avery Dulles noted in 1983, previous Catholic reflection had been mostly apologetic. But *Dei Verbum* is very positively celebratory. "In his goodness and wisdom God chose to reveal himself . . . in Christ who is both the mediator and the fullness of revelation." There are reservations. "Through divine revelation God chose to show forth and communicate Himself and the eternal decisions of his will regarding the salvation of men . . . those treasures which totally transcend the understanding of the human mind." Yet God "can be known with certainty from created reality by the light of human reason . . . [and] through revelation . . . those religious truths can be known by all men with solid certitude and with no trace of error." Such assertions remain currently normative, and there are plenty of recent expositions for your computer search engine to offer. A quick leaf through recent Catholic and Anglican liturgical texts will show a marked increase in the deployment of "reveal," "revelation," and not only around festivals of Epiphany and Transfiguration.

J. L. Schellenberg's 1993 argument over divine hiddenness has occasioned a cluster of journal articles, especially in the relatively recent past.[74] These offerings have tended to concentrate on rebutting the argument that divine self-concealment (from the many) is itself loveless, with little attention to the issues of contradictory diversity Schellenberg also raised (and that I had done earlier in the journal *Religious Studies*, which has since carried much of this current debate.)[75] None that I have met welcomed the insistence that God does not appear to be revealed. (My own discussion constitutes chapter 6 here.)

As I tried to show in the Introduction, some passing attention has, however, been given to some of the issues I and others raised, and some theologians (in response or independently) have avoided such language altogether. In fact, I have not been able to find nearly as many fresh studies devoted to the place of the theme in the canonical texts and/or their interpretation, as were around fifty years ago. But many others (Bible translators, liturgists, and philosophers of religion of the "reformed epistemology" school, in particular) seem to have managed to avoid attention to these critical issues, or not found the arguments persuasive. It seems worth not just returning to them, but fundamentally recasting them, in the light of recent debates over language (summarized in the previous chapter), but also in the light of a wider appraisal of the canonical texts, and later theological reflections (chapters 3, 4, 5).

74. Schellenberg, *Divine Hiddenness*.
75. Downing, "Revelation."

The title I wanted for the earlier study was "Christianity without Revelation." But I was persuaded (and editors can be very persuasive with inexperienced authors) away from it, while allowed to make that the heading for my final chapter. I here offer a summary of some of the latter's main points.

I began with a disclaimer, which still serves:

> It is infuriating to be told that you may not say, 'almost perfect', 'almost complete', because 'something is either perfect or not, complete or not'. Everyone knows what is meant by 'almost perfect', 'almost complete', 'almost full' (even 'the larger half'). This essay is not attempting to impose such a piece of purposeless pedantry. . . . I have insisted, time and again, that 'reveal' *may be qualified,* and meaningfully. All that is demanded is that if the word is intended to express 'theological' (or other) truth, the qualifications should be carefully examined, so that both writer and reader, speaker and listener, may know as precisely as possible, what is being said. . . . the qualifications with which a realistic theologian finds he has to use the words 'reveal' and 'revelation' suggest he would do better, in company with the New Testament writers, to keep these words for the 'future consummation' (however that is understood), and just possibly for the physical seeing of Jesus of Nazareth, long ago.

(Recalling an earlier comment, very often in the New Testament writings "display" or the older "manifest" would be much more appropriate than "reveal." Jesus, God's Christ, God's Son, has been physicallydisplayed, and that has enormous significance: but a significance not handed on a plate, rather a significance to be explored: see, e.g., 1 Jn 1.1–2 with 1 Jn 3.2.)[76]

This was followed by a discussion of "natural" and "historically revealed" "knowledge of God," in the light of common Christian reliance on divine grace/graciousness, God's loving and generous initiative. In brief, a dichotomy of graceless nature versus graced history constitutes a specious limit on divine freedom to be gracious anywhere. Further, those who claim a given divine self-revelation seem to expect it to change people, in specified ways. But where, I ask still, does this seem to have happened to any significant extent in any at all extensive group in which the claim is made?

It had been and still is argued that any divine dealing with us without self-revelation would be lovelessly impersonal. This challenge is discussed

---

76. Cf. Kurek-Chomycz, "The Scent of (Mediated) Revelation," on φανερόω.

here at much greater length than it was then, in chapter 5, in debate with Schellenberg.[77]

(d) Knowledge

(i) Knowledge in Secular Discussion

"Revelation" in much if not all use—for metaphorical "unveiling"—involves claims to "knowledge" imparted. The discussion in the previous chapter takes account of contemporary epistemology, theory of knowledge, and is deployed in what follows.

All of my four sources on "epistemology (chapter 1) accepted that knowledge is to be understood as justified true belief, and discussed suggested ways of justifying assertions of belief so as to warrant using the terms in a full inter-subjectively shared way. Audi included a chapter on "social testimony," but only David Hamlyn of my four argued (with Wittgenstein) that agreement in judgement is necessary if not sufficient to warrant (not prove) claims to knowledge.[78] Audi examined theories of sensory perception in general, as warranting knowledge claims, including claims to religious knowledge, and neither ruled in nor out some "mystical" or more ordinary awareness, say, of God speaking, or just being present, asking only how one might discriminate between that and hallucination. Unfortunately he ignored the issue at the heart of *Has Christianity?* and is so again here: the difficulty of warranting belief in past or current divine (self-) revelation as affording knowledge, propositional or personal, of God in the light of its claimed recipients' disagreements among themselves.

(ii) Knowledge in Theological Discussion

Nicholas Walterstoff has stressed the useful distinction between "make known" and "make knowable," which I also made, but without the clarification that now follows. He and I both left the issue there, without asking how "made knowable" is itself to be validated. He instances "revealing a hiding place" in a then hidden document.[79] I would suggest we imagine that a novelist might suggest some such, and add, "but it was destroyed in the gas explosion." Well, the novelist "knows" that, as do careful readers to whom all

77. Downing, *Has Christianity a Revelation?*, 249–55, with reference to Farrer, "Revelation."

78. Audi, *Epistemology*, and Hamlyn, *The Theory of Knowledge*.

79. Walterstoff, *Divine Discourse*, 31 and 299, n.10.

this has been revealed. But if something is not actually known by anyone in the story, how are we to trust that it is "knowable" at all? In real life, only if the knowledge of the hiding place is gained, and the document found, is it "known" to have been even knowable.

Here I think the Qur'an, and Muslim theologians interpreting it, make more coherent sense than do many of my modern fellow Christians. As already noted, we are assured in the Qu'ran that nothing from God's side conceals God; the only veiling is ours, our ignorance, intransigence, refusal to learn, to comply with God's will. "Whithersoever ye turn, there is the face of God."[80] God is always available: there is no paradoxically "hidden revelation."[81] In the Qu'ran we are given a way to follow, in thought and action, that will change us so that we will be able to perceive God in everything, and come to love God. But nothing is transcendent enough to conceal God from God's side, it is only our obtuseness and stubbornness that curtains him from us. Yet, though Muslims may well believe this, and Christians might do well to concur, at present most if not all of us can still only trust that that is so. We will only "know" the hope as truth if and when we find the coherent and consistent words and actions of adherents who have fully allowed or achieved the transformation.

In actual fact, Paul, of course, much earlier, said something fairly similar, though limited to his situation. Any "veiling" is in the minds of those not allowing themselves to be transformed, as in 2 Cor 3:7—4:4, not in any metaphysical divine shyness. Gregory of Nyssa certainly reads Paul in this way: all of us Christians, not just Jewish contemporaries, have our awareness of God obscured by our own veil. It is that that needs to be stripped away.[82]

Sadakat Kadri has recently catalogued ways in which Muslem internal disagreements have historically multiplied, not least in the current sad and cruel conflicts between Wahabi Sunni factions and Shia. Thus Muslims in general are far from displaying appropriated unveiled access to one coherent deity as has appeared in the tale of Christians past and present.[83]

As already noted in the Introduction and in chapter 1, Timothy Gorringe (though without reference to Wittgenstein) validly objected, "Absence of a particular word from the biblical writings does not mean that the concept is not to be found in them."[84] In the chapters that follow (and despite my unease with "concept") I try to bear that caution in mind. What I shall

---

80. Arberry, *Sufism*, 17, citing Qur'an 2.109.

81. Barth, *Church Dogmatics* 1:2, 84–86, despite the insistence quoted on clarity.

82. Gregory, *Homilies*, 12–13 (Norris, 381–93; Jaeger, 360–73).

83. Kadri, *Heaven on Earth*.

84. Gorringe, *Discerning Spirit*, 8.

ask is whether other things are said that bear on the issue. In part response, I offer Mike Higton's procedure: to qualify any talk of "revelation," of "knowing God who is essentially unknowable," Higton has recently preferred to talk of God as one believed to "identify himself" in loving address, and that phrase, "identify oneself," already discussed above, will be taken up in chapter 3, but critically.[85]

That God had graciously identified himself in various ways, is, of course, what many humans have believed (and have believed they have discerned). In effect, the identification of a gracious (or, of course, malign) act is, observably, something that humans constantly do: they/we take this or that event or insight as a happening or an attitude, say, with which, they/we take it their/our God graciously (or punitively) identifies him/herself. Some Judaean theologians, at least by the fourth century BCE, identified God as graciously identifying himself as, say, the God of Abraham, Isaac, and Jacob, or punitively (and even justly) in the fall of Jerusalem and the Exile. And they take these as indicative in these respects of their God's character. The extent to which these are part of a coherent and fuller characterization of their God remains to be shown. For, as was pointed out in the previous chapter, "self-identification" may be significant, and importantly so, without necessarily implying an extensive revelation of one's true (or "inner") "self," one's character.

Any claim that one may gain knowledge of God from the Jewish and Christian Scriptures must take seriously the sense of the phrase as it occurs there. Anticipating the discussion of the biblical witnesses, which in this volume still lies ahead, I argue here just as I argued back then. Hebrew *yādā*, rendered as "know," seems to serve for something like "acknowledge appropriately," or, more fully, "have an awareness that elicits an appropriate response." There is much more implied in the use of the term than in normal English talk of "knowing" a person, or anything. Thus, a man "knows" his wife in appropriate sexual intercourse with her; a king "knows YHWH" in dutifully ensuring justice for the poor and needy.[86]

In the light of all this,

> Christians cannot claim *any* sort of "knowledge of God" unless they agree about him; they cannot really claim "knowledge of God" [in that biblical sense] unless they act without conflict on what they say they know of him. Nor, of course, till this has

---

85. Higton, *Christian Doctrine*, 31–52.

86. Gen 4:1; Jer 22:16; Downing, *Has Christianity a Revelation?*, 205–6.

happened, can it be said [in that biblical sense] that "God has made himself known."[87]

So, in life at large, we may say we know by revelation (certainly) that sexual relationships are of great concern to God, who has a clear mind on them, and that constitutes an important and integral part of God as a person. No, say some, God is above all that. Or, yes, God not only cares a lot about sexual relationships, but rejoices deeply in loving homosexual relationships. No, God merely tolerates them. No, God tolerates homosexual inclinations, but condemns any genital enactment of them. No, God condemns even the inclinations, and any who harbor them. Surely some of us are wrong, even if we are not all wrong. Some or all of us fail to know God's mind on the issue, and so have, at least here, a very poor grasp of what we style an important facet of the coherent divine mind. It, and God's mind there, have not been made clear, revealed. Or is our God as mixed up as we are? God seems unwilling to reveal definitively, conclusively, which if any is most nearly right and so indicative of the divine character. Even the list of issues we claim are of importance in the divine mind is not made clear, not revealed to us. Nor is the validity, say, of "the just war" (however defined), nor of the "free market," nor female subordination to males, nor whether God micro-manages us, nor of whether God rewards the faithful with physical and financial well-being, so shared disasters prove wickedness, nor whether God cares without intervening, perhaps in love leaves us to work it out among ourselves, remaining in practice quite impartial . . .

Or we wait in faithful impatience with ourelves at least until the transformation of some or all of us together into the likeness of the Son suffices. And then we shall know.

---

87. Downing, *Has Christianity a Revelation?*, 206.

3

Ancient Jewish Scriptures [1]

(a) Canonical Scriptures

As is commonly accepted, Christians claimed the Jewish Scriptures for their heritage. In ways (variously) interpreted by their leaders, these writings were formative and often explicitly taken as in some sense authoritative. For most they comprised the Septuagint (LXX) Greek translations of predominantly Hebrew documents. These dated in their extant forms, some from as late as the early second century BCE, and others from perhaps as early as the seventh (or earlier still, according to quite a number of scholars). In addition to these, the LXX contained a few scrolls that seem to have been composed in Greek. The whole amounted to a much larger set than the Hebrew canon determined by fourth century CE rabbinic authorities, and later recognized (but rearranged) by Protestant Christians since the sixteenth century Reformation as "The Old Testament." Alongside all these, the influence of other extant writings has been discerned and argued or at least considered as illustrative of "ideas in the air" at the time when the Christian New Testament writings were being composed.

> "Revelation implies for the Old Testament *the means God uses to make possible the knowledge of God for men.*" Some such claim about a "concept of revelation" in the Old Testament is often made; we here examine the very slight evidence that might support such a conclusion. [2]

---

1. The sketch opposite represents Abraham offering Isaac, indicating something of the ambiguity of the characterization of God in the Jewish canon.

2. Downing, *Has Christianity a Revelation?*, 20, citing Koehler, *Old Testament Theology*, 99 (Koehler's italics), and half a dozen others in support.

So begins the second chapter of the 1964 volume. The word studies that followed were, so far as I am aware, and so far as they went, unchallenged by, and sometimes actually commended by critical reviewers. However I was, as already mentioned several times, rebuked by one reader, Timothy Gorringe, for assuming that "absence of a particular word from the biblical writings . . . mean[s] that the concept is not to be found in them." Rather than repeat or even widen the word studies, in what follows in this and the next two chapters, I shall chiefly try to show the unlikelihood of any such "concept" being implied by the texts as wholes. Only the conclusions of the original word studies are repeated here.

Has Christianity a Revelation? seemed not a little negative, even destructive, to some readers, although the aim was to recall a richer Christian faith. I argued in fact—and certainly, in intention—for a faith better rooted in the canonical texts and the developing tradition as a whole. Much of the argument back then, and as regularly repeated here, is based on the simple fact that Christians seem to have too much disagreement as to the character of God, and still more as to his specific demands on them, to warrant saying either are revealed, clear to them (or, at least, to any but one cohesive and consistent smaller group of them). If God's (self-)revelation is clear (as the word seems to say), then why the disagreements among separated churches?

The present study argues that in fact such disagreement about God and God's will for humans is already present in the canonical texts themselves. Indeed, there has noticeably grown over the last half-century, among otherwise diverse scholars, a common conviction of the extent of diversity in the sources. For what the confession is worth, I myself cherish the Christian Scriptures, grateful for their Jewish roots (and their "pagan" resonances). But I value them, and commend them, as records of debates and discussions and arguments, inviting us to join in together. We engage with them, not as though receiving a final divine (self-)revealing, but as enriched by a source book of proven worth. As such, it has displayed its value in already shared common reflection and practice, to be accepted as part of our preparation for such divine (self-)revelation as God may fit and enable us ultimately to receive.

(i) Revelation and Knowledge of God

I quote from the 1964 volume:

> To start with, then, we look at *gālāh*. These are the only words at all often used in the Old Testament to convey the same basic

sense as "reveal." When they are used in this way, it is usually to talk of literal uncovering, stripping.

Only *gālāh* is used at all often. It is used to talk about God in four main ways. It can designate a "theophany," God letting himself be seen, as though materially visible. It can be used, more metaphorically, of God's "open" activity. It can describe God providing otherwise secret information about the future, or the structure of the physical world. And there are a couple of idioms in which *gālāh* is used, for the "opening" of a man's eyes to see a vision, or his ears to receive information; and God's communication with men is sometimes described in these ways.[3]

Greek *apocaluptō*, "reveal," is deployed no more frequently in the LXX. God "reveals his holy arm" in and by openly rescuing his people from captivity (Isa 42:10, etc.)

Other terms such as *rāāh*, "to appear," and *yādā* (niphal), "to make known" were also considered. As recalled in the previous chapter, to talk of "knowing God," "knowledge of God," is to talk of obedience to his accepted commands. Nowhere are any of these used for God's *self*-revealing, affording knowledge of his "self." But might more be implied?

I now add talk of God's "face" (mostly *pānîm*, plural form, translated as singular), and especially in the Psalms. There is talk of "seeing" or "seeking" God's face, of God "hiding" his face, or making his face "shine" on a supplant or suppliants. With a preposition, "in," translators prefer "in your presence," (Ps 16:11) rather than "in your face," "from your presence" rather than "from your face" (Ps 51:11). The actual issue is consistently one of well-being, not intimacy for its own sake. You go to the temple as client to patron, subject to monarch, seeking God's favor, rather than as a tourist who has come to gawp, to register a sighting, still less as an intimate. God's face shines on people to grant blessings such as security (e.g., Ps 67:1–2, 6–7). That, basically, is a deity's job.[4] Disaster happens when God hides his face ("self," in some translations; e.g., Ps 89:38–46; 102:1–5).[5] If a king smiles, your request seems to be favored. If he turns his back on you, the petition is refused—or worse. Since you do not in most of the narratives and prayers

---

3. Downing, *Has Christianity a Revelation?*, 21. The older idiom, "man," "men" for human, humankind, now long abandoned by the author are retained in the quotations.

4. Cf. Berleujung's survey of amulets, "Divine Presence."

5. See Curtis, *Psalms*, 139, 186; Eaton, *Psalms*, 245; Rodd, "Psalms," 371–72, 385; Anderson, *The Book of Psalms*, 481; *Psalms 2*, 647, 705; Limburg, *Psalms*, 221, 304, 344; Grogan, *Psalms*, 63, 124, 156–57, 171; Terrien, *The Psalms*, 484.

literally see God smile or frown or turn his head (not even if represented by an image), then here, in effect, good fortune or ill *constitute* the smiling or the hiding. It is possible that Ps 17:15 indicates a hope for an iconic dream-vision of God regarding the suppliant with favor, though some even see it as an unprecedented hope for resurrection.[6] But there is nothing at any point suggesting a deep awareness of God's inwardness, nor, for that matter, of there being an I-Thou relationship valid for its own sake. You do not go to the divine royal court expecting to be as prince Jonathan to young general David.[7]

It must also be allowed that narratives of sightings of a visible, audible YHWH may originally have been intended quite literally, as in Jdg 13, noting verses 18, 22, 23; but also that the canonical narrator is taken to intend "angel of YHWH," and "man of God": verses 3, 6, 8, 9, 10, 11, 13, 15, 16, 20, 21, not YHWH in person; and cf. Ezek 1:26–28.

On the other hand, it is important to acknowledge the significance of open access to God's presence, the sort of access that is expected of an ideal king: only so will either be able ensure justice (Ps 72) for widows and the fatherless.[8] Some kings can be terrifying, one does not approach unsummoned (Esther 4:11). To look on God's face, enter God's presence unbidden, could be terminal. In fact, one may ask God to hide his face, ignore the suppliant's failings; or just leave him alone, stop testing and tormenting him (Job 6:9, 7:19). [9] Standard terms for theophany (*epiphainein*, etc.) are used in the LXX, with still no suggestion of intense intimacy.

It is significant, I suggest, however, that God in these writings refuses intimacy, rather than being ontologically incapable of offering it; though it is tempting to assume that Platonic presupposition.[10]

For sure, it is taken that in all this God has given clear and distinctive instructions (Ps 147:19–20).[11] It would be easy to propose the sequence: God's demands are made clear, his will is made plain, and that must be

6. Curtis, *Psalms*, 32–33; Rodd, "Psalms," 372; Terrien, *Psalms*, 187; Limburg, *Psalms*, 50; Grogan, *Psalms*, 64.

7. *Contra* Cook, "God's Real Absence," who offers the image of lovers whispering sweet nothings (132).

8. Anderson, *The Book of Psalms*, 153, on the poet sleeping in the Temple in hope of a vision, expecting assurance that he will see God's face in the punishment of his adversaries; Curtis, *Psalms*, 149–51; Eaton, *Psalms*, 101; Rodd, "Psalms," 387; Grogan, *Psalms*, 132;

9. Clines, *Job*, 1–20, 166–68, 193–94.

10. E.g., Terrien, *The Elusive Presence*, 65, "the innermost being of God, inaccessible even to a man like Moses"; cf. many of the commentators.

11. Anderson, *The Book of Psalms*, 948; Terrien, *Psalms*, 916; Curtis, *Psalms*, 263.

highly indicative of his character, it must amount to self-revelation. Yet, as
we have seen, the authors of these ancient texts, as we have them, do not
offer that conclusion. Further, it has to be accepted that the ancestors of
our texts, although accepted in some strong sense as authoritative, are not
treated as themselves revealed. For instance, the final form, the wording, is
still to be settled in the first century, other texts besides are taken to be similarly important. Further, it is widely accepted in practice that the import of
the documents themselves was unclear: each needed to be interpreted, even
re-written, in the hope of evoking its "import for our group." The Septuagint
itself shows signs of some of the same apologetic exegetical hermenutics as
can be discerned in *Jubilees* and in *The Temple Scroll*, and Josephus; as well
as divergencies from the later, Masoretic, texts. It is, in our period, all in
flux.[12]

That itself, of course, is just one example among many of the ancient
acceptance that words do not themselves contain ideas, but only may, more
or less effectively, evoke them.[13] What God had in mind for how his people
should live together had certainly not, for the Qumran group, been revealed,
even in the now ancient texts, to the Jerusalem establishment or to anyone
else who had copies. Only now at last, they trusted, had it been made clear,
but to their group alone. The texts were not in themselves being taken as
revelatory (not even in first editions of the groups' own: these too seem to
exist in different versions). Only "our" community interpretation is (and
that only implicitly) taken as such.

(ii) God Identified

In my Introduction and again in chapters 1 and 2 I have noted Mike Higton's
preference for "God identifies himself" in loving address to us; it is this that
constitutes "God's self-identification." Though Higton still uses terms such
as "reveal," "revelation," it is of the God who is in any full sense unknowable,
yet meets us in his loving and demanding address to us.[14]

In chapter 2, Charles Dickens's tale of self-identification was offered
as an example of the importance for some of a very *un*-self-disclosing act
of self-identification. "It was I who did it/me what done it," from a stranger
identifying him/herself as the benefactor or culprit, can be very significant,

---

12. On the canon, Dorival, "La formation"; Zahn, *Rethinking Rewritten Scripture*;
Brooke, "Memory, Cultural Memory, and Rewritten Scripture."

13. Downing, "Ambiguity"; and ch. 1, above.

14. Higton, *Christian Doctrine*, 31–52, 57.

without that in itself telling much of her or his personality.[15] Even when Pharoah's vice-regent identifies himself as their brother Joseph, his siblings do not know whether he is concerned only for vengence on the guilty, or for both that and restoration to his co-maternal brother Benjamin and their father, or for the well-being of the innocents in the family—or for all-embracing reconciliation and unity.[16] A conviction that a divine being has identified his or herself as responsible for some momentous event(s) may matter deeply to those convinced of it, while leaving them "in the dark" as to the character of their patron or judge. (That their God chooses to remain in the dark is, of course, what many ancient Jewish theologians insisted; see further, below.)

In Genesis 1, one spoken of as "God," elōhīm, identifies himself in effective and overtly humane speech as creator, ensuring an earth that could be home for humans, male-and-female, apparently indiscriminately, among other animate and inanimate living things. Humans were made in his own "image and likeness," and thereby seem significantly identified with him. With its plants and animals, and with male and female humans alive and addressed and told to "be fruitful and multiply," and bidden to eat from every plant and every tree, and have charge of all the animals, he rests. All this, of course, affords an indication of this God's character, as tidy-minded, capable, and beneficent, "philanthropic" one might say, in a meaningful measure of self-identification with humans, though not in conversational exchange with them: that much for sure, but no more.

In the next chapter, one spoken of as YHWH God, as every attentive reader knows, makes plants and humankind from scratch, with just one human, for whom animals have to yet to be produced, and with a second human (allowing male/female distinction) to follow. One animal (the serpent) is clearly cleverer than and able to control the humans, rather than be subject to them. This creative deity also identifies himself in address, with a restriction among his fruit trees, threatening one penalty that is not executed, musing compassionately on the first human's need not yet met, and interrogating the couple in person. In that voiced compassion (as in, later, acting as the couple's tailor) he does, but in some quite distinctive measure, identify with his humans. And this split self-identification can get still more difficult.

One with the voice (style) of the first divine self-identifier, after a temporary cosmic reversal to watery chaos, then returns his world to order. He then reaffirms his unrestricted gift to humans of vegetation, extending it

15. See above, chs. 1 and 2.
16. See McConville, "Forgiveness," 643–45; and further, below.

to animal flesh, imposing only one punishment (for homicide, 9:1–7) and vows chaos never again (Gen 9:8–17). The second divine self-identifier, meanwhile, has imposed apparently unlimited penal labor on his first human couple (and the serpent), but only exile on a fratricide. I suppose we could say what they have in common is conditional self-identification with humans, if with rather different conditions.

There is one particular glaring discrepancy that might even leave us wondering whether the intention of the final editor(s) of the Pentateuch, the first five books, was to suggest that we, the hearers/readers, have to make our own editorial choice among the characters portrayed. For while the YHWH of Gen 18 agrees with Abraham that the judge of all the earth should act justly, not killing many innocent with the guilty, yet the ʾelōhīm-YHWH of Gen 22 induces the same Abraham to resolve without demur to kill his own innocent son, and praises him for not demurring.

In yet another passage in our Jewish collection one "named" in the same way as the second divine character in Genesis, here identifies himself as the one who "laid the foundation of the earth" (Job 38:4). He seems to have a rather different memory of the early events, and of his own continuing involvement in them, than either of the previous two; but seems also to imply that he has better things to do than explain even the rationale of his actions to Job, who confesses that it is all beyond his understanding (Job 38–42, with 42:3). Here it seems that this divine speaker breaches his otherness, his refusal to identify with human concerns, only enough to articulate it.

And there is more. Another divine self-identification is given us in Isaiah. Here one seems to have recollections of creation rather more like the above third account (Isa 40:12–14), but emotionally affirming an identity with one group of people, expecting them to identify with him alone as their God (Isa 42:14–17). While alienated from all other people, he affirms at the same time a very close involvement in human affairs in general, summoning a rebel leader of yet another ethnic group to aid his chosen people, keen to restore them after punishment (Isa 40:2; 44:21–28), and willing to explain his intentions and plans (Isa 40:29—45:23, and more in what follows).

The last two self-identifications, we recognize, are in poetic form. So we may well say, as many do, these are simply but splendidly extended metaphors, transfers of words and word-pictures, evoking in a suggestive and irreducible way a response to our earth, our universe, our wonder and awareness and gratitude and puzzlement and even fear.[17] They are thus to be

17. Ch. 1, section (j).

taken as poetic self-identifications of the same God, too far beyond us to be captured in coherent speech.

And, of course, at least since the first century CE it has been possible for a devout reader (e.g, Philo of Alexandria, in his *De opificio*, and perhaps, Paul of Tarsus, at 1 Cor 15:45–49) to recognize but not be fazed by some (at least some) of the discrepancies. At least most hearers or readers cope with these in the divine self-identifications in Genesis, and make coherent sense of both the first two accounts together (and perhaps the others mentioned, and others discernible besides). And many, though far from all Christians today, accept that these are indeed different, thoughtful, and poetic imaginings with most likely a history of reflection behind them. Yet, as self-identifications, they do look very different from each other. What we might like to imagine about creation can be expressed in many different ways. But the character, the ethos, suggested in each individual self-identification is very different from that in any of the others.

The first bespeaks someone orderly and benevolent, in detail attentive to and active in human affairs. The second works by trial and error, imposes arbitrary restrictions, threatens a death that does not happen, and leaves humans (and serpent) in indefinite penal labor. The third is more hands-on than the first, while more organized than the second, is as conversational as the latter, but quite unwilling, too preoccupied, to explain his detailed dealings with humans to anyone. The fourth is as in control as the first, identifies with a favorite people as their God but firmly their only one. He will in their favor manipulate other nations through a foreign rebel leader, but is also involved emotionally (quite unlike the other three). He has imposed limited punishment but is also keen to restore.

In what sense can the same person, the same God be identifying himself as having such different characters, such different personalities, such different willingness to expose himself in any depth, such difference in affirmation or refusal of identification with some or any of them? If there is one pluriform self-identification, it seems to be of a Proteus kind of figure, a shape-shifter, one with an "identity crisis" who does not (in a common phrase) "know his own mind," a multiple personality, one you could not rely on to be the same today as yesterday. And, of course, this fickle character is quite unlike the YHWH who identifies himself as " YHWH, YHWH, a God merciful and gracious, slow to anger, and abounding in steadfast love and faithfulness," at Exod 34:6; (compare Ps 89:24, 33; and similarly diverse self-identifications by other characters in the Psalter.)

If we put narrated, divine self-identification on one side, we have still to consider the ways in which others in this scriptural canon identify God (including identify God as identifying himself).

(1) God is vindictive even with regard to members of his chosen people, identifying himself as "visiting the iniquity of the parents upon their children and the children's children, to the third and the fourth generation" (Exod 34:7, NRSV, continuing the previous passage; and compare Deut 5:9). He also insists on the massacre of many others (e.g., Josh 6:17).

(2) God says, "The person who sins shall die [though with no time limit for execution noted].... But if the wicked turn away from all their sins that they have committed and keep all my statutes ... they shall surely live" (Ezek 18:20–21).

(3) God "does not deal with us according to our sins, nor repay us according to our iniquities ... as far as the east is from the west, so far he removes our transgressions from us" (Ps 103:10, 12).

(4) Isaiah of the exile says YHWH has charged (or, at least, accepted) double from Jerusalem for her sins (Isa 40:2). On the other hand, he identifies himself as one who will give any number of nations as Israel's ransom, while conscripting Cyrus without pay into forced labor for Israel's freedom (Isa 43:3, 45:13). This does seem to contrast with, for instance, Amos's God, who identifies himself as one who demands fair wages and prices (Amos 8:5–6); as well as with the God of Exodus (of the Covenant Code) who gives Moses rules for fair compensation, never more than "an eye for an eye, a tooth for a tooth" (Exod 21–22, noting 21:24–25). By comparison, the God of exilic Isaiah seems capriciously arbitrary. If he reveals anything it is that. "Truly, you are a God who hides himself, O God of Israel, the Saviour!" (Isa 45:15).[18]

We may certainly say, each assertion is clearly and coherently true of the divine figure identified independently in each text on its own. But if we insist on taking texts long bound together as one, then these are true of "God" "revelatory of God" as presented in the Jewish Scriptures but only as identifying a very complex and, it seems, a very inconsistent character. Or we may add into the picture texts from the New Testament, to complicate the aggregate portrayal further. How could we trust one as fickle, untrustworthy, as the composite figure is taken to be?

But for many, "God" in these texts refers to "God who is real outside the texts," and then such believers are faced with the problem of dealing with the discrepancies. Perhaps God-outside-the-texts is mysterious, "uncanny," and we have to leave it to him (probably "him") to reconcile the assertions or to assert his right to be arbitrary—or ourselves to identify with only our own chosen selection, without any definitive revelation of which

---

18. Cf. Blenkinsopp, *Isaiah 40–45*, 258–59.

version is true of him, or at least, least mistaken.[19] Maybe one allows that the various compilers accepted that the real God actually is as fickle as the texts make him seem, and have left their hearers to pick the "face," the divine self-presentation with which each hoped to engage, or felt driven to. Or perhaps God, as at least in some texts, prefers clouds and promises of protective presence to self-revelation, and identifying himself as guarantor, but not unconditionally, of Israel's future wellbeing (Exod and Num, passim; Lev 16:2; Deut 4:11; 1 Kgs 8:10–11; Ps 97:2; Ezek 10:23–4). So perhaps, after all, all that is revealed is our common disqualification so far from receiving any at all deep self-revelation of God—or even God's aversion to self-revelation, a preference for being enigmatic?

For sure, in our English translations we seem to be invited to "know God." As elaborated in *Has Christianity?* God is chiefly known in acts of power (Isa 66:14; Ezek 38:23). But, as explained in the previous chapter, *yādā* covers much more than the kind of abstract cognition that allows you to answer quiz questions, or even anticipate a colleague's reactions. Rather is it to "acknowledge appropriately," or, more fully, "have an awareness that elicits an appropriate-response" (however propriety is assessed). There is much more, lying implicit in the use of the term, than there is in normal English talk of "knowing" a person, or anything. Thus Jeremiah can be assured that God will write his law in people's hearts (reprogram them) so that they will (inescapably) "know [obey] YHWH," not now be able to break his (Deuteronomic) covenant (Jer 31:33–34).[20]

To set against this there is nothing in these texts to suggest a countervailing experience of or hope for a greater intimacy; nor could I find any such in the Septuagint. There is certainly no suggestion that any human may know God's heart; nor in the "apocalyptic" (revelatory) Apocrypha.

To summarize: in most canonical texts that consider the issue, God remains resolutely in his dark cloud or in blinding light, a God who hides (Exod 13:21, 24:15–18; 1 Kgs 8:10–11; Ps 97:2; Ezek 10:3–4; Isa 8:17; 45:15; Lam 3:44).[21] The cloud identifies his active presence as Israel's not unconditional but otherwise quite inscrutable minder.[22]

---

19. Ibid., "uncanny," adducing further Isa 28:21.

20. Cf. Holloday, *Jeremiah 2*, 198.

21. Durham, *Exodus*, 186; "Moses wants and needs to know Yahweh's intention," 446; on the other hand, to explain this in terms of "the gap between finite and infinite" imports too foreign a terminology; better, Hyatt, *Exodus*, 318; on the Psalms cited, cf. Anderson, *The Book of Psalms*, 687; Terrien, *Psalms*, 680, *The Elusive Presence*, 321–26; Curtis, *Psalms*, 197; Eaton, *Psalms*, 343; see also, Fiddes, "The Quest for a Place," 35–39.

22. See the comment in chapter 2, n. 49, on Dalferth and Rodgers, *Revelation*.

Possible exceptions were adduced in the previous volume. Moses is said to have spoken to God "face-to-face" ("eye-to-eye") "as a man speaks to his friend" (Deut 34:10; Exod 33:11; cf. Num 14:14).[23] But Moses is unique (Num 12:7–8); and when he on just one occasion asks for more (greater awareness of God's glory, his effective power), he is still allowed only to see God's back. He is to be made aware only of what lies behind this God, his ways, his promised but not unconditional protective presence, critical, and still enigmatic, arbitrary, in Israel's future ("gracious to whom I will be gracious" (Exod 33:12–23, quoting from v. 19). God positively refuses (without saying it is simply impossible) the level of intimacy that might justify talk of self-revelation. Moses is still in the cloud, no more intimate with God than is Elijah, face carefully covered, when God in majesty passes by and tells of events to come (1 Kgs 19:11–18).[24]

(iii) "Self"

In none of the discussions of supposed divine "self-revelation" in the Jewish Scriptures have I found any attempt to analyze senses of "self" that may be at issue.[25]

Of course "a self" (overt, inner, hidden) may not be in mind at all; "self" may be a simple reflexive ("he hurt himself falling"), or emphatic (it was he, himself, that I saw). But which (any, some, all) is still left unexplained.

In the second chapter here I raised the question as to whether there may be "*in some effective sense a self, an 'I,' that is at least potentially other than its feelings and capable of being in control of them rather than controlled by them (or by any other externality.*" From Galen Stawson's Introduction to his collection, *The Self?* I then quoted:

> It is very natural for us to think that there is such a thing as the "self"—an inner subject of experience, a mental presence or locus of consciousness that is not the same thing as the human being considered as a whole. The sense of the self arises almost irresistibly from fundamental features of human experience,

23. On Deuteronomy, and the reference is to God's choice: Mays, *Deuteronomy*, 414; and Christensen, *Deuteronomy*, 873. On Exodus see Durham, *Exodus*, 443–44.

24. This interpretation (protective presence) is accepted by Soskice, "The Gift of the Name," while still glossing it with an unwarranted "the gift of God's self-disclosure in history," 75. On the enigmatic ambiguities of the Elijah-Elisha cycle, see Feldt, "Wild and Wondrous."

25. Cook, "God's Real Absence," 131–32, simply leaves me puzzled: God speaks as an intimate lover while concealing his "seity . . . inner private actuality," (whatever that is).

and is [in] no sense a product of "Western" culture, still less a recent product of it, as some have foolishly supposed.

This does not settle the question of whether there is such a thing; or, if there is, the question of its nature . . . all six [contributors] allow there is or could be such a thing as the self.[26]

Particularly important is the insistence (against such as Charles Taylor's *The Sources of the Self*), that such talk is not simply Western and recent. I had argued as much some years ago, and have returned to it more recently. In my "Order Within: Passions, Divine and Human. B. Among Late Second Temple Jews and the First Christians" I concluded that in a wide range of writings, including those in the Jewish canon, we may discern an implicit supposition that there is in humans such a "self," able to reflect on and sometimes at least control its feelings; especially in Wisdom writings, but also in some narratives.[27] Divine passions or passionlessness were not my focus. However, on that, indications differ: the "God" of some accounts is wild and fickle, in others has feelings (e.g., of compassion), but they are orderly and controlled. In some narratives (not in my essay) the deity may look back and change his mind; but never does a narrator have God in debate with himself over what to do next. If there is to be a debate, it will be with someone else, e.g., with Abraham (Gen 18:16–33). God can swear by "myself," but that is much the same as pledging his name, his reputation, his holiness.

"Heart" may among humans have something of the sense of "self," at least enough to allow for inner dialogue. So, had any psalmist wished to record or look forward to some deeper, inward awareness of God, the word "heart" (*lěb*) was to hand (and used by many). God knows people's hearts (their minds, thoughts, intentions): Ps 33:13–15; 44:21; 66:18. Yet, while God is said to know what humans have or say in their hearts, he is never said to tell or to open up what is in his own. (Now that would be "self-revealing.") Just twice (possibly three times) an omniscient narrator tells of just one thing in particular that God had in his heart (Gen 8:11; Job 34:14; Isa 21:4) yet no one is said to know God's heart (in its entirety). In fact, elsewhere it is observed that though God knows people's hearts, people do not even know each other's (Jer 17:9–10), not even when they conjecture what a miscreant may have said in his heart (Ps 14:1).

26. Strawson *The Self?*, vi. On "self" as not culturally specific, see also Crabbe, *Soul to Self*. Neither Dainton, "The Self and the Phenomenal," nor Perrson, "Self-Doubt," nor van Inwagen, "Self," in Strawson, *The Self?* cites common usage; Taylor, *Sources of the Self*.

27. Chapter 4 in Downing, *Order*, 103–20.

If, as the proverb runs, "The mind of kings is unsearchable (Prov 25:3) God's heart is hardly less so (Qoh 3:11; 11:5).[28] Perhaps a human king will have an advisor who knows him well enough to anticipate his thinking; but "Who," asks exilic Isaiah, "has directed the spirit of YHWH, or as his counsellor has instructed him?" (Isa 40:13)—and does not expect a claimant, not even from a fellow prophet, one who has stood in God's council chamber (Jer 23:18, 22; 1 Kgs 22:19).[29]

The conclusion for here has to be that in these writings not only is there no overt talk of God's "self," there seems to be no implicit "self-revelation" of God. Or if there is, it has still to be identified and displayed.

(iv) Reconciliation, At-one-ment, and Atoning

The central theme of this study is Paul's thought of reconciliation in Christ to God by God, to make us one in Christ with God, richly, even fully aware of God's triune self. But historically, talk of reconciliation involves us, as we have seen, with "atoning" in the sense of "atoning for," "atoning for sins," not least for sinful guilt inherited from Adam and Eve, very likely evoking ideas of payment and reparation.

On that latter issue, it is worth noting that no passage in the canonical Jewish Scriptures has God unreconciled to humanity as a whole because of some ancient misdemeanor, nor any hint that a once idyllic human relationship with him stands in need of restoration, nor that an original indebtedness needs settling.[30]

In English translations of these canonical Jewish Scriptures, "atonement" is mainly used for the results of sacrifices that deal with the effects of misdemeanors of some kind, mostly accidental (Exod 29–32, Lev, frequent). The Hebrew word is mostly *kāphar*, probably better rendered "wipe away." It is a matter of wiping away the pollution brought upon the temple and themselves by priests and people's mistakes (mostly unawares), restoring purity (e.g., Lev 16:16). To restore purity besmirched, holiness sullied, is an obligation, a debt, incurred, of course. But the *kāphar* is a term for

28. Cf. Prov 25.2, and Murphy, *Proverbs*, 190–91: "God's secret, or unsearchability is proof of divine power—there are secrets that humans cannot even guess. What God does not reveal demonstrates who God really is." On divine inscrutability one may note further Job's speeches; and on Qoheleth/Ecclesiastes (on which, Asurmendi, *Du non-sense*).

29. On Isa 40:13–14 see Blenkinsopp, *Isaiah 2*, 191: God is "inscrutable."

30. Cf. Anderson, *Sin*, 15–110. Anderson perceptively traces how such an idea may seem to have emerged among early Christians—sin as debt-bond in Colossians, and sin originating in Adam, in Romans—but offers no earlier Jewish antecedent.

purification, not for repayment, even though performing it does effect a discharge of the debt of omission. Thus the animal, the meat (which goes to the priest to consume) does not itself discharge the debt of purification owed, only the appropriate manipulation of its blood does that: due purification.

The LXX uses *exilasetai* regularly for *kāphar*. Lev 16:16 LXX reads *exilasetai to hagion*, "he purifies the sanctuary," and that is "because of the uncleannesses of the people of Israel." The verb *exilaskomai* is used in general Greek of propitiating a deity, never, it would seem, a place (which would hardly make sense). Josephus uses it of "purging" Jerusalem with fire (*War* 5:19), and I take it that "purging the holy place" is how he will have understood *exilasetai to hagion*.[31] Similarly, the Philistines hope that returning the Ark with a gift will result in them themselves being purged (*exilsthēsetai*, 1 Sam 6:3/1 Kgs 6:3, LXX; cf. Ezek 16:63).

Though there is talk of reparation for wrong doing in Exodus (Exod 21–22 and elsewhere), and the lifting or removal of the burden of sin, reparation is not the function of meat or other offerings as explained here, or usually elsewhere (save only at LXX Zech 7:2, 8.22; Mal 1:9, where a sacrifice is, unusually, expected to propitiate YHWH).[32] *Kāphar* in Leviticus and Exodus is most like a kindly parent providing a means for clumsy children to wipe away an accidental but disturbing spill—or even a culpable one— but then it would be after human-to-human reparation (Lev 6:1–7). God requires restored purity (at costs graduated by financial ability) to provide the cleansing (Lev 5:7) but exacts no payment, and no tariff (contrast Isa 40:2, discussed above).

One might well, however, conclude further, that restoring purity to God's house as provided for by him is his way of ensuring his continuing benevolent unity with his people, his protective presence.[33] This is not said explicitly: but the dramatic divine departure from his grossly polluted temple, witnessed to by Ezekiel (from much the same date as Leviticus in the form we have it), certainly indicates the temporary ending of any such unity of God and people and land.

As we saw in chapter 2, "reconcile," "reconciliation" in common use do not at all have to imply a return to a broken harmony, nor, indeed, ending any currently active hostility; just overcoming otherness, knitting together what was simply separate, may be the issue (as, it was briefly argued, is the

31. On Leviticus and purgation, cf. Grabbe, "Leviticus," 93–102.

32. In these places the Hebrew does not use *kāphar*. *Exilaskomai* is used of Jacob hoping to propitiate Esau, Gen 32:20.

33. Cf. Terrien, in his entire survey in *The Elusive Present*, though spoiled by positing a desire for the enjoyment of an experience of presence in itself, rather than, simply, a conviction based on events of protection, safeguarding.

case in Paul). If, however, we stay with the long-term Christian use, for "reconciling" as indicating renewal of previous unity, it is clear that there is no instance in the Jewish canonical Scriptures of God in the latter sense reconciling estranged people to himself—at least, not so as to draw translators into English to render it with "reconcile" or "reconciliation." That is so, even though one might have supposed the dialogue in Hosea indicates just such reconciliation of his errant people to himself as YHWH's intention: "Therefore I will now persuade her, and bring her into the wilderness and speak tenderly to her" (Hos 2:14). But no such approach is narrated: rather, "I will return again to my place, until they acknowledge their guilt and seek my face"; and a little later their "Come let us return" is rebuffed as insincere (Hos 5:15—6:1, 4). We may usefully compare Isaiah of the exile's "He will gather his lambs in his arms" (Isa 40:11; cf. 42:16; 43:5–8; 49:6; 54:6–8), where a response, an acceptance of his welcoming approach, is, of course sought: "Seek YHWH while he may be found, call upon him while he is near" (Isa 55:6). Both instances are thus more in line with what one does often find repeated: "Return to me and I shall return to you, says the Lord of Hosts" (Mal 3:7; cf. 2 Chron 15:2; Zech 1:3; Isa 31:6; Jer 31:1, 22; Lam 3:57; Ezek 18:30; and in the New Testament, of course, Jas 4:8.)

There are, on the other hand, quite a few passages where many readers, perhaps most, find some sort of inter-human reconciliation is at issue. (In fact, they anticipate most of the issues canvassed in chapter 2.) There is Jacob's attempt to make peace with his dispossessed brother Esau (Gen 32—33), but he only averts retribution: the brothers then go their separate ways (Gen 33:15–17). Joab attempts to reconcile David and his rebellious favorite, Absolom, the fratricidal avenger of his co-maternal sister's rape. Joab only succeeds in having Absolom's exile ended (even if David's reaction to his son's subsequent violent death suggests the David portrayed would really have welcomed something more: 2 Sam 13:1—19:8, noting 18:33). Particularly significant are the provisions in the Covenant Code (Exod 21–22, noted above) for reconciling people in conflict, with its tariff of reparations and punishments, all within strict limits: "an eye for an eye and a tooth for a tooth" (Exod 21:23–24). Arguably, the emphasis in practice would be on "making good," as in Lev 24:13–23. Thus "making good" would probably amount to an agreed payment in cash or kind; but with a communally agreed limit, restoring unity in the community.[34]

There is one extensive and quite subtle narrative, however, that is often seen as a story of reconciliation, that of Joseph with his brothers

34. On the whole passage, cf. Schenker, *Versöhnung*; Jackson, *Biblical Law*, 71–113; on the *talion*, ibid., 271–97.

(Gen 37–50), but one which seems to take a distinctive route, as helpfully analyzed recently by Gordon McConville.[35] Joseph, his father's favorite and tactless teller of his dreams of eminence, had been sold by ten of his estranged brothers to slavery in Egypt, yet has risen to a prominence where he is confronted by them, in need and at his mercy. He recognizes them, and overhears their "no doubt we are being punished because of our brother," but they remain in ignorance. He could avenge himself, and he does initially subject them to three days in gaol and after that to two harsh tests, but then imposes no further penalty, asking for no reparation, not even for a confession of guilt and a plea for forgiveness. Is it just in concern for his father as family patriarch, concern cleverly aroused by Judah the one who had suggested his sale? The narrative does not tell us, only that the family is in some sense reunited, if with the older brothers still feeling insecure. Thus they ask, but much later, to be forgiven, though with Joseph again doing his best to dispel their anxiety (Gen 50:15–22). Joseph reassures his brothers that the whole drama was God's idea. Might God here, implicitly, be behind this kind of reconciliation?

Putting on one side for the moment key words like "atonement" and "reconcilition," what is on the other hand worth noting again in many of these writings is the common conviction, that the "God" of each wants his people to be one, and himself, it would seem, at one with them: at-one-ment, often "covenanted," but with each narrated God covenanting to his own prescription.

So the God of Gen 1 and 9 makes human people in his own image, gives them a home and a right to sustenance, shares some of his powers and responsibilities with them, and after the purging flood, makes a covenant with Noah and all flesh. A deity with a very similar voice then chooses one human, Abram/Abraham to be the forefather of his special covenant people, prescribing male circumcision, and promising to be their God (Gen 17).

YHWH of Gen 2–4 actually shares the pleasure of his garden with his earth-creatures, making clothes for them even after expelling them, remaining closely in contact (but not in every case imposing the death penalty for homicide), and covenants with Noah before the purging flood. And Abraham seems to be part of his later story, too: here is a deity this-worldly enough to allow Abraham to share a meal with him and his two companions. He then continues as Abraham's minder, and later takes on the same role for Moses: a God, it seems, given to physical appearances.

The God of the Joseph narrative, meanwhile, is also in communication, but only in dreams; active, but less overtly so. If he is, as suggested just

---

35. McConville, "Forgiveness."

above, behind Joseph's kind of fogiveness, he is much less prone to demand recompense or exact vengeance in his concern for unity than is either of the others. The divine covenanting law-giver of Exodus 21–22, as just noted, is concerned with unity and peace in his communities, but his method is to allow for reparations, yet with a strict limit. By contrast, as also already recalled, the God who later in the narrative identifies himself to Moses, and promises his covenanted presence with his people, is to be at one with them as threatening vengeful punishment "to the third and fourth generation." (In footnote 1 in the previous chapter attention was drawn to a rabbinic reading that saw Judah's "drawing near" to Joseph, Gen 44:18 as an anticipation of the future unity later promised by God, Ezek 37:19).

The God of 2 Sam 7:4–17 promises David an unbroken monarchical but not otherwise unconditional succession, later said to be covenanted (2 Sam 23:5), and this seems to be reaffirmed to his son, Solomon (1 Kgs 3:5–14; 8:24). Solomon later reminds him of the promise of his presence, focussed in the temple, for ready access for his people, near and far; "my eyes and my heart will be there for ever" (9:3); but then there are more threats, even against the temple itself (9:6–9). There is also voiced the possibility that God has gone back on his word, that he has unilaterally renounced his covenant (Ps 89, with v. 39; cf. 44:17–22). Implicit throughout, nonetheless, is the ideal of one people, under the one human leader under and loyal to the one God, and so in many psalms (Ps 46–48, 68, 72, 80, 99, 105, 115, 122, 132, 133).

Yet there is another version, already with reference to Solomon's reign: as a punishment for the latter's split loyalty, but postponed for deceased David's sake, the one people will be sundered under Rehaboam (1 Kgs 11:9–14). This split the God of the book of Ezekiel promises to heal, himself cleansing all his people, but from their own sin and that of their rulers (Ezek 37:15–28; cf. Jer 11:13–14; Zech 10:6).

Most clearly in Deuteronomy, but, as noted, widely affirmed, the choice of one people to be at one with himself lies with the God narrated in each case: the initiative lay with him in the first place (Amos 3:1–2; Exod 19:6; Deut 7:7; 10:15; 14:2; Ps 135:4; Isa 41:8; 43:1; 44:1, 21), even if subsequently he awaits that people's acceptance of his repeated call to return. And perhaps, at least in some narratives, the return, the reuniting, the new at-one-ment is the work of that narrative's God, willing to wait no longer: e.g., Jer 31:31–34 (with a new covenant); 32:40; Ezek 11:19; 18:31; 34:24 (apparently a fresh covenant "of peace," 36:26). These are to be imposed, even at the cost of overriding people's free will: a leucotomy (in our terms), an imposed implant of a new heart-mind-will.

Though no narrated deity, identified or self-identifying in these writings, offers self-revelation, many of those who appear do share at-one-ment as their aim, however diversely specified.

Appended Note: The Canon Itself as Conciliating, At-oneing?

Discussion in a recent international seminar attended by the present author prompted the question: might the Jewish canon itself warrantably be seen as an attempt, in effect and even in conscious intention to honor by inclusion some conflicting strands? Thus the emerging collection contains firmly Davidic-Levitical matter (1 and 2 Chronicles) and fiercely Mosaic-Zadokite matter (e.g., the defeated Korah of Num 16). Yet both strands in this conflict of rival scribal groups are intertwined in Ezra and Nehemiah.[36] (Harmony without harmonizing is commended by some of the thinkers instanced in chapter 2, section a.) A suggested socio-political context could be pressure by the Persian authorities for unity in the troublesome province of Jehud.

Another, perhaps complementary suggestion could stem from Jill Middlemas' discussion of multiple metaphors, verbal imagery in place of fixed iconic statutes, or even fixed designations, as a deliberate policy of Hosea and especially of Ezekiel. Their God is in effect trustingly and hopefully proclaimed as real precisely as elusive, un-pin-downable, undefinable and so unclarifiable; revealed, if one must, only as unrevealable. If Middlemas' quite cogent case is accepted, it might even be extended to the collectors, whoever they were: they pinned their hope in an elusive deity, one only ever unclearly, enigmatially glimpsed. Even if I am pressing Middlemas' case further than she would, the suggestion greatly atracts me. It would link with my exploration of metaphor in George Herbert (chapter 7); but might also, just possibly, be seen as a more down-to-earth alternative to abstract arguments for God's "incomprehensibility" (chapter 5 and onwards).

This particular instance, of course, in no way harmonizes the conflicting theologies surveyed above: it specifically resists any systematizing. It is also worth noting that evidenced ongoing further theological variations failed to get included. Enoch traditions in particular get but a single passing reference in the canon: it is diverse but still not all-inclusive.

---

36. Jeon, "Scribal Rivalry"; cf. also MacDonald, "The Spirit of YHWH," on the varieties of "name," "glory," and "spirit" theologies in play in Persian period Yehud.

(b) Non-Canonical Ancient Jewish Writings

(i) Revelation, Knowledge, Self

"None of these works has seemed to suggest a 'revealing' of God himself, an at all intimate 'knowledge of God.'" I can find nothing on "revelation" or "knowledge" of God to alter what was thus summarized in *Has Christianity?*[37] As noted above, I have argued recently that a human "sense of (inner) self" certainly can be discerned in some of these writings.[38] But there is no talk, even so, of God's "(inner) self."

Thus, in the "sectarian" (Essene) writings ascribed by most scholars to the Qumran community over its three centuries' life span (and to the Teacher in particular), as I discerned fifty years ago, there is little if any emphasis on promises of prosperity (apart from ultimate military victory), compared with that in the writings that for us are canonical. The emphasis now is more on "the consolations of religion" and focused on Torah (as interpreted in the community) and the ability to live the divine instruction. There is an intensity of devotion in the *Hodayot*, the hymns, a strong self-identity over against other Judaeans, but still no suggestion of intimacy with God, God opening up his self to anyone. Having recently spent rather more time with these documents than I managed fifty years ago, I can only reaffirm this negative conclusion.

On Philo on Moses's encounter with God in darkness, there is further discussion later in chapter 5.

What has become clearer over the last half-century is the significance for my renewed thesis, of "re-written Bible," especially in *Jubilees* and the *Temple Scroll*, but also in the LXX, and in the Qumran commentary material.[39] As explained above, Torah is given, but the traditional texts do not themselves constitute a definitive revelation of God's will for people (let alone, of God's self). The Scriptures are treated as only a catalyst (albeit a vital catalyst) to enable those using it to discern what God "must" really have meant, and has in mind. That understanding has to be evoked by fresh words, distinct from those of adversaries among fellow Judaeans. Fresh, "sectarian" insights, as noted in *Has Christianity?* are taken as "revealed." But even these have to be re-drafted from time to time, witness the variant successive surviving manuscripts. There is no unambiguous and final revelation in the written words, no inescapable clarity, even of God's will, let alone of God's self.

---

37. Downing, *Has Christianity a Revelation?* 48–62, citing 53.

38. Downing, *Order*, 103–20.

39. On the whole topic, cf. Zahn, *Rethinking Rewritten Scripture.*

(ii) Reconciliation, at-one-ment, identity

An urge to unity was commonplace in the Mediterranean world of the late centuries BCE and the early centuries CE: unity in homes, villages, towns and cities, unity of peoples who had sense of a common heritage. This would often include a drive to reconciliation at all levels of people alienated, estranged from one another. This I have (in conversation with others, especially with Margaret Mitchell in her *Paul and the Politics of Reconciliation*) recently illustrated at some length for Greeks and Romans, Jews, and early Christians.[40] My selected examples for first-century Judaism were drawn from Philo, the Qumran community (centered on the *Yāhad*, "the Unity"), and Josephus.

The latter "boldly maintains"

> that we have introduced to the rest of the world a great deal of what is fine and beautiful. . . . What is more beneficial than being of one mind with one another, to be prey neither to disunity in adversity nor to arrogance nor to disruptive factionalism in prosperity? . . . And to be convinced that everything in the universe is under the eye and direction of God?[41]

Josephus also portrays himself assuring the besieged defenders of Jerusalem that "the Deity is readily reconciled (*eudiallekton*) to those who confess and repent," a motif he seems to have taken from Dionysius of Halicarnassus, *Roman Antiquities*.[42]

The Qumran sect insisted, "All shall be in a Community [unity, *Yahad*] of truth, of proper meekness, of compassionate love and upright purpose." Would-be entrants to the Community received only a very cautious and protracted welcome for testing. Philo and Josephus affirmed a much more open acceptance of whole-hearted incomers, proselytes.[43]

In what follows I venture further back, to "Apocrypha and Peudepigrapha" that could arguably have inflenced early Christians (though some of "Essene" materials themselves also seem to predate the Christians by well over a century).

In some Greek *katalagē* can be rendered either "conciliation" or "reconciliation."[44] In some of the Greek texts to be briefly surveyed here,

---

40. Downing, "Order . . . Jews"; Mitchell, *Paul and the Politics*.

41. Josephus, *Apion* 2:293–294, LCL, adapted.

42. Josephus, *War* 5:415; Dionysius, *RA* 8:50:5.

43. CD 14.4; trans. in García Martinez, *Dead Sea Scrolls;* Philo, *De praemiis*, 152; Josephus, *Apion* 2.209–210.

44. Liddell and Scott, *A Greek-English Lexicon*, 899.

it is rightly translated "reconciliation." Friends, friendly communities, have fallen out and good relations are to be restored. The "re-" is appropriate. But in others, there has been no past unity, and "conciliation" is more apt. There is no "ana-" in Greek to match the latin "re," and it must be context rather than convention that decides.

In 2 Macc 7:33 (c. 124–63 BCE) the youngest of the martyrs insists, "And if our living Lord is angry for a little while, so as to rebuke and discipline us, he will be reconciled [*katallagēsetai*] with his own servants." The agents here, are human, the one to be reconciled is God, who needs to be persuaded to become "gracious," (2 Macc 7:37 [RV; mg., "propitious"]), "show favor" (REB), "show mercy" (NRSV). There is a similar passage in the probably much later (first century CE): 4 Macc 12:17. Here an undefined but positive past for the nation is implicit.

Some of the reflections most akin to the theme here at issue appear in the *Testaments of the Twelve Patriarchs* (around 150 BCE but with later Christian interpolations). Simeon, repentant, admires Joseph's compassion (*TSim* 4:4–6). The author does not say whether the brothers had once been on good terms. Levi looks forward to the time when the Lord will visit (no "re-visit") all the nations with compassion (though a Christian editor has seen a chance to insert "through his son's compassion," *TLev* 4:4), while vengeance against Shechem for sister Dinah's rape/seduction is nonetheless encouraged. Judah takes it that Jacob's peace with Esau was only temporary (*TJud* 9:1). Recovery for violent, sinful, punished Israel is in God's hands (*TJud* 22, 24). Mostly anger and hatred and envy are emphatically discouraged. Issachar works hard and is able and willing to share compassionately, as is Zebulon the fisherman, unasked and irrespective of desert (*TIss* 5:2; *TZeb* 6–8), sure that human compassion will meet with divine compassion. Joseph's compassion follows awareness of God's care for him (*TJos* 1). He did not complain against his enslavement, lest his complaint shame his brothers. Instead he encourages his descendents to mutual love and concealing others' faults (*TJos* 17). Benjamin takes this further: "A good man . . . is merciful to all, even though they may be sinners. And even if a person plots against him for evil ends, by doing good this man conquers evil, being watched over by God. He loves those who wrong him as he loves his own life" (*TBen* 4:2–4).[45] All this out-going kindness is clearly stated to have God's approval; but God does not seem to have the initative, save, by implication, in the case of Joseph.

---

45. Translation here by Kee, "The Testaments"; other references in the following paragraphs to various translators' work, in Charlesworth, *The Old Testament Pseudepigrapha*.

In *Aristeas to Philocrates* (c. 150–100 BCE) conciliatory rule is commended to Ptolemy Philadelphos, with the warning that force on its own resolves nothing (*Aristeas* 187–202). In *Joseph and Asenath* (100 BCE–100 CE), Asenath, a penitent convert to Judaism, and Joseph's new bride, is abducted by his half-brothers, the sons of Bilhah and Zilpah, yet, when rescued, pleads appeasingly for her captors' lives. This plea is taken up by Benjamin and then by Levi, the latter insisting that only clemency encourages friendship (*Joseph and Asenath* 28–29). Again, this is conciliation after increased hostility, with no hint of original fraternal concord restored. *Pseudo-Phocylides* (200 BCE–200 CE) urges making "a gracious friend" rather than an enemy (142), but does not elaborate. There is some similar material in *Sibylline Oracles* 2 (30–70 CE), encouraging outgoing kindness (78–94).

So far the texts cited (save the Dead Sea Scrolls) are in Greek, with the influence on both language and contents of Greek philosophical ethics readily discernible.

In contrast with the above, implicitly identifying a rather different divine character, stands *Jubilees* (pre-100 BCE), more concerned with offenses and their remembrance: Joseph's abduction is recalled, but not his (re-)conciling his brothers (*Jub* 34:10–19). There is no talk of (re-)conciliation, either inter-human or by or with God, in *1st Enoch* (300 BCE–100 CE). The *Psalms of Solomon* (70 BCE–50 CE) insist, rather, on scrupulous behavior, caring for ritual purity, though fasting and abasement will atone, and (interestingly) God will cleanse (3:7–8). Similarly, *Pseudo-Philo* (first century CE; pre 70?) has no room for divinely initiated (re-)conciliation of/with people, nor they among themselves, nor has the (first century CE) *Lives of the Prophets* or *4 Baruch* (70–136 CE), where any restoration of temple and state would seem to await the Torah-observant response of the Jewish faithful.

As noted just above, unity, harmony and (re-)conciliation were important themes in public discourse in the ancient East Mediterranean world, and fuller discussions being readily available, there is no need to repeat them here.[46] But in support I think it worth citing some thoughts of Dio of Prusa (mid first to early second century CE) on concord, its theology, its value and its creation or restoration, in his *Orations* 38–41. Achieving conciliation (*katallagē*) between Nicomedia and Nicaea, at loggerheads over provincial status, he argues, is of such advantage to both as to warrant divine assistance. Concord is at the heart of friendship, conciliation, and kinship (*Oration* 38:9, 11). Refusing it is like being silly children (38:21). Accepting

46. See above and n. 21.

it, you double your strength (38:41). "Will you not look each other in the face? Will you not listen to one another? Will your two cities not clasp hands together, you being the first to extend the hand? By reconciliation, acquire for yourselves all the benefits both enjoy? (38:47).[47] (Some leading families have been allied by inter-marriage, but there is no appeal to renewal of erstwhile inter-city concord.)

It is with this brief reflection on (re-)conciliation, at-one-ment, that we turn to the New Testament writings.[48]

---

47. Trans. LCL, adapted; and see further, 38:49; 39:2; 40:16.

48. There is a recent survey with theological reflections on possible theological approaches to these and more variations in identifications of "the Christian God" in Butler, *Rock of Ages?* My own rather different reflections are displayed throughout in passing, but are concentrated in chs. 7 and 8.

© C.E.Downing 2014

4

New Testament Scriptures[1]

(a) Revelation and Knowledge of God

(i) Introductory

I quote again from the 1964 volume the conclusion of my study of the canonical texts (retaining, with apologies, the non-inclusive language):

> It is perhaps enough to mention a few of the words which the present writer sees as proper keys to New Testament interpretation: not so much the words themselves as the contexts in which they are used. "The (Holy) Spirit," "Spirit of God," "Spirit of Christ"; "sanctification" and "the saints"; "the body of Christ," "the Church," "the people (of God)"; "sons (or children) of God" and "adoption"; "peace," "grace," "reconciliation," "forgiveness," "rightwising" ("justification"); "call" and "calling"; "save" and "salvation"; "redeem" and "redemption"; "lord (Christ)"; and pre-eminently, "love." It is in terms like these that the earliest Christians tried to understand the activity of God in Christ.
>
> As we have clearly seen, none of the canonical writers who use these terms *explicitly* presupposes God's "revelation of himself." Nor is such a revelation even necessarily *implicit* in any of these descriptions of what God *is* believed to have done. It is quite possible to be an enigmatic de Gaulle, and still make for yourself a people; it is only normal to be father to a child long before the child knows you well, if he ever does; you rarely find you "know" a friend's character until you have accepted his

---

1. Recalling John Everett Millais' *Christ in the House of His Parents,* with a larger "holy family" than is often imagined as bringing up the boy Jesus. The older woman: Elizabeth? The boy: John the Baptist? Young man: probably half-brother (late tradition)? Cf. the African saying (I gather): It takes a village to bring up a child.

friendship, and have enjoyed it for a good many years. These (and other) paradigms from ordinary human life are used to describe what God has already done and still does. But he has not yet "revealed himself" and this was not his intention.

"Revelation" is used by contemporary theologians to talk of God's completed "act" in Christ. The New Testament talks rather in the terms we have listed above (and many more) of what God has done and is doing. What he has done and is doing is to prepare a people who may learn to love, be brought to conform to the image of his Son; and only then may God (Father or Son)— some say—be "revealed." Only then will perception of God be made so clear that we would be justified in calling it "revelation of God himself." Already we are "redeemed," "accepted," "made holy." This is as sure and complete as the Cross and Resurrection and presence of the Spirit. It is final. But "revelation" cannot be said to be complete; it is barely begun; it is, we may believe, the ultimate but still very incomplete aim of what God has already done, and still does.

The words in which the New Testament writers choose to talk about what God has done in Christ have the disadvantage of being undisguisably "mythological." A related but not quite identical criticism might be that they do not answer many of the questions that modern theologians would like them to. . . . It seems much easier, superficially, to make good in some way a claim that Christians have a special "knowledge," than a claim that they have been "redeemed," "saved." Saved? What from, what for? Where's the difference? It seems easier to destroy a claim to "salvation." It seems much harder to show that a man has not the "knowledge" he claims, and it is tempting to grasp what seems to be the more readily defensible position.

But I still think that much of the language the New Testament writers in fact use does make sense. It can only make sense (but it does make sense) where people find themselves in a community of those who do love; love and serve each other, and the wider world. Then it, too, is fully defensible.[2]

As intimated, I would today phrase some of that rather differently, but have little relevant otherwise to add. The assessment of the sort of positive "good news" (including revelation-to-come) stands; but so, too, does the

2. Downing, *Has Christianity a Revelation?* 124–25. In the early 1960s I failed to consult BAGD, *Greek-English Lexicon of the New Testament* (1957); had I done so, I would have found already no suggestion that divine self-revelation was indicated in any use of *apokaluptō, apokalupsis,* etc.

insistence on the consistent avoidance of claims to divine self-revelation already.

(ii) Matt 11:25–27; Lk 10:21–22; and 2:30–32

However, I am now not entirely content with my previous treatment of Matt 11:25–27; Lk 10:21–22, Christ's thanksgiving to the Father. The ideas have some parallels in John (and we return to those later), but the language is mostly very different, yet not well matched elsewhere either in Matthew or Luke. Reading each passage respectively in its own gospel context, I would suggest, as proposed by François Bovon, that we discern a reference back to the divine acknowledgment, identification, of Jesus at his baptism. There he is acknowledged as the son in whom his divine father declared himself "well pleased" (*eudokēsa*), just as here the father's "good pleasure" (*eudokia*) is again operative, as the father specifically of this son.[3] What has been "revealed," disclosed in practice, is this son's ability to share with his simple followers ("babes") his power to heal and to exorcize (Matt 11:20–24; Lk 10:12–20; cf. Matt 10:1; Lk 9:1). That these "babes" are Jesus' disciples is explicitly Luke's reading (Lk 10:23–24). In this empowering the divine father has reaffirmed his acknowledgement, identification, of Jesus as his son, an acknowledgment only this divine father can effect. Jesus then, as the only one so qualified, in turn acknowledges his divine father as the source of these delegatable powers. (One may compare the crucial issue of identifying the source of Jesus' power in the Beelzebub controversy in both gospels.) Obviously, these healings also indicate something significant about father and son. But healing is done, according to these two authors, for the sake of healing the sick, not for self-display, self-revelation, which would amount to the hypocrisy, the play-acting that both evangelists condemn (Matt 6:2, 5, 16; Lk 11:42–52).

I also add here a note on another use of "revelation," one left undiscussed in the previous study. In his *Nunc dimittis* Luke talks of God's salvation, and then has, in interpretative apposition, "*phōs eis apokalupsin ethnōn*" (Lk 2:30–32): genitive, "of," not dative "to." Modern translations, including the nineteenth-century RV, have "a light for revelation to the Gentiles," with a footnote in the latter, "Or *the unveiling of the Gentiles*," acknowledging that

---

3. Accepting that some texts of Luke have "today I have begotten you" instead of "with you I am well pleased," but aware also that the latter is what Luke knew in his copy of Mark. And my main argument here does not depend anyway on "well pleased," but on divine acknowledgment in both. In addition to the commentaries cited in 1964, see now, Bovon, *Das Evangelium nach Lukas*, 2.66–79, citing 66; Luz, *Matthew 8–20*, 169; Evans, *Saint Luke*, 450–63.

the genitive does not warrant "to." Theological conviction trumps exegetical nicety. The Isaian passages likely in Luke's mind indicate light as well-being, salvation, *for* others in addition to God's own people: so the older, AV (Coverdale?) translation, "a light to lighten the Gentiles," seems much more appropriate: a light to dispel the darkness of exclusion from YHWH's gift of well-being (and compare Lk 3:6).[4]

(iii) John's Gospel

I was at the time, I confess, least happy with my treatment of the Gospel and Letters of John: there is so much stress there on the vocabulary of "knowing" (*ginōskō* and *oida*). Further, since then I continue to encounter the ongoing conviction of commentators, that (without his using the word "reveal, revelation") the saving mission of Jesus in John is said to be "the self-revelation of God."[5] On the other hand, some recent exegetes have offered analyses of "knowing God" that still often chime in part with what I insisted fifty years ago.[6] However, where they would argue that keeping the command to love your siblings, not some inner certainty, was the *criterion* for genuine knowledge of God, I urged rather that this compliance itself constituted the only true acknowledgement of the God of John's Jesus.

Now I would argue with much more conviction that the evangelist has in effect, if only implicitly, made it clear that "in fact" we do not know Jesus himself sufficiently well to find in him the self-revealing of God (in any deep sense of "self"). In this Gospel, as in the Synoptics, Jesus himself knows what is in people's minds (Jn 2:25; cf. 1:48, 6:61). In the case of the Samaritan woman, he knows, she says, "everything I have ever done" (Jn 4:29; cf. 16:30). Knowing everything in someone's past is at least necessary to, or, very likely constitutes, knowing them fully. If we like to use words like "reveal," we could say, the woman's whole self stood revealed to Jesus. And it is precisely this knowledge of "everything I have ever done" that, the text later tells, we simply cannot know in Jesus' case, for "the many other things that Jesus did" could not be documented even if this whole world were its record office (Jn 21:25). In the sense that the woman's self stood revealed to Jesus, Jesus' self remains undisclosed to us, and as such, leaves his Johannine Father's self equally unrevealed.

4. On Lk 2:30–32, compare the discussion in Evans, *Saint Luke*, 217.

5. E.g., Brown, *The Gospel According to John*, 1:36; Culpepper, *Anatomy of the Fourth Gospel*, 88; Moloney, *The Gospel of John*, 4; Keener, *The Gospel of John*, 1:246; Lincoln, *The Gospel according to St. John*, 70, 75; Scrutton "Salvation as Revelation."

6. Keener, *The Gospel of John*, 1:233–79; Wahlde, *The Gospel and Letters*, 494–503.

If Jesus is styled by us a Revealer, it is as the self-proclaimed revealer of a so far contentless revelation: Rudolph Bultmann's apposite conclusion.[7] If there is to be divine self-revelation, knowing more than just knowing where the knowledge lies, it lies ahead. As the First Epistle of John assures us, when (but only when) we are finally like Christ shall we see him as he is. Meanwhile we go on making ourselves pure (1 Jn 3:2–3).[8] The word (or Word) has been "displayed," *ephanerōthē*, to us (1 Jn 1:1), for us to see and touch, and to be guided in our exploring; but to use "reveal" here (e.g., NRSV) is simply inappropriate; it is only (possibly) appropriate at 1 Jn 3:3: "when he is revealed . . . for [only then] shall we see him as he is."

To reinforce the foregoing argument I offer here a slightly fuller analysis than previously of "seeing" in the Supper Discourses.[9] In John (in contrast with the Synoptists, discussed below) Jesus expresses no uncertainty or ignorance as to his future, as to what the Father has in mind for him (Jn 10:30; 12:27–32; 13:3); yet he still remains stubbornly enigmatic, refusing to reveal what he means by what he says, continuing to refuse any clear insight into the future he (and the Father, we take it) have in mind for others (Jn 21:21–23). Yet by the last night together, have not his disciples known (come to know) Jesus and in knowing him, "known the Father," seen Jesus and in seeing him, "seen the Father" (Jn 14:7–9)? Already, they are told, they do know, have seen. Yet there are indications that John's Jesus is yet again being enigmatically disingenuous. "Do you not believe," he asks, "that I am in the Father and the Father is in me?" (Jn 14:10). It would seem to him to seem they did not. All the way through the final supper the disciples act as though they have still failed to absorb, absorb so as to enact, what Jesus has been trying to share. They have not experienced (perhaps not allowed themselves to experience) what the words should evoke and elicit, even if they have registered the sounds. So Simon Peter persists in misinterpreting Jesus' foot-washing (13:6, 9), Judas is still going to betray him (Jn 13:11), Simon Peter to deny him (13:38). Thomas still fails to recognize Jesus as the way to the Father (14:5). Only when Jesus' followers love him in keeping his word, his commandments, in love for one another, will he be displaying (*emphanizō*) himself to them: in his manifest power then but only then they will be "seeing him." Not keeping his words *is* not loving him, not loving him

---

7. Bultmann, *Theology of the New Testament*, 2:66; Bultmann, *The Gospel of John*, 66 (Jesus simply poses the question, will you accept or reject him); cf. e.g., 119, 499.

8. On which see Painter, *1, 2, 3 John*, 221, "there must be something about him that we do not know"; Lieu, *I, II & III John*, 123–26; Smalley, *1, 2, 3 John*, 145; Kurek-Chomycz, "The Scent of (Mediated) Revelation," 86–87, and 104; comparing also Col 3:4.

9. Downing, *Has Christianity a Revelation?*, 106–13, part of a much longer treatment of the Johannine writings, 97–118.

is, constitutes, not seeing him (Jn 14:21–24); no deeper "seeing" is on offer. But they are still so far from taking on board the Son-and-Father relationship he has tried to share that they are unable to rejoice at Jesus' promised "going to the Father" (Jn 14:28), and, despite further explanation in chapter 15, they are still grieving at Jn 16:6, and confess that they fail to understand him when he talks of being away soon and then back soon (Jn 16:19). In fact they will continue to mourn his absence (Jn 16:20), and that despite the company of his (apparent) *alter ego*, the Paraclete (Jn 14:17; 15:26; 16:7–15). Even when they insist they have at last understood, Jesus tells them, they clearly have not, for they will simply scatter away home (Jn 16:32).

By the time of composition of these dialogues it has been borne in on this author that there has been no effective revelation: there has been physical visibility and physical seeing, but not the sort of deep awareness of the character of Jesus and his relation to his Father that is displayed in appropriate trusting comprehension.[10] As a sociolinguistic analysis indicates, the Gospel is written for the disillusioned, and for all fellow Christians in their failure to see things in this author's way: it does not address an audience of those who have accepted enlightenment by divine revelation.[11] If there is any claim to revelation it is by an author who implicitly claims he alone sees; and what he is sure he sees others have not seen, have not been enabled to see, have certainly not been made to see. And still even what he has understood is far from what would count as a full knowing of Jesus' self, or the Father's.

This, along with the rest of the NT collection and other surviving early Christian writings, still assures us that no revelation of the divine self was believed by "John" to have reached others. And later reception history, while showing John as influential in parts, confirms that it was in no way taken as on its own definitive. Indeed, John was a favorite specifically with those who were convinced that human words and thought forms could not possibly be definitive (see the next chapter). The first letter of John (from the same stable if not the same author) in fact affirms, as noted in the older study, not just that "the world" did not acknowledge Jesus, could not "comprehend"

10. Cf. Lincoln, *The Gospel according to St. John*, 418; on Jn 16:6, "a total lack of comprehension" 422; on Jn 16:19, "heavy underscoring of the disciples' inability to understand," with Keener, *The Gospel of John*, 1043, 428; on Jn 16:32, Jesus has "exposed the groundlessness of the disciples' confidence about their faith and understanding."

11. Culpepper, *Anatomy*, 115. The disciples in the farewell discourse are "surrogates for the church and the reader," and a long paragraph, 118–19. However, although the narrated disciples' failure to understand does allow John's Jesus to explain, this is not in fact all: it is *every* Christ follower's failure to date to understand that is at stake, and it is the reason for writing: North, "Lord, If You had Been Here." Per contra, e.g., Edwards, *Discovering John*, 98–99.

him, but that "we" (even "we in the Johannine community") acknowledge that only when we finally become like him will we be able to see him as he is; and this enhanced seeing is not yet. Even what our change will amount to has not yet itself been revealed. Any appreciable full revelation lies ahead, to be hoped for, expected, but not yet celebrated.

(b) Divine Hiddenness

(i) Gospels and Acts

Further than the foregoing, there seems, then, little to be gained by going back over the evidence for the significant early Christian failure to use the most appropriate terminology available to indicate divine self-revelation already given, received or available, or the imparting of knowledge of the divine self, should those have been in mind. Rather than such repetition, then, and as in the previous chapter, I offer in what follows more positive indications of the opposite, affirmed convictions of divine hiddenness, or of the unavailability of knowledge of God's (or Jesus') "self."

As in the ancient Jewish writings, God remains in a cloud, even when speaking (Matt 17:5; Mk 9:7; Lk 9:34). Cloud indicates the divine presence while still concealing God himself (Acts 1:9; but also Mk 13:26, 14:62, and parallels; 1 Cor 10:1–2; 1 Thess 4:17; Rev 1:7; 11:12; 14:14–16).

Jesus himself, at least in Mark and Matthew, does not know, can only guess, what God has in mind for the world as a whole (Mk 13:32; Matt 24:36). Luke does not allow him such overt ignorance, but if his Jesus knows the Father's mind on this cosmic issue, he is not revealing it (Acts 1:7). In all three Synoptic Gospels he is quite in the dark as to what the Father has in mind for him. He imagines it may well be abandonment to a cup of suffering, but he'll only know from events whether this is the Father's will (Mk 13:32; Matt 24:36; Lk 22:42); John, of course, has Jesus knowing clearly in his own mind (Jn 10:18; 12:27–28). Mark and thence Matthew's Jesus is in distraught agony when he finds such abandonment is indeed God's intention (Mk 15:35; Matt 27:46); though not in Luke,where he is calm (Lk 23:46), nor, of course, in John where he is triumphantly fulfilled (Jn 19:30).

Jesus is constantly allowed in the Synoptics (with John's concurrence, as we have seen) to fail to make his followers understand him, and Peter especially: even the character of his mission, the call to crucifixion, the choice to serve, the refusal to domineer, the call to follow. At its harshest in Mark, it is softened a little in the others: so Matthew insists that Cephas' title for Jesus, *Christos*, came to him "by revelation," yet still accepts that neither the character of the messiahship nor of the anointing deity were themselves revealed. Luke includes some of Mark's critical narratives, omits others, but offers no counter indications.[12]

Luke in Acts is content to display disagreements and misunderstandings, among leaders and ordinary members of the early communities of Jesus' followers, some quite sharp, if not as bitter as noted by Paul. If "revelation" is taken to mean compelling and definitive clarity, there is none suggested by the narrative. Nor is there any "self-revelation" of God offered in the speeches (sermons). It is made clear that an opportunity to change, to acknowledge sins and have them forgiven you is on offer: but even the changes narrated for hearers to admire are left unclear and seem to vary (e.g., the call to a shared purse (Acts 2:43-47; 4:32—5:11, with 5:4). And that is despite a proposed common minimum that "seemed good to the Holy Spirit and to us" (Acts 15:19-20, with 15:28, "seemed good," *edoxen*).

(ii) 1 Cor 13:12 and Other Passages in Paul

Faced, he takes it, with people keen on knowing and confident in what they claim to know, Paul in 1 Corinthians and elsewhere criticizes such assertions, as will be recalled in a moment. Yet early on he seems to undermine his own case by affirming "but we have the mind (*nous*) of Christ" (1 Cor 2:16).[13] However, many recent commentators that I have read agree in calling strict attention to the context. What Paul and his hearers have been given to have in mind is the only knowledge Paul came to share, that the crucified Jesus is God's anointed, Christ, now glorious Lord. This was God's plan, and one that no one could ever have anticipated, for (as Isaiah had insisted), no one shares God's confidence (1 Cor:2, 9, 12, 16, with 1:26-30).[14] We (Christians) can understand "the gifts God has given us," ("wisdom from God, and righteousness and snctification and redemption") but only through the Holy Spirit, who gives us Christ's mind on things, and so is able to shape our living. In practice, sharing Christ's mind, being minded in a manner appropriate to those who are "in Christ," is what we are about, as Paul later reminds the Philippians. There it clearly consists in allowing our minds to

12. "*Christos*," Mk 8:27-33 with Matt 16:23, Lk 9:18-21 spares Peter; precedence, Mk 9:33-41; service, 10:35-45, with Matt blaming the mother, 20:20-28, not Lk, but cf. Lk 22:24-27 and Jn 13:3-11; following boldly, Mk 14:53, with parallels including Jn 18:17, 25-27.

13. Interpreted so by Héring, *Première Corinthiens*, 29: it is said to mean that a Christian can explore the divine essence.

14. Cf. Downing, *Has Christianity a Revelation?* 63-65.

go on being transformed (Phil 2:12–13; cf. Rom 12:1–2). Sharing Christ's mind, being appropriately minded is not, in these instances at least, having mystical or even otherwise enlightening experiences: it means avoiding self-ish ambition and conceit, jealousy and quarrelsomeness (Phil 2:1–14 with 1 Cor 2:16—3:4). We are not "being puffed up" (1 Cor 8:2, as in what follows), we live together in love (as detailed in Rom 12:3—15:13).[15]

Even without the benefit of modern discussions of epistemology, in general Paul is very uneasy with talk of "knowing God." "Knowing" some-one in Paul's Jewish literary context so much suggests choosing, acknowl-edging, as by a superior whose acknowledgment of us is what really matters, that Paul prefers to switch to the latter:

> Now concerning food sacrificed to idols: we know that "all of us possess knowledge." Knowledge puffs up but love builds up. Anyone who claims to know something does not yet have the necessary knowledge; but anyone who loves God is known by him. (1 Cor 8:1–3)

We may compare Gal 4:9, "now you have come to know God, or rather, to be known by God."[16] The commentators cited all link this with the still more explicit 1 Cor 13:12, to which we turn in a little more detail in a moment; for Paul any knowing "Christ Jesus my Lord," any knowing worth terming such, remains to come. This he still makes clear some years later, explaining from prison to his friends in Philippi, "I want to know Christ and the power of his resurrection and the sharing of his sufferings by becoming like him in his death. . . . Not that I have already obtained [better, so some commenta-tors, "grasped"] this or have already reached the goal. . . . I press on" (Phil 3:10–14).[17] He does not immediately say when he expects this conformity to be perfected, but it is certainly not before the final deliverance (Phil 3:21).[18]

15. On 1 Cor 2:1–3:4, see, e.g., Soards, *1 Corinthians*, 62; Collins, *First Corinthians*, 137–38; Schrage, *Korinther*, 266–68; Ciampa, *1 Corinthians*, 137–38; Perkins, *First Cor-inthians*, 63. On Phil 2:1–14, Bonnard, *Philippiens*, 40–52; Beare, *Philippians*, 73–88; Hawthorne, *Philippians*, 70–101.

16. On 1 Cor 8:1–3, Plummer, *Corinthians*, 164–65; Héring, *Corinthiens*, 63–64; Conzelmann, *1 Corinthians*, 140–42; Soards, *1 Corinthians*, 171–72; Ciampa, *1 Cor-inthians*, 375–79 (but missing "known" as "chosen"); Perkins, *First Corinthians*, 114.

17. On Phil 3:10–14, Beare, *Philippians*, 122–23; Hawthorne, *Philippians*, 143–47 (but both want to stress Paul's present awareness more than Paul does). More recent commentators are readier to allow that Paul meant what he said: Fowl, *Philippians*, 159–63, aligns the logic of "grasping/being grasped" with Paul elsewhere on "knowing/being known"; Silva, *Philippians*, 173–74, notes the "intriguing parallel with 1 Cor 13:12, 174; Sumney, *Philippians*, 84–87; Witherington, *Philippians*, accepts that Paul waits to be "fully conformed."

18. Stephen Fowl and Ben Witherington both note the importance to such as

For the argument of this book, the most significant passage in Paul is, of course, 1 Cor 13:12:

> At present we see only puzzling reflections in a mirror, but one day we shall see face to face. My knowledge now is partial; then it will be whole, like God's knowledge of me.[19]

Commentators agree that Paul expresses the certainty that "then" will be very much better than now, but are on the whole less ready to allow for his current uncertainty. Many note the use of *ainigmata*, puzzles, in the LXX of Num 12:6–8, where God says he does not communicate in riddles with Moses, but speaks face to face, so that he may see the appearance (but hardly "the self") of God. And a few of the commentators also then refer to later rabbinic midrash on the passage, where the unpointed word for "appearance" can be interpreted as "mirror," so even Moses's awareness was not immediate. A few of those I have read have noted the use of this imagery by philosophical Greeks, even Paul's Jewish contemporary, Philo of Alexandria.[20] A couple of those listed in footnotes here refer the reader on to 2 Cor 3:18 and 4:6, where again Paul deploys the metaphor of seeing in a mirror (Schrage, dismissively).[21] And some discuss the supposed poor quality of ancient polished metal mirrors, culturally distancing themselves from Paul.

In fact, though Plutarch agrees that poor reflection is useless, he takes it that a good one is normal. This comment occurs in his encouragement to a wife to ensure that her facial expression reflects her husband's moods (of course, not vice-versa).[22] One face can mirror another, as Paul allows (2 Cor 3:18 with 4:6, as just noted); one's behavior, says Philo, Paul's contemporary, can hold up a mirror to others.[23] Not only can you reflect someone else's reality, by introspection you can reflect on your own, as Philo explains; but also, you can reflect divine reality.[24]

Gregory of Nyssa of this "not yet"; see the next chapter.

19. REB. On this passage, and implications still to be spelled out in following chapters, see Downing, "Reflecting."

20. E.g., Conzelmann, *1 Corinthians*, 227–28; Soards, *1 Corinthians*, 278–79; Collins, *First Corinthians*, 486–87; Schrage, *Korinther*, 308–16; Ciampa, *1 Corinthians*, 658–60 ignores the Greeks, apart from Philo.

21. Plummer, *Corinthians*, 299; Schrage, *Korinther*, 311; positive, Perkins, *First Corinthians*, 155.

22. Plutarch, *Coniug. Prae.* 14, *Moralia* 139F–140A; cf. Lucian, *De historia*, 50; Epictetus, *Diss.* 2.14.21.

23. Philo, *De ios.* 87.

24. Philo, *De opif.* 76; *De dec* 105; *De mig.* 98; *De fuga*, 213; *De mos.* 2.137–39; cf. Epictetus, also contemporary, *Diss.* 2.22.51. On this compare Heath, *Visual Piety*, 226–39; she rightly focuses on seeing in Paul, but the whole section seems to include

Philo picks the reference to *ainigmata*, puzzles, in Num 12:6, 8; and while he does not, I think, combine *ainigmata* with mirrors, there is a passage where he treats the words of Scripture as a covering, or a shadow-shape, one that obscures their true function as a mirror of divine reality.[25] The terms are combined by a near contemporary, Plutarch, in an explicitly "theological" discussion. Inanimate things afford only a puzzling clue to the divine (*ainigma tou theiou*), live beings are clearer mirrors.[26] That some later rabbis speculated in these terms with reference to Num 12:6–8 simply adds reassurance.

In the light of this usage, we seem bound to take it that Paul is sure we are already in some puzzling way face to face with Christ, in him beholding the divine glory (2 Cor 3:18, 4:6). This assures us of being in the divine presence without allowing us (yet) to penetrate it, even though we are already being changed increasingly towards becoming ourselves true images of God. Seeing the change in and among us is our assurance that God has welcomed us, God acknowledges us, knows us in a full and positive sense. In and among ourselves we must, then, already be glimpsing more of the divine reality, but it is still unclear, puzzling: which aspects, which parts, of what we see really mirror God? If we knew that, there would, at those points at least, be no puzzle: yet puzzling it still was for Paul. I suppose we could say, well, at those points, in those "parts," we were right, we actually did know after all, only just did not know that we knew. But, as argued in chapter 2, it is misleading to claim that you know at a time when you cannot show you really do know. Knowing God in any full sense, knowing God as God knows us, "divine self-revelation" in anything like that sense, we trust lies ahead, but, according to Paul (if we want to take notice), is certainly not yet given, is not yet ours.

(In later Christian reflection there is a close link between God's "unknowability" and his ineffability, "unsayability." Ineffability also seems to appear in Paul, at 2 Cor 12:4, at least as recently and persuasively argued by Cosmin-Constantin Murariu.)[27]

Divine self-revelation, if it is to happen at all, is not, for Paul, a given past event: any unveiling (re-velation) must happen in the minds of those refusing to be transformed (2 Cor 3:7—4:6). If there is a "veil" that needs removing, it is in humans who allow the "the god of this age" to blind them; it is not around God.

"any" who are in Christ.

25. Philo, *Leg. all.* 3.103, cf. *De spec. leg.* 1.26; *Quis haer.* 262; *De vita cont.* 78.

26. Plutarch, *De is. et os.* 76, *Moralia* 382A; cf 80, 384A.

27. Murariu, "Impermissibility or Impossibility?"

Then in further support we may compare 1 Jn 3:2, touched on earlier, as evidence for a similar early Christian agnosticism, insistence on our not yet knowing.

(c) Identification

Compared with the older Scriptures, God in the New Testament collection is very rarely narrated as identifying himself in speech. He does so in all three Synoptic Gospels at the baptism of Jesus, and once more at Jesus' transfiguration, specifically as the father of this son, the son to whom he on the mountain commands his hearers' attention. "The Father" identifies himself quite distinctively in John in response to a request from Jesus, that he glorify his own name, reputation. A voice from heaven assures some perceptive bystanders at least that he has done so, and will again. Jesus says this is announced for the hearers' sakes; he himself did not need it (Jn 12:28–30). Then, according to John the seer, "the Lord God" identifies himself with "I am the Alpha and the Omega, who is and who was and who is to come" (Rev 1:8), but where and when and to whom are not explained. Nowhere is God identified as yet self-revealing in any full sense; nor does any such clarity seem to be implied.

"God" is variously, if only implicitly, identified as the certain or likely cause of events, such as exorcism (Matt 12:28; Lk 11:20), or storm-stilling (Mk 4:41 and parallels, with Jesus as divinely empowered) or healing (Jn 9:30–33; cf. 14:11; Acts 4:30). God is taken as the agent in the tearing of the temple curtain at the death of Jesus (Mk 15:38–39; Matt 27:51, 54; Lk 23:45, 47); and in punishment of individuals (Acts 5:1—11; 1 Cor 10:5; 11:30) and communities (Mk 12:9 and parallels; Mk 13:20 with Matt 24:22; Rev 6; 14:8; 18—punishments past or prospective, or both).

God is also identified on a few occasions as refusing to show favoritism: he displays no "respect of persons," *prosōpolēmpsia* (Rom 2:11; Col 3:25; Eph 6:9; Acts 10:34; and cf. Gal 2:6). Perhaps better, however, in the light of the various contexts, would be, "is not influenced by status." Fellow Christians are also enjoined to avoid any such regard for status as ungodly (Jas 1:1, 9; Jude 16), and Jesus is flattered by their ackowledging his customary refusal of any such favoritism (Mk 12:14; Matt 22:16; Lk 20:21). Jesus as sketched in the Gospels does seem to avoid it: if he heals a centurion's favorite, it is the latter's faith, not his rank, that impresses the healer. And if he restores the daughter of a synagogue leader, he takes time out to assure a hemorrhaging woman that her faith was instrumental. Paul's gentile mission evinces his acceptance that this is God's ethos (Gal 2:6, Rom 2:11). I think Luke's

Acts is less consistent: though ethnic status is ignored, other social status is emphasized. And, embarrassed, it would seem by divine choice (Rom 9:14 through to 11:36), Paul simply replies, it is an arbitrary making of favorites for a purpose, so (implicitly) still displaying no attention to status.

One may reflect further on God as ignoring status. Unless one takes a "universalist" line on life after death (in accord, just possibly, with Rom 11:25–26), the problem remains. And even with a post-mortem universalism, divine providential care in this life still seems to have favored Europe.

Mostly the one who is narrated as identifying himself, or identified by others, is Jesus; his identification as son by God (Mk 1:11) has been mentioned above. In what follows I summarize the rest of the first eighth or so of Mark, usually with quite or very close parallels in Matthew and Luke. Jesus identifies himself as herald of God's rule, demanding change and trust (Mk 1:15 and parallels); as an exorcist (Mk 1:23–26 and parallels); and then is more specifically but variously identified by the unclean spirits (but he objects to such disclosure). He is displayed as a healer by healing (Mk 1:41 and parallels), and, as such, as one authorized to remit sins (Mk 2:5–12 and parallels) and to befriend sinners, and that as itself therapeutic (Mk 2:16–17 and parallels). He is a metaphorical bridegroom (Mk 2:19) ushering in the new, with authority as Son of Man to redefine Sabbath observance: as life-enhancing, not threatening (Mk 2:21—3:5; "Son of Man" being explained later as also a title of glory).

In Matthew and in Luke, rather than relying on the Father to identify him, at one point Jesus, as recalled above, identifies himself as alone able to identify the divine father; but elsewhere he also identifies himself as one greater than Jonah, greater than Solomon (Matt 11:25–27; 12:41–42; Lk 10:21–22; 11:31–32). Yet he also identifies himself as one who, as Son of Man, inevitably must sustain humiliation and death, called to serve in liberating the majority, at least, of people (Mk 8:31 etc., and parallels; and 10:45, with Matt 16:21, 20:28; cf. Lk 22:27). Intriguingly, in Acts the risen Jesus identifies himself as suffering with his followers (Acts 9:5; 22:7; 26:15). The same, similar, and different positive and exalted identifications are offered by others (for instance, in the birth narratives in Matthew and in Luke), besides malign ones by a few opponents.

Much the same can be said of the Fourth Gospel. God's sole self-identification (as self-glorying) was noted earlier. There is a significant difference, in that the Word who is divine and agent in creation is identified with Jesus from the start, to be followed by Jesus in turn identifying himself with echoes of divine self-identification ("I am") drawn from Exod 6:14 and Isa 41:3, etc., at Jn 8:58 etc. And here, rather than God identifying the son as his, as in the synoptic baptism and transfiguration accounts, it is Jesus who identifies the Father as his. Yet he does this by subsuming himself in the Father, making himself, as is often said, "transparent" to the Father. He can do nothing on his own accord (Jn 5:19, 30–33; 6:38; 7:17–19; 8:50, 54; 12:44; etc.), seeking only to glorify the Father. You look at Jesus to look through him to the Father, and if you do see the Father you will know that you do; you will bear unspecified "fruit" (Jn 15:1–5). The only criterion for the appropriateness of the disciples' response is their unity, unity in love for one another, a unity, it would seem, mirroring that of Father and Son (Jn 17:21–23). As argued earlier in this chapter, the text as it stands makes it quite clear that there is no deep self-revealing by God as yet. There is only an invitation to engage in John's kind of rhetoric, clear of rival reflections, as a shared waiting, waiting to be made like Christ when he does finally manifest himself.

That must suffice as a sketch of something of the range just in the gospels and Acts, and already some variations among them have been noted. It was suggested in the previous chapter, that many narrated divine self-identifications and identifications of God by others in the Jewish canon clashed too seriously to allow us to take them as identifications of the same person; or, if of one person, then only as a very mixed-up and inconsistent and unreliable one.

We need to ask now how coherent are the foregoing and other New Testament identifications of God and of Jesus. But before that there are two preliminary questions. One was touched on in the previous chapter: are we in this collection, then, to expect God as narrated to be trustworthy, faithful, consistent? The answer from some at least is affirmative: with God "there is no variation or shadow due to change" (Jas 1:17; cf. Rom 9:6; 1 Cor 1:9; 2 Cor 1:18; 1 Thess 5:24; Heb 6:18; Tit 1:2). The second is, are we expected to be like God, is our behavior to be modeled on his, so that what is morally expected of us can be expected of actions and attitudes ascribed to God? In Paul, for sure, we are explicitly urged to imitate Christ, as Paul does (1 Cor 11:1; 1 Thess 1:6), and so, implicitly, imitate God whose image Christ is. Imitating God is also implied by our being urged to welcome, accept one another, as God has done (Rom 14:3). We should emulate the valuation implicit in God's choice (1 Cor 1:26–29 and 12:24); God's peacefulness (1 Cor 14:33); faithful consistency (2 Cor 1:17–18); unfailing generosity (2 Cor 9:6–15); refusal to be law-bound (Gal 3:5).[28] At Eph 4:32 we are urged to "be kind to one another, tender hearted, forgiving one another, as God in Christ has forgiven you" (cf. 2 Cor 2:10; Col 3:12–13). Matthew 5:48 urges hearers to "be perfect as your heavenly father is perfect," where Lk 6:36, in

---

28. See the discussion in Downing, "One God, One Lord" ch. 7, in Downing, *Cynics, Paul*, 204–49, citing 207.

a similar context of kindness to enemies, has "be merciful [compassionate] just as your Father is."

(d) Diversity in Identifications

Many at least apparent inconsistencies in actions ascribed to God cluster around issues of responses to offenses, sins, and especially sins seen as debts. Both Matthew's and Luke's Jesus urges the hearers not to "judge," not to condemn, we may take it, by their social actions (Matt 7:1–5; Lk 6:37); a stance echoed by Paul (Rom 14:4, 13; cf. Jas 2:12–13). Yet Matthew's Jesus himself appears extremely judgemental in chapter 23, with vituperative woes against Pharisees and scribes as "children of hell" (condemned to indeterminate punishment). Luke's Jesus is only a little briefer in his vituperation (Lk 11:39–52). One may compare Paul (Rom 1:18—2:34; Phil 3:2). And yet Matthew's Jesus himself also forbids even vituperation (Matt 5:22); compare Paul, "bless, don't curse," (Rom 12:14b; also, perhaps, Jas 3:9–10; 4:11). Of course, we may try to follow the ascribed ideal rather than the ascribed practice. So we might hold the writers, not Jesus, responsible, and try to excuse the former for their apparent inconsistency. Perhaps those who show no appreciation of tolerant non-judgementalism and goodwill can be held to have brought the contrary on themselves, and deserve it. I doubt if that will convince the reader; it certainly fails to persuade me.

Even more emphatic than eschewing condemnatory judgement is the positive insistence on forgiveness. Jesus is portrayed as extending forgiveness, and freely. He not only declares it, but by his removal of what would be likely to be perceived as punitive illness, he strikingly enacts forgiveness; and he also forcefully enjoins it. Later followers repeat the lesson (as already illustrated above). An emphasis on interpersonal forgiveness is particularly strong in the teaching of Matthew's Jesus, with prompt reconciliation urged (Matt 5:23–24).[29] Yet, as we have just noted, Matthew's Jesus and Luke's display quite the opposite in their attitudes to Pharisees and Scribes (contrast also Mark's Jesus to a scribe, at Mk 12:28–34).

Furthermore, right through the New Testament collection communal and private disasters are unquestioningly identified, with very few exceptions, as acts of an apparently very unforgiving God (again, as illustrated earlier).[30]

---

29. Cf. Downing, "Forgiveness"; but especially Mbabazi's, *Interpersonal Forgiveness.*

30. A selection: punishment for individuals, Acts 5:1–11; 1 Cor 10:5, 11:30; communal, Mk 12:9 and parallels; Mk 13:20 with Matt 24:22; Rev 6; 14:8; 18 (punishments past or prospective, or both). Exceptions: Matt 2:16–18; Lk 9:54–55; 13:1–4 (but cf. v.

Then, is one told to repent to qualify for the remission of sin as debt, or is repentance expected as one's grateful response? Jesus in the Synoptic Gospels is certainly portrayed as demanding repentance as a trusting response to the rule of God (heaven) proclaimed by him and his twelve closest followers. (Both John's Jesus and his Baptist, avoid "repent, repentance," *metanoiein, metanoia*, though both enjoin change.) But in none of the four does Jesus make a change of mind-set, let alone of practice, a precondition for healing, or for acceptance as disciple or friend. Luke's parable of the spendthrift son "coming to his senses" is often interpreted as emphasizing contrition, especially in the light of the refrain ending the first two parables in Lk 15. But Luke does not repeat the term "repents," and when elsewhere he uses "came to himself" it is of Peter coming to his senses (Acts 12:11). Forgiveness terms are rare and only incidental in Paul; and when Paul celebrates God setting us right with himself, there is no hint of a prior qualifying change on our side, only an insistence on our trusting acceptance. We are "reconciled," "at-oned" (God unites us with himself) while we are still enemies. Change, transformation are certainly expected, but as following, not preceding.[31] Yet Mark's and Luke's John proclaims repentance "for" forgiveness (Mk 1:4; Lk 3:3), and at Lk 24:27 Jesus does the same. Later, at Acts 2:38 (cf. 3:19; 5:31; but contrast 10:43–48) Peter demands repentance (still undefined) as a condition for forgiveness. Whether God has a preference, and if so, which it is, does not seem to have been revealed, then or now.

The Jesus of each of the four Gospels inculcates service, by word and by example; and in the first three contrasts this with what is expected of emperors and other great men (Mk 10:42–45; Matt 20:25–28; Lk 22:24–27; cf. Jn 13:1–17, including the contrast with what might be expected of a "Lord and master"; and cf. Phil 2:6–11. Yet there remains much in the collection that seems to portray God as an unreformed Hellenistic king or Roman emperor (Matt 13:49–50; 18:34–35; 22:13; Mk 9:42–47; Lk 12:4, 46–48; 19:27; Rom 2:5–11; Gal 6:21; 2 Thess 2:9–12; Heb 10:26–27; 2 Pet 2:1–10; Jude 14–15; Rev 6, and 8–9; 19:3; 20:15 (even if enigmatically balanced by such as 21:24, where the condemned seem to find themselves accepted). If God the Father is like that, then Jesus as son in his this-earthly life must seem to have signally failed to emulate him, and thus to have completely failed to reveal him. Instead Jesus must seem to have contradicted him in word and deed.

5!); Jn 9:2–3.

31. See the discussions on "faith," "trust," noted in Downing, "Ambiguity"; and on "Setting right," in Downing, "Justification."

There are other discrepancies. I note here encouragement to pray repeatedly at Lk 11:5–8; 18:1–8; Eph 6:18; with Matt 6:7, where heaped-up words are disparaged. I include attitudes to Torah in Matt 5:17–20 on righteousness and in Paul, "If righteousness/justification comes through the law, Christ died for nothing." (Gal 2:21, cf. 3:19, read as "the law was added for the sake of transgressions," *tōn parabaseōn charin*, Gal 3:19.) Or, important for many Christians, Jesus as of the seed of David in Paul and elsewhere (Rom 1:3), entailing Joseph as father; over against Luke and Matthew, where Joseph is only an adoptive parent.[32]

In Rom 1:24–27 God is seen as opposing any (sexual) deviation from "nature," whereas in Rom 11:13–24 God is seen as himself doing something at least analogous to transgressing nature (in grafting Gentiles into the cultivated Israelite olive tree).[33]

Or there is the God-given and God-backed authority of first century CE Roman emperors and their deputies (Rom 13:1–6; and that as a guide to politics today), over against Rev 13. (Or is Paul, as some aver, being ironic, himself sure there is only one God, one Lord [1 Cor 8:6], so Caesar is neither and his adjutants' authority spurious?)

The "Erastian" reading of Rom 13 is often backed by Mk 12:17 (or, Mk 12:17 is traditionally interpreted to suit that reading of Romans). Yet if Mk 12:17b ("to God what belongs to God") is taken in the light of the Psalter's, and exilic Isaiah's, and Paul's own insistence that "the earth is the Lord's, the entirety of it" (1 Cor 10:26), the question seems to be thrown back at the hearers. What size God does these Pharisees' and Herodians' question indicate; what God of everything, or relegated Godlet, will they acknowledge?

Obviously Christian leaders and Christians led have made choices among these conflicting assertions, ignoring what does not suit them or persuade them or baffles them. Perhaps the focus is on different strands at different periods, and ignores discrepancies not then in view. Or having chosen what persuades them, Christian leaders have reinterpreted more or less drastically what may seem to be in conflict so as to give a semblance of harmony. But what best represents God, God's character, God's self, remains a puzzle, still quite unclarified, unrevealed.

My own proposal, for what it is worth, is to choose boldly. But then I still choose to retain the remainder to keep me from quiescence, and to maintain a base for discussion together with others who are held by different Bible-stimulated versions of God in Christ in the power of the Spirit.

32. Downing, "Women and Men," 182–87.

33. Rogers, "Same Sex," argues that here Paul retracts Rom 1; I wish I were persuaded.

Togetherness, a trust that this enigmatic God is with us, has united us to himself, is the most prevalent common motif, it was argued, in the Jewish canon; and perhaps it is so in the Christian one, even if the character of the one who is elusively present and at-one-ing us does remain unsettled.

(e) God's "Self"

As in the previous chapter, I have to confess, I have not been made aware of any attempt, scholarly or otherwise, to clarify let alone specify what may be understood by "self" in talk of "the self-revelation" of God. Again, while there is plenty of material that can validly be read as indicating a sense of a human "self," it does not seem to be echoed or mirrored in talk of God.[34] The discussion earlier of the Fourth Gospel on knowing someone well as contrasted with lacking any such knowledge of Jesus, the Son, is more widely indicative. "Heart" and "mind" could have been used for God's inner self; but are not. God reveals specific plans, wishes, and demands; but not his whole heart, mind.

(f) Reconciled by God to be at One with Him

(i) Paul

> If anyone is in Christ, there is a new creation: everything old has passed away; see, everything has become new! All this is from God, who reconciled us to himself through Christ, and has given us the ministry of reconciliation; that is, in Christ God was reconciling the world to himself. . . . So we are ambassadors for Christ, since God is making his appeal through us; we entreat you on behalf of Christ, be reconciled to God (2 Cor 5:17–20; NRSV).

This passage, where Paul uses the words *katallasso, katallagē,* "reconcile," "reconciliation," with emphatic repetition, is the one most often quoted when ideas of reconciliation, becoming at one with God, are discussed by Christian theologians (as already noted in the second chapter). Theologians often observe that Paul uses these terms, of God with humans, only elsewhere in Rom 5:10–11, 11:15, though *apokatallassō* is used at Eph. 2:16, and Col 1:20–21. It has also been noted that William Tyndale's sixteenth-century English translation offered the words "atone," "atonement," an older

---

34. Again, see Downing, "Order."

term signifying making one, "at-one-ment." That might well seem closer to general Greek usage, which deploys these terms (and others with *allassō*) to talk of kinds of change, changing money, but often change from apartness to togetherness, unity.[35] Whether that means a return to an older but currently broken unity depends on the context. It is so at 1 Cor 7:11, where *katallagētō* is used for "let a wife be reconciled with her husband." It is shown clearly not so when Paul uses this terminology again at Rom 5:6–11, for it is enemies (v. 8) who are granted peace, made at one with God; not erstwhile friends. Only one of the five recent commentators consulted on the passage in 2 Cor introduced the thought of restoration, and that without relating it to anything in the text.[36]

It is often mistakenly asserted that the Greek usage is purely secular; but Dionysius of Halicarnassus and Josephus, for instance, readily talk of Gods or God being easily reconciled to penitent humans. Here, too, a prior, in this case recently disrupted harmony is obviously in mind.[37] Paul, however, emphatically insists that something very important and quite new has happened, not that some erstwhile togetherness has been restored. This is the beginning of the process of reconciling, uniting "the world" to himself, the basis of the appeal "be reconciled," "be at-oned," to those who obviously still are not. Others, however, it would seem, in Corinth, as later in Rome, have already gained this new, shared identity, accepting the invitation and from being enemy aliens have become friends, set right with God. These Gentile outsiders are now accepted (Rom 11:15), at peace with God, his love for them flooding their hearts, their minds (Rom 5:1–11, noting 1 and 5).[38]

There is no suggestion here that any of those addressed (even in the distant past) were once in harmony with God, at one with God. Later Christian reflection, however, decided that in the instance of Adam and Eve, humankind as a whole had indeed briefly been at one with God, in a unity now being restored. One may note the Latin translations, always using *reconciliare*, with the *re-* seeming to convey the (inception of) a renewal of

35. Liddell and Scott, *A Greek-English Lexicon*, 898: *katall-* etc.

36. Harris, *Second Corinthians*, 436, though fully aware that no original friendship is implied; Héring, *La Seconde*, 53, can only bring Adam in with the help of Col 1:13 and 2:14–15.

37. Dionysius, *RA* 80.50.4; Josephus, *War* 5.416, using the cognate εὐδιάλλακτον.

38. Compare the discusssion in Thrall, *2 Corinthians 1–7*, 420–38; Harris, *Second Corinthians*, 424–49; Roetzel, *2 Corinthians*, 78–82, God dealing with humans who are alienated, not humanity having become so; Martin, *2 Corinthians*, 138–58; Lambrecht, *Second Corinthians*, 96–100; and Esler, *Romans*, 196–99; Witherington, *Romans*, 131–40; Dunn, *Romans*, 244–69; Jewett, *Romans*, 344–68, preferring (against most commentators) the 5:1 reading, "let us have peace"—although that conflicts with the already shared assurance of this passage as a whole.

an earlier, now broken harmony, even though *conciliare* would have been closer to the openness of the Greek. Certainly, Paul *could* have supposed a restoration of Eden, or of one or more of the covenants (compare again, his talk of the reconciling of a separated wife and husband), but he does not say so here: it is "new creation," not restored creation. We may compare his sharp contrast elsewhere between the old and the new Adam: Christ is the second, and new; not the first, the earthly one, reborn (1 Cor 15:45–49). And even if Paul could have supposed that God with Abraham had anticipated such reconciliation, at-one-ment, he does not talk of a broken previous covenant being reasserted, but of a previous one that brought death, not life (2 Cor 3:7). There is no suggestion that any of those fellow Jews currently being invited were being invited to come back, return to a unity they had relinquished. In terms used in Romans, "all (Jew and Gentile) have fallen short": all are enemies, all have fallen short, not some fallen short, some fallen away.

When Paul talks of "new creation," and "all things," it seems to me, here against my commentators, unsafe to exclude the possibility that a cosmic scope could also be in mind (compare Rom 8:20–23, and the deutero-Pauline Col 1:20–21, Eph 2:16): but the focus here, is for sure, on current humankind. That God has reconciled, united the whole cosmos to himself is, of course, a bigger and riskier claim than that of the reconciliation of humankind. Do we, and even more, does the physical world look reconciled, united with God? George H. van Kooten cogently argues that the author of Ephesians is firmly qualifying the more exuberant claims of Colossians.[39] The issue remains for further reflection in the final chapter.

There is, then, widespread agreement, albeit with differing nuances in detail, that Paul invites hearers and readers to reflect on a new and positive relationship with God they already share, one that offers them along with Paul himself the possiblity of a continuing transformation (e.g., 2 Cor 3:18 with 5:15 and 6:1; Rom 5:3–4, with 12:2).

There is also widespread and age-long theological attention to the metaphors that Paul deploys in these and other affirmations, and deploys without further elaboration. Yet instead of allowing Paul to be allusive, and intending to be, there is a wide but not universal agreement among Christian commentators that his metaphors must be delimited and turned into precise similes for the rationale, almost the mechanics, of God's setting right, reconciling, accepting, saving, at-one-ing.

Thus in one of the passages discussed above, Paul asserts his conviction that Christ "died for all, therefore all have died" (2 Cor 5:14; for the first phrase, cf. 1 Cor 15:3; Rom 5:8). He takes this solidarity as intelligible

39. Van Kooten, *Cosmic Christology*.

without, it seems, seeing any need to explain how it happens or has happened, only generalizing its implication, a reciprocal "living for him who died and was raised for them" (2 Cor 5:15).[40] It has turned out that the death—now, death and resurrection—of Christ has in practice enabled this experienced solidarity. It is, it seeems, potential for all, and is actualized, it is suggested elsewhere, in the experience of Holy Spirit (Gal 3:3), and/or in baptism (both, 1 Cor 12:4–13; Gal 3:26–29; Rom 6:3–11). With "for" (*huper*) the "how," or the "why," how or why the death or the life benefits the target persons is not specified; nor, it seems, does it need to be. If it happens, it happens. And if it happened, why would it require an explanation? Ralph Martin, however, (citing many others) insists on a "substitutionary" sense for *huper* to explain how Christ's death benefits others. This Margaret Thrall cogently rejects, as all are specifically *included* (or may be) in Christ's dying, not substituted for. Further, Harris points out that Paul has Christ raised "for" (*huper*, again) those for whom he died (2 Cor 5:15), which here is certainly not "instead of." Even so, Thrall and Calvin Roetzel, for instance, both introduce "sacrifice," "sacrificial," but without further elaboration, though Harris does avoid it.[41]

I have yet to find a commentator asking, or noting colleagues asking how neutral aliens were made into friends, or enemies were (re-)conciled in Paul's world. Plutarch claims that Alexander refused Aristotle's advice:

> Have regard for the Greeks as friends and kindred, but to conduct himself towards other peoples as though they were plants or animals, encumbering his leadership with battles and banishments and seditions . . . instead he brought together into one all people everywhere, uniting and mixing in one great loving-cup, as it were, people's lives, customs, marriages, life-styles.[42]

Plutarch's Alexander himself adopted a sort of "composite dress," Persian and Macedonian: adopting and encouraging a sense of solidarity. Elsewhere on Alexander, Plutarch has him not seizing loot, rather himself obedient to, conforming to his announced ideals, striving to make all peoples into

40. The centrality of this solidarity, of being "in Christ" is itself fully noted, e.g., in Thrall, *Second Corinthians*, 433–34; Harris, *Second Corinthians*, 255–56, 431–32; and in Gorman, *Inhabiting the Cruciform God*. On "for," ὑπέρ, as "for the benefit of," not "instead of," see Bieringer, "Dying and Being Raised."

41. BAGD offers a substitutionary sense specifically for this passage; checking one example offered from elsewhere, Jos. *Apion* 2.142, I drew a blank. Liddell and Scott, *A Greek-English Lexicon*, give none. Marshall, *2 Corinthians*, 130–31; Thrall, *Second Corinthians*, 408–9; Roetzel, *2 Corinthians*, 80, adding "Rather than a theory of atonement."

42. Plutarch, *De Alexandri* 6 (*Moralia* 329 BC), LCL, adapted; see the discussion in Downing, *Order*, 13–16.

one. (The resonance with Paul's Christ in Phil 2:5–11 has been noted.) Roman emperors claimed Alexander as their forebear, though usually created peace by sparing from total destruction those who surrendered abjectly and encouraging a foreign aristocracy to adopt a degree of "Romanitas," while devastating all resisters. Plutarch implicitly contrasts the Romans with his idealized Alexander. In Paul God (re-)conciles, unites with himself by his Christ's own solidarity with sinners, in it enabling and inviting and encouraging solidarity with himself.[43] Not holding against us past hostile acts, trespasses, and, instead, solidarity with us, is a way of conciliation that could make sense in Paul's world without further analysis or explanation.

That such a sense of solidarity is logically implicit throughout Paul's surviving letters has been argued in effective detail by Daniel Powers, looking at the implicit acceptance of solidarity in phrases such as "died for us," "raised for us" to share his new life, his being right with God, "given/ giving himself, for us, for us to share in, have communion in his body. Christ lives, died, was raised to include us in his life, in himself, and in no way as a substitute for us.[44]

Christ's solidarity with sinful humanity is noted by Paul in various brief phrases. He was, as just noted, with us in his death "for us." "For us, God made him to be sin who knew no sin, so that in him we might become the righteousness of God" (2 Cor 5:21). In their commentaries, Thrall and Harris both offer a thorough discussion of suggested interpretations.[45] None of them persuades me: they all propose an underlying theological position ("sin-offering" or "penal substitute") for which there is no explicit evidence in Paul's surviving letters. Even Powers seems to supposed that for Paul Christ suffered alienation from God in his solidarity with us, was "made to be sin for us" (2 Cor 5:21a). Rather, I suggest, we should take it that treating Christ as a sinner, by crucifying him, was for Paul a mistake made by the ruling powers (1 Cor 2:8), albeit permitted by God. Instead, and quite simply, we may take it that Christ crucified seemed to be but was not an epitome of sin, his whole life there identified with alien humanity. Yet in imagined reality, for Paul, he was and is all the while the focus of God's ending alienation, now denoted as conciling, setting us right with himself by our acceptance of identification with Christ, our solidarity "in him" (v. 21b). If more needs adding in support, we may note that elsewhere Paul says,

43. Cf. Thrall, *Second Corinthians*, 442; cited with approval by Powers, *Salvation through Participation*, 64–67; earlier, Whitely, *The Theology of St. Paul*, 130, 155.

44. Powers, *Salvation through Participation*; see his summaries, e.g., 56, 84–85, 109–10, 142, 166, 191; Gorman, *Inhabiting the Cruciform God*, 3n6, and 68n75.

45. Thrall, *Second Corinthians*, 439–49. Though she rightly emphasizes identification with Harris, *Second Corinthians*, 449–56.

"Christ became a curse for us" (Gal 3:13): in the eyes of fellow Jews, and perhaps the wider world (1 Cor 2:8), the whole of Jesus' life stood condemned
as sinful, apparently shown under God's curse, by his crucifixion. That this
was mistaken, a false impression, and not in fact God's view, was shown by
his raising Jesus to glory, as his Christ, his anointed. What seemed to display
an epitome of sin, of alienation by God from God, itself turned out to have
been all along a display of God's righteousness, God's setting people right,
uniting them with his Son and so with himself (2 Cor 5:21b, again, with v.
11; cf. also Rom 3:26).[46] Then much the same is said later in Rom 8:1–4,
where vv. 3–4 run:

> For God has done what the law, weakened by the flesh, could
> not do: by sending his own Son in the likeness of sinful flesh,
> and to deal with sin, he condemned sin in the flesh, so that the
> just requirement of the law might be fulfilled in us, who walk,
> not according to the flesh, but according to the Spirit.

("The just requirement of the law," as Paul has argued, being, so the law itself
implies, to trust God, not law, for being right with God.) Metaphors such as
those in Rom 3:24–25, 8:3, with their talk of redemption and propitiation/
expiation, or 1 Cor 1:30, 6:11, may be taken as intentionally left open by
Paul. Being set right by God seems somewhat like having been liberated
from slavery or the debt that might end you in slavery; it is a bit like the
experience of having had a purifying sacrifice offered for you (while noting
how infrequently are purifying terms used by Paul generally), and so on.[47]

And perhaps we should appreciate the identification implied in "taking the form of a slave" (Phil 2:7) read with Gal 4:8–10: Paul's Christ, "born
under the law" shared our slavery to elemental forces. This then might encourage us (but hardly oblige us) to allow that Jesus will have been, like us,
bound up in an unjust society. We might still imagine that, for Paul, Jesus
never deliberately did or entertained the idea of doing anything he saw as
alienating him from God as he perceived God (Paul's "who knew no sin").
Paul's Christ is thus taken to have accepted solidarity with other humans as
an involuntary captive enslaved to communal sinfulness, while leaving his

---

46. On taking "justification" as overlapping, at least, with "making one," "at-one-
ment," Tanner, *Christ the Key*, 256.

47. Gorman, *Inhabiting the Cruciform God*, 102, taking such terms as about results
in us, not explanations of means; cf. Tanner, *Jesus, Humanity, and the Trinity*, 39 and
87–89; *Christ the Key*, 247–61. For very clear surveys of atonement/salvation/redemp-
tion "explanatory" models/metaphors, Dillistone, *Atonement*; McIntyre, *The Shape of
Soteriology*.

overt relationship with his Father intact. Well, at least that's one possible interpretation of Paul's very condensed affirmation.[48]

So much for Paul's Christ's solidarity, identification with fellow humans. Our solidarity with Christ is expressed by Paul in the repeated phrase "in Christ." I quote part of a good summary in Harris:

> So ubiquitous (over 160 uses) and the person of Christ so central that, not surprisingly, some scholars see this as the central or unifying motif in Pauline theology. Of the main interpretations of the phrase—the local or "mystical," the ecclesiological, the eschatological, the soteriological, the representative, and the personal—the approaches that accommodate the largest number of uses seem to be the personal and the ecclesiological. That is, "in Christ" often means "in personal union with the risen Christ" or "in the body of Christ" (= the church).[49]

My own interpretation here is that these, together with talk of "being the body of Christ" (e.g., 1 Cor 12:12–27; Rom 12:4–5) constitutes also the heart of Pauline soteriology. It seems to me that Ben Blackwell amply justifies his recent coinage, "Christosis," in interpreting this strand in Paul, but also in noting considerable overlapping (not identity) with "deification" themes in Ireneus and Clement of Alexandria.[50] It is by allowing ourselves to be drawn to identification with Christ, living as his body, that we enjoy "salvation," wellbeing with God. I can then also accept Michael J. Gorman's earlier argued choice of the term "theosis" ("divinization") to summarize what is implicit in what Paul attempts to share. Gorman offers this definition of his use of the word:

> Theosis is transformative participation in the kenotic cruciform character of God through Spirit-enabled conformity to the incarnate, crucified and resurrected/glorified Christ.[51]

Later he conlcudes

> . . . we may propose theosis, rather than, say, justification or reconciliation, or even participation, as the centre of Paul's theology.

---

48. Cf. the discussion in Tanner, *Jesus, Humanity, and the Trinity,* 52, 75; more fully, in *Christ the Key,* 170–71.

49. Harris, *Second Corinthians,* 431; he lists a number of writers in illustration; I add from the more distant past, Kramer, *Christ, Lord, Son of God,* 114–46, with 177–79 ("in the Lord").

50. Blackwell, *Christosis.*

51. Gorman, *Inhabiting the Cruciform God,* 162. "Kenotic" refers to Phil 2:6–11, presented as Paul's "master story" in detail in ch. 1.

Justification and its Pauline synonym reconciliation [2 Cor 5:21, etc.] are, as we have seen, a large part of theosis. And theosis is certainly a soteriology of participation. But "justification" and "reconciliation" are terms that are a bit too narrow to indicate the heartbeat of Pauline soteriology, while "participation" is inevitably a bit vague. Theosis is a better choice. It is, of course, *cruciform* theosis.[52]

It is precisely these strands of forensics ("justification") and suffering that Blackwell notes are not taken up by Clement or Ireneus, but that we might well wish to retain.[53]

Christ's solidarity with us as a fellow human is narrated in the Gospels, most explicitly in Jn 1:14, "the Word became flesh and dwelt among us," itself echoed in 1 Jn 1:1–3; 4:2. Elsewhere it is most clearly emphasized in Hebrews (Heb 1:9–14; 4:14–16; 5:7–8).

(ii) Other New Testament Writings

Much more briefly I now offer a survey of the promise or hope of unity with God as expressed by other authors in the New Testament collection.

Matthew offers "God with us" Matt 1:23, and Jesus "with us" (Matt 18:20; 28:20), but also in needy followers (Matt 25:40, 45). Mark (followed by Matthew and Luke) has Jesus invite an ongoing costly following (Mk 8:34), and, enigmatically, the risen Christ's presence "in Galilee" (Mk 14:26, 16:7). Luke's Christ promises the Holy Spirit, and seems in touch "from heaven," as well as being identified with suffering followers: in persecuting them Paul was persecuting him (Acts 9:4, 22:8, 26:15).

Mutual "abiding in," as deployed by John, comes close to Paul's "in Christ," especially in Jn 15, while it is then paralleled, not necessarily strengthened, with "abiding in my love." However, at Jn 17:21 Jesus prays, "As you father are in me and I am in you, may they also be in us," (unparalleled in Paul) and this and the abiding language recur in the first epistle (1 Jn 2:24; 3:24; 42, 16).

Colossians and Ephesians, as deutero-Pauline writings, continue with the phrase "in Christ," with much the same range of senses; including churchly (e.g., Col 1:18, 24, 27; 2:19; 3:15; and Eph 1:13; 22–23; 2:16;

52. Ibid., 171. It is only here (though this is the thrust of the study) that I claim support. Gorman is, though only incidentally, too ready to talk of Paul's (supposed) conviction that talk of " the light of the knowledge of the glory of God" (2 Cor 3:18) as "God's self-revelation," (120).

53. Blackwell, *Christosis*, e.g., 262.

4:15–16; 5:30). Christ's ongoing solidarity with us is most strongly emphasized in Hebrews, Christ as the leader who continues to take his people into heaven with him (Jack McKelvey). With John's Apocalypse one has to decide whether God's dwelling with humans is purely a future hope, or already anticipated (Rev 3:6 and 21:3). (Be it recognized, most, but not every New Testament writing articulates this double motif.)

That God enables us together to identify with his Son, his Christ, to be united with him, leads, as noted, into the patristic reading of the New Testament documents in terms of *theiosis*, "deification," our formation, our readying for divine self-revelation, for a final face-to-face knowledge of God; or at least for massively increasing such awareness. Second Peter, talking of Christians as "sharers in the divine nature" introduces that terminology, to be explored further in the next chapter.[54]

And that shared hope then prompts the argument of the final chapters. Together, in all our variety, we may trust we are in Christ in the power of the Spirit already beginning to be fitted for God's self-revelation, or at least, for fuller readying.

---

54. See Starr, *Sharers in the Divine Nature*.

5

Ongoing Christian Tradition [1]

(a) Revelation and Knowledge of God

Has Christianity? surveyed, in elements of ongoing Christian tradition, claims of "revelation" of or by God: that is, claims of knowledge of God, enablingly granted by God. Included were eleven sources from the first five centuries, and then two leading theologians from later years (Thomas Aquinas and John Calvin), leaving a more thorough account of recent thought to Hugh D. MacDonald in his *Ideas of Revelation.*[2]

On the one hand we have easy and unself-critical assurance that God through Christ has revealed himself to us. On the other are the leading Christian thinkers of the early centuries who never made any such large and encompassing claim, but rather insisted very seriously that God in himself remained beyond their comprehension.

There follows here in brief some of the conclusions drawn previously.

(i) 1 Clement

That 1 Clement [90 CE?] contains an outlook very similar to that of the Pastorals is almost a truism of New Testament research. Clement's understanding of the purpose of Christ is just one instance of this. Jesus came to make God's demands known, the real point at issue . . . being God's will for the ordering of his community. Obedience to his will (an obedience that is "not through ourselves or through our own wisdom or

---

1. Traditional Orthodox "the hospitality of Abraham" taken as God's self-presentation as Triune, inviting us in.

2. McDonald, *Ideas of Revelation*; cf. his slightly later *Theories.*

understanding of piety or works," 32.4) is the way of life and salvation. It is "knowledge of God's wishes" that Christ came to impart. He did not, does not "reveal God" or "knowledge of God himself."

"In regard to faith and repentance and genuine love and self-control and discretion and patience, we have exhausted every topic" (62:2), is Clement's own concluding catalogue of the contents of his letter.[3]

(ii) Ignatius of Antioch

For Ignatius, God through Christ, and Christ through the leaders of the community, has made his "mind" known, for the ordering of the life of the church and individual; and God also empowers the obedience he demands (*Smyrneans* 11), which is conformity to the life of Jesus. At best this takes the form of a "martyr's" death. And so the Christian may "attain God" (*Romans* 8, *Trallians* 13, *Magnesians* 14). Not even this does Ignatius explicitly call "revelation of God."[4]

(iii) Barnabas, Hermas, The Didache

There is a fair amount of agreement in the use of words like "knowledge" (as given by God), "manifest" and (though it is rarely used) "reveal." The "knowledge" God gives is how to please him and qualify for immortality. . . . Christ himself was "manifested" to impart this "knowledge" of how to please God, and perhaps also to enable its use. And at the end of time, Christ will be "manifest" again. . . . There is nothing that can clearly be called "revelation of God himself."[5]

---

3. Downing, *Has Christianity a Revelation?*, 129–130. On Clement, Clarke, *First Epistle*; Elliott, "Extra-Canonical," 1314; Frend, *Early Church*, 52–53.

4. Downing, *Has Christianity a Revelation?* 132; cf. Williams, *The Wound of Knowledge*, 13–21.

5. Downing, *Has Christianity a Revelation?*, 135.

(iv) The Letter to Diognetus

This letter does outline, for the first time, something like a "theology of revelation." "No man has either seen or recognized Him (God), but He revealed [*epedeixen*] Himself." "For what man at all had any knowledge of what God was before He [Christ] came?" (8 [8:5, 8:1]). And now it is possible to apprehend "full knowledge" of the Father (10 [10:1]).

There are only a few qualifications to note. The "full knowledge of God" that is now possible is propositional—it is "knowledge about God," "what God is"; it is the ability to make correct statements about him, such as "For God loved men for whose sake he made the world . . ." (10 [10:2]). And the purpose of this revealing is to enable our imitation of the love of God.

"Revelation" is still only one aspect of God's purpose in Christ; by itself it would not have been enough; men had to be fitted, made able.[6]

Nowhere in this is there any delving into God's "self." It is also worth adding, on the basis of more recent discussions, there seems little sign of this work being influential at the time or later; it seems to have been widely ignored until a single manuscript was discovered and copied in the sixteenth century. What was more generally significant, I suggested then, was the letter's acceptance of a popular philosophical definition of the human as a mind-soul battling with, even imprisoned in, a distracting body. Thus,

If you start off with a view of man in which ratiocination, or even, more widely, conscious cognition, is his esse, then the situation with which you believe God in Christ has dealt is defined in advance in these terms, and you are almost certain to look for knowledge of or about God as the saving results of Christ's coming and life.[7]

(v) Justin Martyr

Among surviving evidence for ongoing Christian tradition, Justin's works are the first to cite Matt 11:25–27 (or its Lukan parallel). It meant that Jesus "revealed therefore to us all that we have understood from the Scriptures by his grace" (Trypho 100:2). In fact, it is revelation of knowledge about his

6. Ibid., 135–36; Grant, *Greek Apologists*, 178–79.

7. Downing, *Has Christianity a Revelation?*, 137.

role and status. To know how to designate God correctly, and the obedience he demands—this is the knowledge Justin is concerned with. Compliance should follow; but the two are distinguished. God reveals, not himself, but commands and indications of the future, and how to respond to the saving events of Jesus' life, death, and resurrection. And, perhaps surprisingly, becoming a Christian actually made Justin less confident in any human capacity to "know God," less confident than he had been as a Platonist.[8] I shall return to this, below.

(vi) Irenaeus

In polemical opposition to those who claim to "know," Irenaeus insists, frequently and emphatically, that what he holds to be true has been revealed (e.g., *Adv. haer.* 4.6.5). This revelation of divine truths is to humans, for whom "the body cannot make the soul lose its power of knowing" (*Adv. haer.* 2.33.4). Significantly, what is held by those who agree with him does not display the dissensions that undermine his "gnostic" opponents' credibility (*Adv. haer.* 4.35.4). For all that, Ireneus nonetheless strongly affirms Phil 3:12 with 1 Cor 13:9–10, "not that I have already attained . . . for we know in part and we prophesy in part . . . but when that which is perfect is come, things which are in part shall be done away" (*Adv. haer.* 4.9.2; cf. 5.7.2). Anything that counts as "seeing God" remains for the future.

As I wrote previously,

> Irenaeus is being driven to talk a great deal about "revelation" (but only in this limited sense of the "revelation" of propositions that make clear the identity of the Creator with the Father of Jesus) because of its denial by his opponents. But it is not a belief that God has "revealed his self" that he is defending. It is the total Christian experience of acceptance and renewal, while comprehension of God is still dim. To this Christian experience, its continuity with pre-Christian Jewish, and total human experience is integral.[9]

---

8. Downing, *Has Christianity a Revelation?*, 138–41; Grant, *Greek Apologists*, 50–73; Osborn, *Beginnings*.

9. Downing, *Has Christianity a Revelation?*, 141–45, lightly recast; Frend, *Early Church*, 77–83; and now, for Ireneus, see also Williams, *Wound*, 25–31; Blackwell, *Christosis*, 35–70.

(vii) Origen and Chrysostom

From Origen, quoting "No man has seen the Father . . ."

> "Knowledge of God" is made possible through the coming of
> the Logos; and this is salvation: "Accordingly, if Celsus asks us
> how we can come to know God, and how we imagine we shall
> be saved by him, we reply that the Logos [intelligence] of God
> is sufficient; for he comes to those who seek him, or who accept
> him when he appears to make known and reveal the Father, who
> before his coming was not visible (sc. to the eyes of the soul).
> And who but the Logos can save and lead the soul of man to
> the supreme God? (*Celsum* 6.68). [But] Only after troubles and
> strivings here shall we come to the topmost heavens . . . and then
> see face to face" (*Celsum* 6.20, 7.38).

That God had revealed himself, so that we could know God as he
knows himself was never suggested until it was proposed on the extreme
Arian wing of Christian debate in the second half of the fourth century CE,
with Eunomius as its leading spokesman. According to him (as polemically
summarized by his opponents), the word *agennētos*, "unbegotten," labeled
and evoked in human minds an awareness of the unique God as clear as
God's own self-awareness. To illustrate the response that became formative
for the Eastern Christian tradition, and rather than the Cappadocians, Basil
the Great, Gregory Nazianzus, and Gregory of Nyssa, I there chose John
Chrysostom, who interpreted Matt 11:25–27 as indicating the *limitation* of
human knowledge of God, for (much as in Origen) we do not yet even know
the Son as he should be known; quoting in support 1 Cor 13:9, "we know in
part and prophesy in part," (*Homily on Matthew* 28:2). And even the "face
to face" of 1 Cor 13:12 does not actually mean that we shall know him as as
well as we are known by him, but only with the same intensity and self-
giving (*Homily on 1 Cor* 34:2–4).[10]

(viii) Augustine of Hippo and Thomas Aquinas

For Augustine the limiting factor is present human sinfulness rather than
finite intelligence as such, though sin is itself seen as unreason. However,
when, but only when we have accepted the cleansing made possible in the
self-giving of Christ, then our justification will be complete, "we shall be
like him, for we shall see him as he is" (*Sermon* 3:11; *De trinitate* 4:3, 15:11):
in clear contrast with the Eastern tradition. But for now humans are too

10. Downing, *Has Christianity a Revelation?*, 147–49; cf. Williams, *Wound*, 37–46.

irrationally wicked to receive a self-revelation of God, even though the love for him and for one another that God elicits from us and enables in us nonetheless affords already a very positive relationship with God.

Thomas Aquinas agrees with Augustine (explicitly against Chrysostom), that human intellect is such that it allows and even demands the final beatitude of seeing the essence of God; even if that is still less than God's own self-knowledge. For now, however, we are joined to God as to one unknown (*S.T.* I 12:1, 4–5, 13). But still, even more firmly, it seems, than in Augustine, "Now it is love that unites us to God . . . since he that abides in love abides in God and God in him" (S.T. II/2 184:1).[11]

(ix) John Calvin

Calvin, educated in the humanist tradition, saw humankind in terms of intellect, knowledge taking precedence over righteousness and holiness. And Jesus mediates the full knowledge of God in a form we can appreciate (*Inst.* II.10), and the whole of salvation is understood in terms of "revelation." Here and now, "As soon as the minutest particle of faith is instilled in our minds, we begin to behold the face of God placid, serene and propitious; far off, indeed, but still so distinctly as to assure us there is no delusion in it" (*Inst.* III.2). As noted in the previous study, this contrasts with Augustine's exposition of Paul's "in a glass darkly," Augustine insisting it can *not* mean we see from a distance, clearly.[12]

It still may be worth repeating that an insistence on "revelation" seems to arrive at times of bitter controversy, reflecting and reinforcing Christian division. It does so with Irenaeus, with Eunomius, with the Reformation; and again in the Enlightenment, as noted in the final pages of chapter 4 in the previous study.

I still trust that the original survey of past discussions of "revelation of God," taken as the imparting in current experience of "knowledge of God," showed effectively how small a part, but also, how heavily qualified a part such ideas have played in the books of the Jewish and Christian canons, and then in ongoing Christian reflection, as more briefly reviewed in the foregoing. That was a case for an absence, noting what is not said, or not without heavy qualification. What I add now, as in the two current preceding chapters, is a fuller account of what is present, what is overtly and often

11. Downing, *Has Christianity a Revelation?*, 149–55.

12. On God's hiddenness in some western mediaeval mystics, and then in Luther, McGinn, "The Hidden God."

emphatically stated, on these issues of revelation and knowledge, both in clear negative assertion and alternative positive affirmation.

(b) Divine "Incomprehensibility"

At first sight, and even on further reflection, "incomprehensible" can sound negative and forbidding. If the word is used at all, it can be in protest: "the Secretary of State's decision is quite incomprehensible." But as used in early and ongoing Christian reflection it is not an authoritarian put-down, "Yours not to know the reason why." Rather is it a confident shared insistence: "We are all in the dark together, but walk assured. We—the believers in our group, at least (or alone)—have been given a trustworthy glimmer to show us the direction to move towards the light." "And when we arrive, what then?" "Maybe we'll find we can see; or may be we will find we can see with greater clarity that there's still more ahead."

The assurance that we are on the right road would seem to entail, as we have seen, at least implicitly, and often explicitly, that the way forward had been revealed. But that did not mean that the goal itself (him-/herself) is clear: the divine reality towards which we move or are being moved remains only hinted at. The way to knowledge of God, to divine *self*-revelation is indicated in trusting hope; divine self-revelation as such remains a promise awaiting fulfilment. And then one must these days ask critically whether even the way ahead was really clear, "revealed": could it really, indefinitely include as the divinely revealed path the rightness of the subjection of women, of the institution of slavery, of the conviction that one person could own another and bindingly commit another, of guilt as inheritable and transferable, of Christians deploying state power to enforce subscription, of witchcraft as real, to be purged by burning?

And, further, if the right way is not itself clearly given but has to be accepted on trust, we do not "know" which ways are wrong, or so wrong as to be surely self-stultifying. We may hope, trust, insist that we are right; but if we cannot warrant such a claim to know, we may be wrong and those with whom we disagree may be right. Yet, for good or ill—ill according to the present writer—the ancient fathers in their unknowing could still imply that they knew enough to exclude many rivals. . . . A close companion to talk of divine incomprehensibility was an insistence on ineffability, "apophasis," the assertion that we have no adequate words for talking of God. And that conviction was regularly, but I suggest, inconsistently accompanied by the insistence that they did know and could find valid words to designate what stood in the way of being able to justify a claim to knowledge. To pretend to know clearly what it is that precludes knowing is incoherent.

One outstanding example is that we "know" that God is infinite, and we know what such divine infinity means, we "know" what it precludes us from saying of God. God must be unlike, so we know that the boundless deity is bounded by divine boundlessness? By definition—ours!—God cannot be (rather than may not be) at all like anything we can imagine. The God we—perhaps still sustainably?—term "infinite" is restricted by difference.[13]

As I argued fifty years ago, rather than start with abstract definitions of one we have already decided is undefinable, is it not better to look at the evidence. So, does Christian history convincingly support the claim that our God has achieved a self-revelation in any full sense, something that we know and can show that we know? The evidence suggests that s/he has not. Either that was not God's intention or God failed. Until God has succesfully transformed us—those claiming to be his—God, yes, does and will remain incomprehensible to us. But that is a deficiency in us, not in God. Untransformed, for now, as Paul said, we see but puzzling reflections in a mirror. And, as a consequence, if we are moved at all to move in the directions we variously deem appropriate, we are moved to explore in trust, not warranted to claim to have arrived or even discerned the only path.

That we cannot hope, now, or even ever, to get our minds round God, as it appeared in Philo, and then from Justin onwards, was touched on already in the previous work, and some of that will be recalled shortly. However, it seems to me that its appearance in Philo and its later adoption need to receive rather more attention that I accorded these matters fifty years ago. Especially does this (negative) conviction need to be seen in context, not as an isolated and arbitrary definition.

(i) Philo

In Philo's Stoic-tinged Platonism, ideas in our minds stem from our senses. Sense experience is not sufficient, but it is necessary.[14] We need sense experience to get our embodied minds working at all. Then, perceiving things with our senses, and noting similarities and differences among them, and

---

13. A confident assertion, with Dionysius, of divine infinity as though meaningful as a basis for further reasoning is widespread, for instance, as found in many of the essays in Boesel, *Apophatic Bodies*; e.g., Keller, "The Cloud of the Impossible," 31, and 35, citing Cusa; Faber, "Bodies of the Void," 201; Dickinson, "Emptying Apophasis," 269.

14. Philo, *De opificio* 139; *De somniis* 1.186–87; *De congressu* 17; cf. Dio, *Discourse* 12.65, cited in Downing, "Ambiguity," 154.

discerning what is in common, what is generic, we have an awareness of the "idea" (the "ideal idea," *eidos*; or the "form," as in Aristotle) that these individual things represent. Thus we can give the idea a "name," *onoma* (even if today, we might prefer to conclude that we tacitly come for the most part to start with the words in common use around us).[15] The "idea" (or, the family resemblance) is not itself contained in the word/name (as much modern discussion, ignoring Wittgenstein, still supposes). For the ancients, the name can only, and at best, evoke the idea in our minds, call it to mind.[16]

So, once you take it that there is only one God, and he is not available to the senses, you have no comparisons to allow you to discern a common "idea" of God, a definable common idea you could evoke (or label) with a name. God is not in a genus, not a nameable one of a kind. (This view of language is common to all the authors surveyed here.) God, in Philo's version of Jewish tradition, can be addressed with a name (one that he authorizes), but that cannot *in the nature of language as understood*, evoke any valid idea of the God-who-is-unique, invisible, and incomparable.[17] Thus, while what God's effects, through his powers at work, can be known in sensuous experience, he in himself is incomprehensible, *akatalēptos*: you have no way of distinguishing him and calling him to mind. What your mind can only (but usefully) "apprehend," "get your mind round," "grasp," "master," is that it is *unable* to master, grasp, apprehend, what God is (*katalabein hoti akatalēptos ho kata to einai Theos*). This Moses learns when he enters the darkness, the dark cloud, on the holy mountain (Exod 20:21; cf. 33:13); Philo's interpretation then being recalled in this connection by many Christian commentators.[18] All that we can perceive is the working of his "powers" (*dunameis*), as in the passage cited, and often elsewhere—a theme also expanded by later Christians, though soon *energeiai* (still usually Englished with "powers") is preferred.

It is not clear whether Philo supposed any other wise person will ever enter the cloud as far as Moses did. While the quest still remains eminently worthwhile, yet God remains elusive, always ahead, never reached. The "endless vision of God" promised elsewhere is still only a vivid awareness

15. On necessary sense-experience, *Leg. all.* 2.71; 3.56–58; *De sobrietate*, 52; on similarities and differences (oppositions), *De cher. 64*; *De ebrietate* 187; *Quis haer.* 207–14;

16. Argued with sources by Downing, "Ambiguity," in reliance on classicists, but not finding discussion elsewhere among other commentators on early Christian thought.

17. *De all.* 3.206; *De praemiis, 40*; *De mut. 12–15*.

18. *De post. 14–16*; *katalambanō* being the verb that provides the adjective *akatalēptos*; cf. also *De post. 169*; *De conf. 136–38*; *De somniis 1.67*.

of his existence; "to God alone is it permitted to apprehend God."[19] However, Peter Schäfer, reading the Armenian translation of Philo on passages in Exodus, deduces there the possibility that Philo may have allowed that death for Moses, if for no other, meant translation from created duality into divine unity, approaching identification with, while still not assimilation into God.[20] Others may, with divine help, make similar initial progress, but still, it would seem, to very limited vision, and no more.[21]

(ii) Clement of Rome, again, and the Apologists

The word *akatalēptos*, "incomprehensible," is not used in the New Testament writings, even of God; *the* nearest to such usage is Jn 1:5, "the darkness has never mastered it [the light, the Word]" (REB), *ou katelaben*. Clement of Rome, again, does talk of God's "incomprehensible wisdom" (33:3), but without actually saying that God is himself ungraspable. Justin (c. 110–165 CE) mocks Plato for supposing that the *human* mind can "perceive being," and insists that the Father is ineffable (which, I take it, amounts to the same conclusion: there is no word that can call the being of God to mind). Athenagoras of Athens (c. 177 CE) writes of God as "invisible, impassible, incomprehensible, apprehended by the understanding only."[22]

(iii) Irenaeus

Ireneus, from the east Mediteranean, bishop of Lyons (177–202 CE), as noted just above, and fully illustrated in the previous study, vigorously insisted on the scriptural revelation of divine truths received by his kind of Christian. Yet despite this, as also already observed, he qualifies such claims with 1 Cor 13:9–10 and Phil 3:12; and elsewhere is even more scornful of those (his "gnostic" opponents), who claim to know so much more. In support of his reservations he cites passages from Isaiah, Jeremiah, and Ephesians, concluding that "God cannot be measured in the heart, and is incomprehensible to the mind . . . but if a human fails to comprehend even the fulness of God's hand, how can he be held to understand such a God or

19. *De post.* 17–21; *De praem.* 27, 40; cf. Schäfer, *The Origins of Jewish Mysticism*, 155–74, citing 156, where he summarizes *De spec. leg.* 32–49, on even God's "powers" being beyond human comprehension.

20. Schäfer, *The Origins of Jewish Mysticism*, 166–67.

21. Ibid., 168–72, citing further passages, including *De somniis* 2.232–33.

22. Justin, *Trypho*, 4; Athenagoras, *Legatio* 10:1. For these writings, Elliott, "Extra-Canonical"; Frend, *Early Church*; Grant, *Greek Apologists*; Hazlett, *Early Christianity*.

know him in his heart? . . . As regards his greatness, then, it is not possible to know God." "In respect of his greatness and his wonderful glory 'no one shall see God and live,' for the Father is incomprehensible; but in regard to his love and his goodness, and as to his infinite power, even this he grants to those who love him, that is, to see God." The one who spoke "face to face" with Moses was the Word, and he it was, not the Father, who allowed his back to be seen (Exod 33:20–24).

Though there are similarities with Philo in the allegorical methods deployed, there is no sign of direct dependence, and Ireneus (like Justin, but also like Clement of Alexandria who does seem to attend to Philo) pays much more attention to the prophets along with the Pentateuch, the books of Moses, than Philo does. Actually, Irenaeus's insistence on the immeasurable greatness (and so, incomprehensibility of God's creative work) might seem a still more cogent argument for divine incomprehensibility than Philo's linguistic one. Though both are metaphysical, Philo's Platonism is prescriptive (of how we should talk of "being") while Ireneus's is descriptive: if you believe in a God who contains and pervades everything, implicitly you believe in one whose mind contains immeasurably more than a human brain could. You could not comprehend such a God as that God comprehends him/her self. This argument can be further strengthened by the appreciative discussion of prophetic rhetoric in Middlemas, as touched on in chapter 3. The elusiveness of God could likely be better expressed by imaginative use of multiple metaphors than by prescriptive metaphysics.[23]

However, now, fifty years on, and having read further among Middle Platonists, and even a little of Plato, it does seem to me that we may well have more in common with other aspects of Platonism that once my erstwhile authorities led me to think imaginable. We might well agree that common sense experience makes verbal agreement on most topics much readier. Thus, lack of such agreement in most God-talk, even supposedly experiential God-talk, makes it difficult to get such talk under way.

But even if we doubt the cogency of a Platonizing reification of absolute and so ineffable "being," we still might well accept the Platonic idealization of harmony, unity. That challenges any equally ready acceptance of conflict, disharmony, as an inescapable fact of life. Much Christian hope is for experienced unity with God, and how to adapt, allow ourselves to be unified, "reformed" to meet or match God's unity with us, begun in Christ. This we may trust, surely must remain something that still has to happen more fully among us and in each of us for us to begin to reach any agreed inkling of it.

23. Middlemas, "Divine Presence."

(iv) Clement of Alexandria

Clement of Alexandria (c. 150–215 CE), omitted in the previous study, is, as noted above, clearly dependent on Philo. Despite overlooking the latter, along with Christian predecessors, it has been helpful to have available Henny Fiskå Hägg's study of apophaticism, the speechless (ineffable) way to God, in Clement, with its attention to near contemporary Middle Platonists such as Alcinous and Eumenius.[24] In this Hägg also does allow for something of the relevance of ancient Mediterranean ways of thinking about language, sense-perception, and meaning. But he fails to allow for words being taken as names to evoke idea in the mind—where meaning, in contemporary reflection, simply does not reside in the words themselves. Clement is as sure as Irenaeus that some valid knowledge is attainable; but not of God as God is. God, as Philo had affirmed, "always retreats from him who pursues him. . . . He is far off in his ousia (for how can that which is begotten ever come close to that which is unbegotten?)."[25]

For this book's argument, at least, it is important to draw attention to Clement taking and citing Plato, but Plato taken (as in Philo's presentation) as a pupil and expositor of Moses:

> "For both is it a difficult task to discover the Father and Maker of this universe and having found him, it is impossible to declare him to all. For this is by no means capable of expression, like the other subjects of instruction," says the truth-loving Plato. . . . For he had heard right well that the all-wise Moses, ascending the mount for holy contemplation, to the summit of intellectual objects, necessarily commands that the whole people do not accompany him. And when the Scripture says, "Moses entered into the darkness where God was," this shows to those capable of understanding that God is invisible and beyond expression by words. . . . For since the first principle of everything is difficult to find out, the absolutely first and oldest principle, which is the cause of all other things being and having been, is difficult to exhibit. For how can that be expressed which is neither genus, nor difference, nor species, nor individual, nor number; nay more,

---

24. Hägg, *Clement of Alexandria;* and on Clement and Philo, see Osborne, *The Philosophy of Clement,* and Trigg, *Origen,* 54–66.

25. Hägg, *of Alexandria,* 212–13, citing his own translation of *Stromata* 2.5.3–4. However, I think he is mistaken to suggest in Clement an "absolute gulf" between Creator and created. The other way round, between us and knowledge of God, yes; but not of the middle platonic God who has no limits in any direction; see Downing, "Ontological Asymmetry." See also Osborne, *The Philosophy of Clement,* 23 (on Philo).

is neither an event nor that to which an event happens? . . . And therefore it is without form or name.[26]

For anything that cannot be apprehended by analogy, signs, or the senses, is incomprehensible, and hidden from us.[27] We reach towards the reality, the essence of things, by the method of abstraction, removing incidentals, the things of sense, till we reach the (supposed) common essence. But with God there are no such incidentals for us to get started on.

For a relatively modern defense of such classical "negative theology," we could turn to Ian T. Ramsey, on "models and qualifiers." But the trouble today is that this process of abstraction and negation so as to reach the "essential nature" of something, albeit endorsed by Aristotle, has long ceased to be an accepted procedure. Now if we completely discard the words of sense-experience we are simply left with no common language at all: what we say dies "the death of a thousand qualifications." That does not at all preclude metaphor as open-ended; but it cannot be both open-ended and objective, interpersonally testable truth.[28]

For now, Clement assures us, we have received the visible Son, who sets us on our way, while, as Paul said, "we see in a glass, seeing ourselves in it by reflection, and simultaneously contemplating, as we can, the efficient cause, from that within us which is divine." For now we rely on present training in love for our perfecting after physical death.[29] The Son, the divine Word, is the power of God in action, the unitive focus, the prime instrument of plural perceptible and nameable divine powers. These *dunameis* (again echoing Philo) bring us towards our salvation (well-being), our perfection, towards an ultimate fuller awareness of God.[30] As a near synonym to *dunameis* Clement can also use *energeiai*, energies, the word that will be taken up and elaborated in later reflections: "we have as our teacher him that filled the universe with the power of his energies in creation, salvation, beneficence, legislation, prophecy, teaching: we have the Teacher from whom all instruction comes."[31]

---

26. *Strom.* 5.12, ANF, slightly recast; Hägg, *Clement of Alexandria*, 217.

27. *Strom.* 8.9.

28. Ramsey, *Religious Langauge*, 49–89; Flew and MacIntyre, "Theology and Falsification"; on Aristotle, Hägg, *Clement of Alexandria*, 218–19, referring to *Metaphysics*, 1016–65.

29. *Strom.* 1.19 with 4.8; Hägg, *Clement of Alexandria*, 220–30.

30. Hägg, *Clement of Alexandria*, 230–34.

31. *Protrepticus* 11.

(v) Origen

Joseph Trigg notes that Origen claims to have read Philo, and himself insists that Origen must have known Clement, and not just his work, though there is no direct evidence for that. Certainly Clement and Origen have much in common: thus for Origen, too, God is unmeasurable, incomprehensible, pure unity.[32] So convinced is Origen of this that he deduces it, remarkably, from the Great Thanksgiving:

> Although a derived knowledge is possessed by those whose minds are illuminated by the divine Logos himself, absolute knowledge and understanding of the Father is possessed by himself alone, in accordance with his merits, when he says, "No man has known the Father save the Son, and him to whom the Son will reveal him." Neither can anyone worthily know the uncreated and firstborn of all created nature in the way the Father who begat him knows him; nor can anyone know the Father in the same way as the living Logos who is God's wisdom and truth.[33]

What each can look forward to is a gradual, and, it would seem, open-ended process of reconciliation to happiness with God in place of hostility.[34]

(vi) The Cappadocians

As already recalled, a concentration on divine incomprehensibility was triggered by the contrary affirmation of Eunomius that a valid idea of God could be evoked by a readily available word, *agennētos*, "unbegotten." Here, rather than resort to Chrysostom's somewhat later polemic, I offer some slightly earlier material from two of the Cappadocians. Basil (the Great), elder brother of Gregory of Nyssa, had written to oppose Eunomius, and the latter had responded vigorously in two works, and, according to Gregory, mostly in vituperation, not in theological argument. Gregory responded, initially in defense of his brother, but then massively in philosophical detail, reflecting on contemporary understanding of the way words, including metaphors, work. We can understand creation through differences and similiarities in the attributes of things; but God's being "does not present signs

32. Trigg, *Origen*, 54, 95; *De principiis*, 1.1.5–6 (from Rufinus's Latin translation).

33. *Contra Celsum* 6.17, as quoted in Downing, *Has Christianity a Revelation?*, 147. Clement had also qualified this assurance of knowledge of God with just "as far as human nature can comprehend," *Strom.* 1.18.

34. *De principiis*, 3.6.6.

of its inmost nature . . . it is too high for any distinctive attribute." We may in thought catch a glimpse of the divine nature, like seeing a distant ocean, but when we try to grasp it, comprehend it, we find it always eludes us, always moving on beyond us.[35]

His position is presented much more positively in his *Life of Moses*, with very clear dependence on Philo; but also elsewhere, e.g., in *Homilies on the Song of Songs*. Gregory allows that initially as a Christian one seems to be enlightened by comparison with the pagan darkness around one. But then as one, like Moses, progresses, one comes to realize that the divine nature is invisible, beyond not just physical sight, but beyond what our minds can suppose, finally attaining a full awareness that what one seeks is beyond knowing, beyond grasping, beyond anything but an awareness of its complete incomprehensibility. And he cites Jn 1:18, as an eternal truth: no one is ever in a state of seeing God.[36] In effect, asserts Gregory, God lures Moses (and us) into an endless pursuit, a desire never to be satisfied. If you decide you have seen, then you have passed from the life-giving quest to a spiritual death.[37] (In 1964 I cited Chryostom to a similar effect.)[38]

In further illustration, I cannot forbear quoting from Nan Shepherd's account of her lifelong pilgrimage into the Cairngorm range in the Scottish Highlands, where one ascent discloses another:

> At first I was seeking only sensuous gratification. . . . But as I grew older and became less self-sufficient, I began to discover the mountain in itself. . . . This process has taken many years, and is not yet complete. Knowing another is endless. And I have discovered that man's [sic] experience of them enlarges rock, flower and bird. The thing to be known grows with the knowing.[39]

Fifty years ago I preferred on this issue Augustine, who trusted that we would know as well as we are known; and I have since noted that Gregory

35. Gregory, *Contra eunomium* 1:373, 368 (Migne), 26 (NPNF, adapted), Jaeger, *Gregorii* 1:137, 135; see also 1:7–4 (NPNF); and NPNF 2:276. See also, Williams, *The Wound*, 52–67.

36. Gregory, *Life*, 2:162–63, 376C377A, in Danielou, *Vie*, 80–81; *Homilies* 6 (Norris 193; Jaeger, 181).

37. Gregory, *Life*, 2:233–34, 404AB, and 304–7, 424D425AB, in Danielou, *Vie*, 107; *Homilies* 5 (Norris 151; Jaeger, 138), 8 (Norris 259; Jaeger 245–46).

38. Downing, *Has Christianity a Revelation?*, 148, citing Chrysostom, *Homilies on 1 Corinthians* 34:2–4.

39. Shepherd, *Living Mountain*, 107–8. For Shepherd this was a Buddhist kind of "journey into Being," while, as Robert Macfarlane in his "Introduction" points out, her Presbyterian background also shines through.

Nazianzus, though equally sure that God is incomprehensible for us in this life, is convinced we shall finally know as we are known.[40] But now, on further reflection, in preference I commend Gregory of Nyssa, if still not for his prescriptive metaphysics, yet certainly in respect of his conclusion.

Often Gregory, like the others, bases his conclusion on abstract Platonic reasoning. When in support he and the rest quote Jewish Scripture on God's unfathomable ways as creative and sustaining ruler of all, I find the argument much more meaningful. Any attempt to comprehend in any detail "even" the physical universe seems beyond us. Yet just such a detailed comprehension by God seems implicit in any trust in God as creative sustainer of all there is. The God who comprehends in detail all there is seems, then, likely set to be always incomprehensible for us, even if, as we may trust, always luring us on.[41]

Whether any of these arguments persuade—or even make sense—I leave the reader to decide. But what does seem clear—"revealed," even—is that to no one in the early days (not even to Eunomius) did it occur to claim that God had revealed his "self." No one before Eunomius seems to have challenged the common assertion of divine incomprehensibility, and even he did so in terms of word-usage, not claimed experience of divine face-to-face self-revealing.

But also in this connection we must critically attend to the apparent loneliness of both Gregorys' quests, insisting that every quester, like Moses, obviously has to leave "the people" behind.[42] While in Gregory of Nyssa's *Homilies* there is quite frequent reference to the church as the context for the quest, awareness of the divine encompassing of all still does not seem to be considered as belonging to the goal.[43] (On this topic, see further, below.) I would rather suppose that the God who sustains a loving awareness of each of us in our interconnections cannot even be approached without others in mind and in view

---

40. Gregory Nazianzus, *Discourse 28 (First Theological Discourse)*, 1–6, with 17, 25C32A, 48C; 32:15, 192 AB.

41. Most recently for me, Scharf, *Gravity's Engines*.

42. Gregory of Nyssa, *Life*, 2:160–61, 376BC in Danielou, *Vie*, 80; Gregory Nazianzus, *Discourse* 28:1–6, 25C32A.

43. Gregory, *Homilies* 7 (Norris 229; Jaeger 217); 8 (Norris, 269; Jaeger, 256); 12 (Norris 361–63; Jaeger 341–42); 15 (Norris 495; Jaeger 466–67).

(c) Identifying

In his very carefully argued discussion of Gregory Nazianzus on the knowledge of God, with close attention to the text, Christopher Beeley insists repeatedly that Gregory's "apophaticism" should not be overestimated.[44] In response, it seems to me obvious (and explicit, and for good or ill see further below) that none of those surveyed espoused a systematic agnosticism. They were sure they had been and were continuing to move in the appropriate direction. Taking up the contrast, they had identified and were aiming for the true "mountain" and the right cloud (not the false cloud of pagan ignorance). Taking their stand with "the rock," Jesus, they were convinced they were in the right place to be enlightened, purified. It is God himself that the cloud identifies, that all creation points to. This is particularly clear in Gregory of Nyssa's Homily 11. Just when the Bride seems to have arrived, we find "she has not yet . . . enjoyed a face-to-face revelation" (*oude tēs kata prosōpon emphaneias katatruphēsasan*).[45] Nothing in all this warrants Beeley's claim (itself without textual backing or further discussion) that this denotes "God's self-revelation"—at least, not if any strong sense of "self," as discussed in chapter 2, is intended.[46] But "self" as posited in the theology of the early Christian centuries warrants further discussion.

(d) "Self"

In what follows I refer to a recent two-part discussion of my own, "Order Within: Passions, Divine and Human." Against Charles Taylor, *Sources of the Self*, I had earlier argued that Epictetus and Paul clearly each thought they could reflect on a "self," and that hearers would understand.[47] In my more recent treatment I was able to use wider reading to set the issue in its socio-cultural context. I quoted from Malte Hossenfelder,

> It was a time when even free male Greek citizens were politically powerless, when a basic shared principle was an acknowledgment of those needs whose satisfaction lay in one's own

---

44. Beeley, *Nazianzus*, 98–99, 105–6.

45. Gregory, *Homilies* 11 (Norris 337; Jaeger, 320).

46. Beeley, *Nazianzus*, 98, 106, 107, 111. This casual use of a theological catchphrase is uncharacteristic in Beeley.

47. "Self" is discussed earlier and noted (ch. 3 and ch. 4n20); Taylor, *Sources of the Self*, discussed in Downing, "Persons."

power, and unruly emotions could be seen as threatening that autonomy.[48]

Reflections on "the self" thus arose in conditions of powerlessness, and of inner division between a "self" affirmed: the (at least potentially) controlling self and a repudiated self of passions thought of as fighting for that control. And in no way were philosophical Christian theologians of the first few centuries (or even later) going to think of their God in these terms, the only context for introducing "self" talk into God-talk. God was absolute unity, and absolutely in control of everything. Even the few who could allow that some "passion" words could rightly be applied to God did not think of them as threatening the absolute divine unity. Any suggestion to the contrary in inherited Scriptures had to be understood in some other way. The nature of human selfhood as analyzed by Plato, Aristotle, the Stoics, and Paul (if one may summarize them so) is to be divided, prompting inner reflections of self on self. The nature of divine selfhood is precisely what remains hidden in the cloud, certainly other than ours, and incomprehensible. While fourth-century theologians, such as the Cappadocians and Augustine, are content to reflect on and share accounts of their own inner, otherwise very private thoughts and feelings, in apparently very "self-revealing" ways, I find no suggestion that God is taken as doing anything similar. God is taken as identifying the way to identify with himself. To term that "self-revelation" is simply slipping in a standarrd catch phrase unreflectively. Rather, what God in Christ in the power of the Spirit is taken to offer and enable is our progress Godwards, ultimately to ready us for face-to-face revelation, knowing as we are known, or, with Gregory of Nyssa, at least to continue approaching such awareness.

With Marcion and most conventionally styled gnostics refusing, the Christian thinkers acknowledged by later orthodoxy identified the creator God of Jewish tradition as their God, the Father of Jesus, the source of the Holy Spirit. There were very diverse identifications of God in the Jewish Scriptures glossed over, with the help of Philonic allegory and perhaps as (also Philonic) concesssions to human ignorance. That this was at the cost of more humane (anthropomorphic) identification was part of the bargain that most accepted. One particulary interesting exception, in terms of theologians noted in this chapter, is Gregory of Nyssa. In his *Catechetical Discourse* he offers a stipulative definition of *pathos*, "passion." Most physical phenomena are activity, *ergon*, not *pathē*, not passions, in a pejorative sense, and certainly not in the life of the incarnate Word. He, it would seem,

48. Hossenfelder, *Die Philosophie*, 24 (trans., Downing); in Downing, "Order Within. A," 86.

had intentionally and virtuously agreed actively to experience human physical sensations. Passion is primarily a voluntary surrender of control, from virtue to vice, not bodily exierence as such. But in our authors the often passionate divine characteristics identified in the Scriptures are not accepted as options to be considered.[49]

(e) Becoming Divine

In the previous chapter, adumbrations of ideas of divinization in the New Testament writings were sketched, with the help of such as Daniel Powers, Michael Gorman, David Litwa, and Ben Blackwell. This is the very positive side of the insistence that we have not yet arrived, and God remains incomprehensible, whether just for now, or endlessly emergent into our awareness. We are seen as being in the process of being assimilated to God in Christ: in that inceptive sense we are already coming to share the divine life. We are being readied for God's self-revelation, face-to-face, to know as we are known, or at least moving more appreciably towards that goal.

Such a claim, that we not only can be changed, but are being transformed, is risky. Is it really happening in me, in you? Does it look as though it is? But by the same count, as experientially falsifiable the claim is at at least meaningful. It has seemed (especially to many more recent Western Christians) safer and easier and even more impressive (in a reinforced guilt culture) to propose an undemonstrable "objective" atonement for guilt inherited/incurred: a hypothetical penalty borne, a theoretical debt paid, as a gift given. But then the same critical question recurs: do I, even if persuaded, and grateful, now as discharged debtor, experience *and evince* a richer and growing awareness of unity with God? We have a gift from God in Christ, say these theologians. But it is a gift we acknowledge and accept only by allowing it to change us. It is nothing other than a deepening relationship with God, initiated by God who becomes human to lure humans into transformation.

The Hellenistic (including Jewish) context for reflections on divinization are treated at some length, and usefully, by both James Starr and David Litwa, and also in a collection edited by Stephen Finlan and Vladimir Kharlamov. All emphasize the ethical quality of such assimilation, along with a

---

49. Various exceptions noted in Downing, "Order Within. A," 98–100, Gregory Thaumaturgus, Lactantius, and Gregory of Nyssa, as summarized, in *Catechetical Discourse* 15–16 and 24.

promise of immortality with God, in Jewish and other authors, as well as Christian.[50]

(i) 2 Peter

Although James Starr places this tractate in the 90s CE, and so contemporary with other New Testament writings as they are often dated, I take it to emanate from well into the second century CE, with a general ethos much closer to that of the early apologists than to Paul or even John, especially in its treatment of desires (which, I regret, I overlooked in my "Order Within"). But in general Starr's treatment is persuasive: for 2 Peter the goal of human existence necessarily includes a progressive moral transformation that results in a virtuous character, which increasingly resembles divine virtue, and so approaches incorruption. There is, however, no suggestion of a future, let alone already anticipated, face-to-face awareness of God.

(ii) Irenaeus and Clement of Alexandria

Blackwell succinctly guides us through "deification" in Irenaeus's *Adversus Haereses* and *Demonstration of Apostolic Preaching*. Christ became human so humans could become like him. He recapitulated and restored, by his obedient life and death, what Adam lost, drawing us into his own perfect obedience, and so sharing his immortality, though not divine creative power. We have noted Ireneus' insistence on divine incomprehensibility; and while he does on occasion quote 1 Cor 13:13, he does not cite verse 12, only looking forward to a contemplation of God in which our love for him will continue to intensify.[51]

Clement, as summarized by Eric Osborn, also trusts that humans made in the divine image can have the originally intended likeness to God restored by God.[52] The true gnostic seeks to imitate God, encouraged by pagans willing to call the virtuous godlike and equal to the gods, divine in a sort of outsider's inkling of what is asserted in Gen 1:26. The guidelines for assimilation to God are mildness, love of neighbor, eminent piety. That way Clement's gnostic reaches the heights, becoming "perfected to have converse with God . . . embracing the divine vision, not in or by mirrors,

50. Starr, *Sharers in the Divine Nature*, 92, 116, 142–43, 165–66; Litwa, *Being Transformed*, 85, 106, 116, 195–206; Finlan and Kharlomov, *Theōsis*.

51. Ireneus, *Adv. haer.* 4.12.2.

52. Osborne, *The Philosophy of Clement*, 88–89, citing *Strom.* 2.131, 2.185, and *De princ.* 3.6.12; and Osborne, *Beginnings of Christian Philosophy*, 116–19.

but the transcendently clear and absolutely pure insatiable vision . . . being made like the Lord, to the extent of each one's capacity."[53]

(iii) Gregory Nazianzus

I quote from Christopher Beeley's very thoroughly researched study, including his translation of Gregory:

> Poised between heaven and earth, the human being [Adam] was created to be "a ruler on earth yet ruled from above, earthly and heavenly, temporal and immortal . . . a living being cared for (*oikonomouein*) in this world, then transferred to another; and—the final stage of the mystery—made divine (*theoumenon*) by his inclination towards God" (38:11).
>
> As Gregory analyzes it, the very nature of creation, reflecting God's infinite goodness, is designed to provide for the growth of human beings toward God and their final divinization. We have been created, in other words, in a state of dynamic movement toward God, so that the process of divinization is rooted in the structure of our existence. . . .
>
> Both before and after the fall, the incomprehensible God lifts us up to himself through the illumination of his own light, causing us to ascend beyond the fleshly veil of our human existence, "to hold communion with God, to be associated with the purest light, as far as human nature can attain," and to be divinized through our union with the Holy Trinity (21:1–2).[54]

Beeley is careful to add, "this still does not mean becoming God in the full sense of the word." And this becoming is still seen as God's initiative, God's fresh gift: "Although divinization is rooted in creation, our knowledge and experience of this transformation occur exclusively through the reformation of *theosis* that Christ effects."[55]

As noted earlier, Gregory Nazianzus trusted that we would finally come to a face-to-face vision, while Gregory of Nyssa disagreed (see just below).[56]

---

53. *Strom.* 4.26; 7.3; compare the whole of 7.11.

54. Beeley, *Nazianzus*, 118, citing *Discourse* 38.11, 21.1–2; Gallay, *Grégoire*, SC.

55. Beeley, *Nazianzus*, 120, citing *Discourse* 38.2–4; Gallay, *Grégoire*, SC.

56. Gregory Nazianzus, *Discourse 28 (First Theological Discourse)*, 1–6, with 17, 25C32A, 48C; 32.15, 192 AB (Gallay, *Grégoire*).

(iv) Gregory of Nyssa

Gregory saw created life as essential mobile, either moving towards but never reaching divine perfection, or slipping back into error and non-being. He found support for this in Phil 3:13, "reaching out to what lies ahead":

> If nothing from below interrupts the soul's impulse towards the Good, whose nature is always to draw to itself those who focus on it, the soul always raises itself beyond itself, drawn by a desire for the things of heaven, "what lies ahead," the flight always taking the soul higher and higher. The desire not to forgo the heights above, just for the sake of retaining what has already been gained, makes for an endless upward movement, with what has been gained itself prompting the impulse to mount ever higher still.[57]

For the moment we have only sense experience, images, *fantasiai*, a term which slides easily into "imagination.[58] But, of course our imagination cannot hope to encompass the only true reality, God.

Significantly, this upward movement is not presented as an encapsulated mental exercise for Moses. It began with repudiating Egypt and royal status, living quietly as a desert shepherd, the shoeless approach to the bush on fire, liberating his people, escaping the sea, enduring the thirst and hunger; all this as well as entering the cloud and penetrating the true sanctuary, always in motion. Yet there is also a stability (*stasis*) of sorts, precisely in the constancy of ascent.[59] When he ends this life Moses's "eye is not dimmed nor his appearance [LXX] marred, for how could an eye always in the [divine] light be veiled by alien darkness, or anyone working ceaselessly for incorruptibility experience decay? Moses is truly the [being restored, still human] image of God, as never turning his attentive gaze away."[60] Although he does not here use the term *theiosis*, this is, for Gregory, what it amounts to.

For us the human life, death, and resurrection of the divine Word were needed to draw us back to what God intended. It is not that the incarnation in itself saved us (as a sort of forced re-programming). It is the effects of the

---

57. Gregory of Nyssa, *Life of Moses* 2:401A, 225–26; cf. *Catechetical Discourse* 6.53–79, 28B; 8.155–170, 40B (Danielou, *Vie*); *Homilies* 1 (Norris 43; Jaeger, 39); 5 (Norris, 151; Jaeger 138); 6 (Norris 187; Jaeger, 174); 8 (Norris 259; Jaeger 245–46).

58. Gregory of Nyssa, *Contra Eunomium* 1, NPNF 26; Jaeger, *Gregorii* 1, 364/365, 134.

59. Gregory of Nyssa, *Life of Moses* 2:401B, 223–35, with 405C, 242–43 (Danielou, *Vie*).

60. Gregory of Nyssa, *Life of Moses* 2:429A, 318; cf. *Catechetical Discourse* 38.112–20, 97A (Danielou, *Vie*).

human life, including death and resurrection, for which various metaphors are available, effects we can accept or reject, that show God's loving reasons: our diseased nature needed a physician, our fallenness needed someone to stand us back up again, our lifelessness needed one to revive us, our poverty someone to enrich us, our darkness someone to give us light, our captivity needed one to release us, our servitude a liberator.[61] But for now we have to move on, come more fully to enjoy the benefits, till we may be in a position to understand the hows and whys. (I note a comparable but even fuller passage in Gregory Nazianzus.)[62]

(f) Alone or Together?

The earliest Christians had a strong sense of solidarity, solidarity with each other with Christ, or so it was concluded in the previous chapter, with the help of such scholars as Blackwell, Letwin, and Powers. It is most explicit in Paul and John, but arguably implicit in many of the other authors represented in the New Testament Scriptures. And increasing solidarity with Christ clearly meant being transformed to become increasingly Godlike, well before Christ's own deity was being overtly asserted by these pioneering authors. What seems (to my mind, regrettably) to have happened, is that the more our potential "deification" is proposed, the more any sense of human solidarity in the process is of being lost. The end in view, as displayed above, is to become individually so Godlike as to be able to sustain a face-to-face awareness of God as God is; or at least (with Gregory of Nyssa) to make unending but appreciably increasing progress to that infinite end. It is obvious to me that a full, or at least a massively fuller, awareness of God as God must include an awareness of divine loving awareness of our interrelatedness. But of this I found not a hint. No such sense of God's solidarity with us has appeared in any of the texts I have read over the years, nor in any of the secondary literature. Of course, it may be displayed in writings from the ancient authors that I have not read, or may have been there and simply overlooked by me. But I have tried to find anything of the sort, without, so far, any success. Certainly I have found no extensive and explicit affirmation of any such trust in our potential clear or clarifying detailed awareness of God's continuing alert and loving solidarity with us. (That God as Trinity

---

61. Gregory of Nyssa, *Catechetical Discourse* 15.1–30, 48AB, with all of 16–17 (Winling, *Discours*); cf the discussion in Downing, "God with Everything," 242–44, 256–57 .

62. Gregory Nazianzus, *Discourse* 31.21 (Gallay, *Grégoire).*

has such awareness Gregory of Nyssa takes for granted; but not for us to share in.)[63]

It is not as though these writers eschewed or despised loving inter-human relationships, as can be seen in Gregory of Nyssa's *Life* (or, for that matter, Augustine in his *Confessions*); or in Gregory's sympathetic imagined portrayal of the bereaved widow of Nain, or his appreciation of the joys of "comfortable" marriage in contrast with his bleak arguments for virginal celibacy.[64] Yet when Gregory expounds Paul's love that abides (1 Cor 13:13) it is a love that is captivated, contemplates and adapts. There is no sign that I can detect of our response as being thought to affect God. We are enriched, but God is not (perhaps cannot be). There seems to be no reciprocal exchange, nothing *we* might term "interpersonal," no sign that God is imagined as valuing (as a gift to be enjoyed) the responses we humans make.[65]

Nor, of course, is any such interchange posited within God, despite the contrary reading by some who would like to find ancient support here for a social doctrine of the Trinity. When the Cappadocians and their successors talk, for instance, of Father and Son as relational terms—that is of a purely formal, logical relationship—one term implies the other (just as "great-great-grandparent" and "great-great-grandchild" are relational terms, although those so styled have never even met).[66] Although I think the Cappadocians and others could have defined Christian *agapē*, love, in interpersonal terms, as love willing to need others (for instance, with the help of ancient analyses of friendship), they seem not to have done.[67] That would have meant forego-ing a standard axiom of divine perfection as necessarily without needs.[68] It is only if one defines love in two-way relational terms that one allows that to affect reflections on divine love. We have to wait till Richard of St. Victor (albeit influenced by ps.Dionysius in turn influenced by Gregory of Nyssa), it seems, for the light fully to dawn. It needs to be seen that love is best when multiplied interpersonally: it can only fully happen, be realized, in actual ongoing interpersonal relationships. Unless God is thought of as *in se*—persons in love needing persons—God cannot be thought of as love,

---

63. Gregory of Nyssa, *On "Not Three Gods."*

64. Gregory, *Life of Macrina*; *De viginitate* 3; *De opificio* 24.10.

65. Gregory of Nyssa, *De anima et res.* Much the same is said in Dionysius, *The Divine Names* 12, 709C, in Luibhead, *Pseudo-Dionysius.*

66. On which see essays in Coakley, *Rethinking Gregory*; and the discussion in Downing, "God with Everything," 254–55.

67. On "friendship" in each, with Trinitarian implications, see now, Downing, "Friends in God," and chapters 7 & 8, below.

68. See the discussion in Downing, "God with Everything," 256–57.

able in love to love into being persons open to being loved into inclusive loving—as we may trust we are. That is "the logic of love."[69]

Conclusion

I would suggest, for what my suggestion is worth, that these theologians of the early centuries were right in denying that we have any clear knowledge of God, right not to consider that God has revealed God's "self" (in any full sense of "self"). They were also right to insist that we will need to become much more divine, Godlike, before we can hope for a complete, or at least appreciably richer, awareness of God. But they were wrong to limit their expectations with individualistic restrictions derived from contemporary (Middle/neo-) Platonism. I would suggest that they were also misled in their insistence that the words and patterns of disciplined activity were so clearly God-given that any one disagreeing must obviously be wrong, and excommunicated.

Rather, may we prefer to choose in faith to hope to share the very earliest (New Testament) appreciation of our diverse solidarity with each other in Christ: sharing that loving solidarity together in and with God in Christ in the power of the Spirit.

However, I have of late discovered a renewed challenge to any claim that a so far un-self-revealing God could count as loving in any meaningful sense. I had met it argued in the 1960s by a fellow Anglican Christian, Austin Farrer, and have of late found similar thought had been expressed forcefully around the same date by C. S. Lewis.[70] More recently still it has beeen deployed since the 1990s, yet more trenchantly as an atheistic argument by J. L Schellenberg, already mentioned in passing. To that and my own response I now turn.

---

69. Richard of St. Victor, book 3 of *The Trinity.* On "the logic of love," cf. Downing, *A Man for Us,*" 52–70; and Brümmer, *Model.*

70. Austin Farrer, "Revelation"; C. S. Lewis, *Till We Have Faces,* 258.

Rebels Go On Rampage

Thirteen Years a Sex-Slave

Sea Levels Threaten Millions

Renewed Deforestation

Rebels Go On Rampage

More Floods Forecast

"Iran Still Threatens Israel"

Tribal Massacre in Sudan

Oil Threatens Wildlife

Water Wars Foreseen

Rape As Weapon of War

Resistance To Antibiotics Increase

More Race Hate Crime

Landmines Kill Children

Ebola Outbreak in West Africa

HUNDREDS BURIED IN AFGHAN MUDSLIDE

Girls Gang-Raped and Hanged

All We Can Do is Pray

Pit Rescue Called Off

Earthquake in Turkey

Kidnapped Schoolgirls On Video

Aid Dwarfed by Debt

6

Hide and Seek with the God of Love[1]

Introduction

The argument so far has been that God has not revealed, does not reveal him/her self in any deep sense of "self" or in any full sense of "reveal." Rather, we are invited to trust God to lovingly transform us into persons capable of face-to-face loving intimacy with God. But is this initial reticence, concealment of God—the source of all good—not itself ungenerous, unloving?

That God is or has or had been hidden or thought to be so is clearly noted, often deprecated but sometimes desired, in the recorded traditions of Abrahamic theism, whether eliciting rebuttal or reassurance. It figures from at least the fifth century BCE if not earlier (as was illustrated above in chapter 3) in the Jewish canon of sacred Scripture, most frequently in the Psalter.[2] There what is said to be at issue is Israel's God's ascribed failure to ensure his client's or his client people's success in harvest, health, battle.[3] The topic of divine hiddenness then recurs on occasion in ongoing Jewish and Christian reflection, and in the Qur'an (though with explicit, if qualified dismissal; see further, below).

Its emphatic reality is still penetratingly conveyed in the anguished protests of R. S. Thomas. With, I guess, both Plato and the biblical Elijah in view, he recounts:

1. The montage opposite simply illustrates the at least apparent hiddenness of any just and loving deity.

2. For an independent brief survey of the Jewish Scriptures, Fiddes, "The Quest for a Place."

3. Ps. 89:46 (RSV); see Pss 10:11; 13:1; 27:9; 30:7; 69:17; 104:29; Isa 54:8 and 64:7 in the context of the whole chapter. The *locus classicus* for the *deus absconditus*, Isa 45:5(Vulgate), perhaps requires a different translation, "mysterious"; so, Blenkinsopp, *Isaiah*, 2, 258.

> I emerge from the mind's
> cave into the worse darkness
> outside, where things pass and
> the Lord is in none of them.

Or, here, Moses:

> He is the shape in the mist
> on the mountain we would ascend,
> disintegrating as we compose it.[4]

As some readers may possibly recall, about twenty years ago God's hiddenness was made the focus of a full-scale atheistic argument by John L. Schellenberg.[5] His case may have made an immediate widespread impact of which I am unaware, but it received only a "Book Note," not a full review, from Peter Byrne in *Religious Studies*, and less than a page in Charles Taliaferro's *Contemporary Philosophy of Religion*.[6] However, in the last decade or so, attention seems to have increased considerably: counter objections have been raised, and Schellenberg has riposted in detail to many of them.[7] In a recent skeptical theists' attempt to show that Schellenberg's case lacks the force of certainty, Justin P. McBrayer and Philip Swenson, for instance, raise questions over steps 2–5 of his case, cited below, but take it that the first step is uncontroverted. It is so, because it is uncontrovertable that "God is perfectly loving" *in Schellenberg's stipulated sense* of "perfect love." A perfect lover cannot hide him/herself. That there is a God so loving, they accept, cannot be denied "without giving up traditional theism."[8]

Yet it is precisely this first step of Schellenberg's, as elaborated by him, that this chapter challenges (in passing, thus also challenging McBrayer and

---

4. R. S. Thomas, "Threshold," *Later Poems*, 155; and, with no title, in *Counterpoint*, 15. In this latter poem occurs the oft repeated image of a "black hole."

5. Schellenberg, *Hiddenness and Reason*. At the time of drafting I had overlooked Cupitt, *Christ and the Hiddenness of God*; so has Schellenberg, it seems.

6. Byrne, "Book Notes," 570–71; Taliaferrro, *Contemporary Philosophy*, 332.

7. In chronological order, e.g., Snyder, *New Essays*; Evans, "Can God?"; Poston, "Divine Hiddenness"; Westphal, "The Importance of Mystery"; Henry, "Reasonable Doubt"; Tucker, "Divine Hiddenness"; Cordrey, "Divine Hiddenness"; Dumsday, "Free-will," "Divine Mercy," and "Responsibility"; McCreary, "Schellenberg"; McBrayer, "Scepticism"; McFall, "Can We Have a Friend"; and entries here in the bibliography under Schellenberg.

8. McBrayer, "Scepticism," 130; Poston and Dougherty, "Divine Hiddeness," 188, and 194–95, and Tucker, "Divine," 281 and 284–85, do suggest cogent qualifications to the model; see further, below.

Swenson's assurance). Rebutting this premise, of course, rebuts the "atheistic" conclusion.

I reproduce the basic argument, as presented by Schellenberg and then further supported and refined in his rejoinders to specific critics.

1. If there is a God, he is perfectly loving.

2. If a perfectly loving God exists, reasonable non-belief does not occur.

3. Reasonable non-belief occurs.

4. No perfectly loving God exists. [from 2, 3]

5. There is no God. [from 1, 4][9]

Schellenberg stipulates, then, that perfect love entails the lover making herself totally available to the loved one, and, since such a God has obviously not made himself [sic] totally available to us humans as a whole, such a perfectly loving God does not exist.

From the start it should be clear that this chapter, like the book as a whole, is written in agreement that, yes, there is no such God *apparent to all of us humans*. There is no God—that is, fitting the given description—of one revealed to all as loving. Indeed, I would assert further that there is no God matching any widely accepted precise and informatively detailed description "revealed" to us humans as a whole, or even to those of us who assert a Jewish, Christian, or Moslem "ideal traditional theism." It is, however, already on his specification of "ideal traditional theism," and its implications, that there seem nonetheless to be good reasons to disagree with Schellenberg, as well as with all of his critics who accept his specification.

My objections are three. The depth and extent of self-exposure purportedly entailed by perfect love is not validated in the human experience and aspiration to which Schellenberg appeals in support. Further, this specification of divine self-giving love does not represent the actual claims of the lived "traditional theism(s)." And, thirdly, theistic "faith" can be more effectively freed from making or implying unsubstantiatable claims than by Schellenberg's deconstruction of the ontological assertions of an abstract (and factitious) theism.

I begin with the second strand, "traditional theism," as defined by Schellenberg. He quite justifiably takes issue with those who counter his

---

9. Schellenberg, *Hiddenness and Reason*, 83.

argued conclusions on the basis of their own paraphrases of them, rather than on his own carefully chosen phrasing of his proposals. As it is some of the most fundamental of the latter that I find unconvincing or simply in factual error, it is now appropriate to cite some relevant instances: "God, if loving, seeks *explicit, reciprocal* relationships with us. . . . If I love you and seek your well-being, I wish to make available to you all the resources at my disposal. . . . I must also make it possible for you to draw on me *personally* . . . the resources of an intimate personal relationship with me . . . self-giving [where] the self is the totality of what a man has and is." This relationship is further designated as "experiential," "communion," and "achingly beautiful."[10] Schellenberg allows for (freedom for) growth into and out of the ideal relationship by the one loved, but the loving parent ("mother" specified) will never take steps to preclude the inception or renewal of that deep, reciprocal relationship; it will always be overtly and in its entirety possible, albeit at the level appropriate to the one loved.[11]

At issue, then, is a deeply "personal" relationship with a loving deity. It is not a relationship of the sort afforded, for instance, by an impersonal, ever-ready neighborhood and obvious ATM or an inexhaustible unlosable credit card. (On the other hand, physical care and physical contact as an integral part of embodied relating do not seem to figure in the model, either.) Yet let it be accepted for argument, at least, that there is no sign of a God openly and obviously offering without forcing such loving intimacy, in a manner essential to that God's being. If that is the theoretical essence of that deity, then that deity is notional, not real. No God under that description actively exists. Common experience "reveals" his/her/its/their non-existence.

So what? Schellenberg's essentially never deliberately occluded self-offering of a truly loving God does not happen, does not "exist" in human experience, so the one whose hard-to-escape self-gift is of his essence, does not exist. But does the non-existence of Schellenberg's God have any wider implications? Does it have anything to do with any currently instantiated traditional theism? On one hand, quite early in the renewed debate, Schellenberg allowed that his arguments allowed for some other kind of God existing. Nonetheless, a little later, refusing to be bound by some aspects of tradition (e.g., patriarchy), he insists that in this discussion he is focussing on the fundamentals of traditional theistic belief. And the drift of his case on divine hiddenness is one among a number of others he advances

10. Ibid., 18–22; See also Schellenberg's *The Wisdom to Doubt*, 201–4; "Argument. I," 208; "Response to Tucker," 290.

11. Schellenberg, "Argument. 1," 203 and 208; he properly allows for the (theoretical) possibility of infinite development in a human relationship with an infinitely rich God: "On Unnecessarily," 201; and " Response to Tucker," 290.

"for atheism" unqualified; the non-existence, if would seem, of any divine being.[12]

(a) Traditional Theism

It is then relevant to consider actual traditional theisms and their actual use of affective, "love" language in their God-talk.[13] Is Schellenberg's characterisation of a loving God as having to be deeply and inescapably self-revealing to count as truly personal and genuinely loving and instantiated, in fact really "normal" ("usual" or "normative") in traditional theisms? The nonexistence of Schellenberg's God would be widely significant if he—and the handful of (Christian) theologians and philosophers he cites—were right in taking it that the God of potentially immediate, overt, and intense loving personal interaction were in fact the God claimed by major traditional theisms. In his earlier writing on the theme only Christians (mainly Anglican) are mentioned; later he lists (without further quotations) Jews and Moslems as well. Whichever it is, at least the evidenced canonical Scriptures and formative traditions of each must surely be deemed relevant.[14]

He and his handful of Christian theological "authorities" (W. H. Vanstone, R. Adams, B. Mitchell, B. Hebblethwaite, M. McCord Adams, G. Jantzen) together with his later critics, are clearly agreed on such characterisation of "traditional theism." That they very likely are or were mistaken in any such implicit or explicit claim must now to be summarized: summarized rather than, in a single chapter, proven. Tradional affective theisms, it appears, can readily be seen to be quite different from Schellenberg's, and the ontological failure of his deity's logically necessary effect to be instantiated can have no ontological significance for the God of any of these others.

Clearly, traditional Abrahamic faiths do deploy an effective vocabulary of "love" in major strands of their God-talk, but that is without supposing the degree of constant intimacy Schellenberg insists is necessarily implied by talk of a God of love. A casual reading of Martin Buber on "I-and-Thou" might nonetheless suggest otherwise for traditional Judaism(s), since Abraham and Moses, at least, are designated "friends" of God, with Moses

---

12. Schellenberg, "Collaborative," 60; *The Wisdom to Doubt*, 196, 192–93, 297; cf. "Argument Revisited. I," 201, 209; "Response to McCreary," 227, 232.

13. Schellenberg, "Now, a theological agnostic could concede . . . that a loving personal God-wherein 'love' and 'personal' are given their usual meanings-does not exist," ("Collaborative," 60). The question then is about what "meaning" is "usual": how is Schellenberg using "traditional theism" in this section, and "love," here and later?

14. Schellenberg, *Hiddenness and Reason*, 18–29; Schellenberg, *Prolegomena*, 19.

(uniquely) speaking to God face to face, "as a man speaks with his friend." And this merciful God is on occasion accorded a tender motherly or fatherly love for his people.[15] Yet even Moses is refused any deep face-to-face encounter, as was discussed in chapter 2; and, as there further explained, it is obvious in many different canonical Jewish writings that no one is thought to have "known the mind of God": God's inner self remains impenetrable. The (still effective) relationship is, ideally, as with a benevolent and just and effective king, one who can be approached, humbly, with requests for aid, justice, and pardon for real or imagined misdemeanors.

When Philo of Alexandria, first-century CE philosophical theologian, imagines Moses's exceptional relationship with God, it is, as recounted earlier, as a journey into thick darkness. When Philo expresses his own most intense awareness of God, it is of God as creator, Philo "a fellow traveller with the sun and moon and the heavens, the whole universe."[16]

Among some Jews there developed later a *merkevah* mysticism attempting to view the divine chariot (and charioteer?) of the prophet Ezekiel's vision. But that was only for the few, and it was not seeking to encounter a deity making the resources of his inner self available; and it was also imagined that such attempted proximity could be fatal rather than heartwarming.[17]

Martin Buber in the mid-twentieth century, by no means speaking for all Jews, did encourage the readers of his *I and Thou* to accept,

> Of course He is the *Mysterium Tremendum* that appears and overthrows; but He is also the mystery of the self-evident, nearer to me than my *I.* . . . There is no such thing as seeking God, for there is nothing in which he could not be found. . . . Every relational event is a stage that affords [one] a glimpse of the consummating event.[18]

For Buber, such coming into relationship with God, if and when it occurs, is also explicitly reciprocal, we respond to God "as helpers and companions." But this available God is far from the inescapably obvious and immediate figure Schellenberg posits. An "I-It" relationship is always much readier, and the experience of the divine "Thou" as such seems always mediated, even though taken by Buber as never deliberately hampered by God.

---

15. Buber, *I and Thou*; see further, below.

16. Philo, *De spec. leg.* 3.1; cf. *De spec. leg.* 1.36; *De ebr.* 147.

17. On *merkebah* see Rowland, *Open Heaven*, 275–81; on Jewish mysticism in general, Schäfer, *Origins*.

18. Buber, *I and Thou*, 78–83.

Christians inherited much of their practices and beliefs and attitudes from a variegated Judaism that had for three centuries engaged diversely with its multi-faceted Greek world, where friendship with the Gods could be claimed by some (for instance, Cynics), but still only in the sense in which Dio of Prusa could claim to be a "friend" of the Emperor, one who might enjoy table fellowship, and could risk not just giving advice asked for, but even offer it, yet hardly as a soul-mate.[19]

Friendship motifs appear in Paul's writings, where, as explored in chapter 4, we are accorded "the mind of Christ," know and share a significant attitude of his; and we have more than Moses's boldness in approaching God. Yet for now, even in our very privileged Christian relationship with God "we see puzzling reflections in a mirror"; now we have partial awareness, knowledge: only then shall we see face-to-face, and know God as God already knows us.[20] Friendship language is still more pervasive in the Gospel according to John; yet when John's Jesus says to his disciples they are his friends, not his slaves, still "You are my friends," applies only "if you do what I command you": they are "friends" in a contemporary, heavily qualified sense.[21]

I could, on the other hand, offer a limited set of further New Testament passages that might seem to support at least elements of Schellenberg's claim to represent "traditional theism." On models of human parenting, Jesus in Matthew and Luke assures his hearers that God's care for them is like, but surpasses, best human parental care. Schellenberg insists that faith in God involves "belief that," to wit, "existence" claims: "that God exists." In fact a Letter to Hebrews has confidently asserted, "whoever comes to God must believe that he exists." However, in context "belief" in Hebrews seems also to imply the whole range of trust, faith, trustworthiness, without the primacy of *de dicto* ("belief that") on which Schellenberg insists. It is "good things" from God as caring divine Father that Matthew's Jesus promises, while in Luke what is promised is the gift of Holy Spirit. For neither is there any promise of self-revelation. Matthew does have Jesus claim the power to "reveal," the Father; compare Luke, "who the Father is." Here, as was argued in chapter 3, the focus is on "identifying."[22] In none of these passages is an unmediated personal interchange proposed.

19. For a useful sketch of the Aristotelian basis of this understanding, see McFall, "Can We have a Friend."

20. 1 Corinthians 2:16, for "mind of Christ"; 2 Corinthians 3:12–18 for boldness, with 1 Cor. 13:12, for "puzzling and partial"; cf. 1 John 3:2 and 4:12; see ch. 4.

21. See van Tilborg, *Imaginative Love*; along with McFall, "Can We have a Friend"; and John 15:14–25.

22. Hebrews 11:6 in the light of Still, "Christos as Pistos," 764–75, taken with

It is perhaps worth adding, from Luke's Acts of the Apostles, the words he ascribes to Paul, words that in turn prompted the title for this chapter: humans were "to seek God in the hope that, groping after him, they might find him, though he is not far from each one of us, for in him we live and move and have our being, as some of your own [Greek] poets have said"; the themes seem also to echo the first century BCE Wisdom of Solomon, but also resonate with Luke's Jewish contemporary, Flavius Josephus. Though "seeking God" is enjoined in some of the Jewish Scriptures, the authors just cited, as is widely recognized, echo Stoic (pan)theism. Thus it is more a matter of hide-and-seek, or even of blindman's bluff with God, "faith seeking revelation," than of instant, still less constant reception of divine self-disclosure.[23]

The ongoing patristic Christianity of the early centuries, accepted as formative and normative by the later "Great Church" (including more recent Reformed off-shoots) resolutely interpreted Paul's "puzzling reflections" and "partial knowledge" in terms of divine "incomprehensibility," as was extensively evidenced in chapter 5, noting its immediate origins in Philo's Platonic Jewish theism. The loving God of these writers is too transcendent for us to even hope to get our heads round him. Even readings of the intensely experiential biblical Song of Songs, by such as Origen, Gregory of Nyssa and (much later) Bernard of Clairvaux, as an allegory of engagement between the divine lover and the enraptured believer, remain within the same constraints.[24]

It would seem obvious that any talk of "traditional theism" must also include some awareness of Islam, as listed by Schellenberg in passing. And although the debate at issue has focused in practice on Christian theism(s), these, both Western and Eastern Christianities, have been affected by Islamic theology and practice, and particularly by Islamic philosophical theologians' interpretative transmission of Greek philosophical reflections.

We are assured in the Qur'an that nothing from God's side conceals God; the only veiling is ours, our ignorance, intransigence, refusal to learn, to comply with God's will. "Whithersoever ye turn, there is the face of God."[25]

Schellenberg, "Unnecessarily," 199–204; and Matt 7:11 and 11:25–27, with Lk 11:13 and 10:21–22.

23. Acts 17:27–28; Wisdom of Solomon 13; Josephus, *Antiquities* 8:108–112 (Josephus' version of Solomon's speech, 1 Kings 8); "seeking God," e.g., Psalm 27.

24. See, e.g., Westphal, "The Importance of Mystery," but also Fiddes "The Quest for a Place," and McGinn, "The Hidden God."

25. See Arberry, *Sufism*, 17, citing Qur'an 2.109; and Nasr, *Ideals and Realities*, 21; Chittick, *Self-Revelation*, 21, 46, with reference to Ibn Al 'Arabi; Kadri, *Heaven on Earth*, 82, with reference to Al Ghazali.

In the Qur'an we are given a way to follow, in thought and action, that will change us so that we will be able to perceive God in everything, and come to love God; and in that loving, but only then, we will find that now—but only now—are are loved by God.[26] (It was noted in earlier chapters that Paul, too, could say that the only "veil" between humans and God was refusing transformation, as in 1 Cor 4:1–6; and this is elaborated at least by Gregory of Nyssa, in his *Homilies on the Song of Songs*.)[27] Very recently Claudia Wetz has provided a reminder from Abraham Heschel of a Kabbalistic insight: "It is not God who is obscure. It is man who conceals him." His hiddenness "is due to us who have forsaken him."[28]

Nonetheless, an Islamic philosophical theologian, such as Ibn Al 'Arabi, reflecting on the reality of divine self-disclosure, insists that even negative terms cannot capture the divine essence. Reminiscent of Philo, it is in contemplating the cosmos that one can see the face of God in its beauty. Or, echoing Matthew's Gospel, Ibn Al 'Arabi takes it that "When one of His servants is hungry, He says to the others, 'I was hungry, but you did not feed me. When another is thirsty . . . if you had given him to drink, you would have found that you gave to Me.'"[29] It is such perceptive action and reflection, it would seem, that constitutes seeing the unremittingly disclosed face of God.

Very rarely, even among Sufi mystics, is this relationship seen as analogous to inter-human reciprocity. Even Mohammed receives the Qur'an by angelic mediation. Heaven, Paradise, allows, not interchange, but our unveiled contemplation, no more if no less.[30] Sadakat Kadri cites as exceptional, a mystic who hears God call,

> "Do you want me to tell people what I know of your sins, so that they stone you to death?" "O Lord," he whispers back, "Do you want me to tell people what I know about your mercy, so that none will ever feel obliged to bow down to you again?" "You keep your secret, and I will keep mine," replies God.[31]

26. Arberry, *Sufism*, 27, citing Kharrāz, *Kitāb al-Sidq*.

27. Gregory, *Homilies* 12–13 (Norris 381-93; Jaeger 360–73) again.

28. Welz, "Resonating and Reflecting," 182, citing Heschel, *Man Is Not Alone*, 153–54. Or one may compare Francis Thompson's couplet in "The Kingdom of Heaven": "'Tis ye, 'tis your estranged faces, / That miss the many-splendoured thing."

29. Chittick, *Self-Revelation*, xvii, 28 and 348.

30. Nicholson, *Mystics*, 47; Ibn Al 'Arabi clearly insists there is no equality, that divine love is very one-sided (Chittick, *Self-Revelation*, 76).

31. Kadri, *Heaven on Earth*, 110, from Nicholson, *The Mystics of Islam*, 136. The stoning would be for heretical assertions.

No more than in traditional Jewish or Christian effective theism do we find here in Islam the ideal of divine, love-laden, outgoing, universal self-gift as an ideal, one that Schellenberg can show to be unrealized by its failure to make itself obvious to all.

Thus, as suggested, the non-existence of Schellenberg's deity, demonstrated by the failure of that deity's necessary open self-presentation (as stipulated), has no ontological significance for traditional theisms that classically entail no such definition.

So much for his insistence that his is a general atheistic argument. (Of course, if Schellenberg's ideal monotheism were somehow shown true, with such a deity effectively existing, then these other *mono*theisms would, by definition, be discounted as oddly unperceptive.)

However, although the non-existence of Schellenberg's deity may thus be agreed to have no ontological import for traditional theism(s), the failure of his ideal to be instantiated might still have critical implications for instantiated theisms. For Schellenberg's specification does echo, as he claims, the ideal theologies of some mid-twentieth-century Christian theologians (whom I value, though not uncritically). There may incidentally be implications for the persuasiveness, attractiveness, even ethical propriety of the divine character as traditionally presented and trusted. Perhaps Schellenberg's recent exposition of an ideal but uninstantiated divine love shows the poverty, the emptiness of traditional theisms' accounts of the love they ascribe to the God whose reality they proclaim? The God of actual instantiated theistic traditions could perhaps seem by this comparison as made to look so poor, so loveless, so uninviting as not to warrant allegiance, thus encouraging a practical atheism.

(b) Models of Loving Relationships

The question is not, then, about the propriety of effective language in God-talk: as noted above, some seems to be endemic in the canonical writings. The question is over the particular model of loving relationships proposed as ideal.

My 1964 study attempted a short rebuttal of a vigorous insistence on divine love as entailing divine self-revelation. Austin Farrer had argued that a God believed only to "deal in us," "impersonally," and not self-revealingly to "deal with us," could not be seen as loving at all: Farrer insisted, "Now, 'dealing with' involves two parties who must be aware of each other's actions."[32] I responded:

32. Farrer, "Revelation," 100

But as an analysis of the term as it is normally used this is just not true. A teacher "deals with" rowdy pupils without trying to increase their "awareness" of himself, personally. Perhaps Farrer understands a more refined sense of "deal with personally." But a parent can "deal with" a child tactfully, with every respect for the emerging personality, long before the child can be aware of many of the actions [let alone inner thoughts] of the parent as a person at all, or be at all able to respond on a personal level. Compared with God as "a person" (if that be a proper phrase), the most fully personal of us, I think a Christian would want to say, is very much a child, to be "dealt with" as a child, and not be expected to see the full "personality" of him with whom we have to deal. In fact, the parent who tries to "reveal himself" too soon, who tries to elicit a precocious personal response, is not acting "personally" at all; he is not looking for a personal relationship, but just a foil for his own personality. This is not God's way with us.[33]

Schellenberg, as sketched in the introduction to this chapter is not blind to some of the kinds of points I made. But his argument for the openness of real love is somewhat more elaborate.

The account offered by Schellenberg, asserted by those he quotes, and accepted by his critics seems to be, even more distinctly, a very modern one, of the mid-twentieth century for its full flowering, even if with earlier adumbrations, and doubtfully appropriate in a discussion of "traditional" anything. Schellenberg's ideal presupposes a trust in a common humanity, with the rejection of slavery, and its inherent racism (both still cruelly with us), and a fuller (if still quite incomplete) acceptance of equal rights for women and men: all of these needing to be widely accepted before children could have ascribed the right to such parental openness, self-sharing. In the English reading world one sees it as an idealization of strands in John Bowlby, *Child Care and the Growth of Love* (1953), based on his World Health Organisation 1951 report, *Maternal Care and Mental Health*; or David W. Winnicott, *The Child, the Family, and the Outside World* (1964), based on two earlier Tavistock reports of 1957 (North American readers and others might add William Spock).

Schellenberg's model clearly condemns all three traditional theisms from the start, for not having jumped straight into twentieth-century enlightenment: for proposing a loving God without realizing what "love" "must really" mean today. This leaves no instance of his kind of "traditional

---

33. Downing, *Has Christianity a Revelation?* 250–51, again with the original uninclusive language, and an addition in square brackets.

theism," and so nothing to fail to be instantiated. Perhaps 1 Corinthiaans 13, with its "not yet face-to-face" simply illustrates Paul's antique obtuseness. And of course, Schellenberg is free to condemn actual traditional theisms for their ancient obtuseness, in company with those who in much the same way condemn these theisms for their failure to make intially or very early this prescient leap on the prior issues of slavery, racism, sexism, patriarchy and women's and children's rights. (Schellenberg categorizes "patriarchy" as only a peripheral flaw.) So, too, in the same way, the God of traditional theisms, even as modified by Schellenberg's modern "authorities"—Vanstone, Adams, Mitchell, Hebblethwaite, McCord Adams, Jantzen—would stand condemned for his/her creative adoption of evolution. For that allowed millions of ancestral humans (humanoids?) to emerge as beings whose best relational aspirations have fallen signally short of the enlightened twentieth century ideals espoused by Schellenberg.

But the more weighty question that faces us concerns the ethical and psychological validity of the model proposed, that of unrestrictedly constantly accessible self-giving love. In response we need first to determine whether his is a free-standing "thought experiment" (of the "brain in a vat" kind), or is it supposed to represent actual aspiration tested by experience? Schellenberg's talk of thinking "free" of inherited concepts might suggest the former; his early dismissal of "brain in a vat" in favor of trusting perceptual claims, suggests the latter.[34] Even thought experiments are expected to relate to an imagination formed by our actual ordinary world, and Schellenberg certainly makes frequent appeals to the validating responses he expects to be forthcoming among his readers.[35] We may take it that he/his text intends his sketches to represent our common aspirations and experience.

Room is carefully left in his model for the loved one's growth, and for freedom to accept or reject, to move in and out of the relationship offered. The lover her/himself seems, however, to be "passionless," immoveable. Nothing the loved one does has any effect. The beloved is quite powerless, cannot in any way cloud the sunshine of the love outpoured. The loving parent, sibling, friend seems oddly akin to the passionless, unmoved deity of some Aristotelian- and Stoic-influenced theism (there have been other kinds), or its emulating philosopher. The loved one can do nothing to the lover to show that s/he matters to the lover, who frustratingly maintains a

34. Schellenberg, *The Wisdom to Doubt*, 190–91, with "Experience," 157.

35. Schellenberg, *Hiddenness and Reason*, 23. See also his "Collaborative," 41; *The Wisdom to Doubt*, 203. Among responses I have encountered, only a review by Alan Padgett of *Divine Hiddenness*, and quoted by Charles Taliaferro, *Contemporary Philosophy*, 332, seriously questions the model itself, rather than just details of its supposed implications.

fixed affectionate stance (even smile?). All that really matters to the lover, or so it must seem to the victim of such love, is the former's maintaining an unshadowed consistently loving attitude, impervious. I find it hard to believe that I am unique in my rather different experience of being a twentieth-century English child and then parent. The realization that not only can one "freeze" one's response to a parent (for which Schellenberg allows), but one can also freeze the parent, is itself a part of growing up and into a potentially richer and adult relationship. A realization of the other's genuine vulnerability—vulnerable love—is part and parcel of coming to some sort of adult-to-adult engagement of genuine giving-and-receiving, needing and being needed.[36]

But still more basic, it might seem, is the need of the child to be different, and in that sense free of the parent (lover of lover), by *not* being exposed to the unrelenting and potentially overpowering splendor and richness of character that Schellenberg implausibly imagines in his ideal deity. *The Guardian* has for some years been publishing a family Saturday supplement. Nowhere that I can recall over many years has the kind of persistent self-revelation by parent or other indicated by Schellenberg been either celebrated or its lack lamented. I can think of aspects of my wife's and my own "selves" that we could in no way have revealed nor now think we should have revealed to either of our children in earlier days, but some of which we have now been able to share since they were in their forties. I think of my father's devoted grief at my mother's attitude to him, a sadness I only came at all close to comprehending in my forties, and would have found it hard or even impossible to live with earlier. Nor could I have appreciated something of my mother's struggles, though my older sister, growing close to our mother later, recently shared with me some insights. Thus it is hard to imagine how one could be faced by a divine person immeasurably rich, deep, compelling, without being constrained, either positively or negatively, in one's quest to be free, independent, other. And one finds an awareness of this aspect of childhood, its independence, its creativity, its inquisitiveness, not just in the last century, but already in ancient writers, such as Cicero and Quintilian. There is heart-breaking evidence in the resistance evidenced by Victorian accounts of the vicious measures needed to "break the child's will."

In adulthood we do not impose a total awareness of ourselves on each other, not even in the closest of human relationships.

Schellenberg's deity also seems to be a creator who should from the start have made humankind with at least an inalienable potential for an intimate awareness of that God's self, so that any refusal could be the

---

36. Compare Tucker, "Hiddenness," 281, 284–85.

responsibility of the loved one, not of the divine lover.[37] That would seem, as already noted, to preclude evolution. Those loved by Schellenberg's hypothetical God still seem bodily and finite (they grow), but the deity at least is omniscient and ubiquitous: they are ill matched. Then, to be aware of him/her would seem to demand being aware in some detail (how much?), not just in general, of God's relationship with others: that is surely integral to this divine self's richness. This wealth Schellenberg would have fully available, demanding "self-giving [where] the self is the totality of what a man is." So we ourselves need to have been made, at least potentially, omniscient? These imagined beloved persons seem from the start to be disembodied (angelic?) beings, yet with a mental-and-effective capacity greater than any imagined even in traditional Christian angelology. They are clearly not restricted by the tally of synapses in a modern physical human brain. These objects of love do not seem to be constituted by any sort of physicality that we are aware constitutes each of us. They seem to be on equal terms with their deity, just like supposedly ideal grown up children with a parent, and with ideal adult friends, but with an immeasurably greater openness themselves, as well as an unlimited, infinite responsive capacity. So we do actually seem to be dealing with a thought experiment, a model of relationality detached from human life as we know it. Human life as we know it seems to resonate much more readily with traditional theism than with Schellenberg's imagined perfections.[38]

Further, let us entertain, at least for argument's sake, recent theologians' talk of "the pain of God." That is a theme certainly integral to the reflections of many of those whom Schellenberg cites, but with some roots, though not undisputed, in Christian and Jewish tradition, if not in Islam. One would then have to ask how being exposed to that omniscient or at least multiscient divine level of grief could be advantageous or even sustainable?[39]

37. Schellenberg, *The Wisdom to Doubt*, 205n11, happily dispenses with the guilt word, "inculpable," of unbelief, in favor of "non-resistant."

38. While drafting this, I gathered from my son that working out a critical awareness of the functions of scientific "models" at secondary school gave him confidence in his critical abilities. This he might not have gained had I shared with him at that stage what I had published on "models" years earlier. Having the Creator's mind open to us would seem even more potentially stultifying than having constant and automatic access to an infallible Wikipedia.

39. See Heschel, *The Prophets*, for ancient Jewish reflections; see Gregory Thaumaturgos, *Ad Theopompum* and Lactantius *Institutes* 6, for a more open strand in early tradition; Kitamori, *Pain of God*; Sarot, *God, Passibility* and Pinnock, *Most Moved*; Downing, "Order A," 95–101; and "Order B," 103–6.

(c) "Belief"and "Faith"

But perhaps the trouble lies, not in Schellenberg's model of self-giving love, but in our or my failure to deploy his distinction, noted earlier, between "faith in" and "belief that."[40] Schellenberg's "faith in" has to be private, not uttered publicly: so avoiding any impression of asserting a proposition for which probative evidence is required but unavailable (such as, "that a deeply, unmissably self-displaying loving God exists"). In reponse I allow that an author may stipulate a preferred usage of which a reader must then take careful account if sincerely trying to understand what that author's work intends. But I here see no good reason for accepting that restriction in my own attempts to communicate. It seems to me (*contra* Schellenberg) that the "family" of English terms: "believe," "believe in," "finding believable (that)," "trust," "trust in," "putting trust in," "trust that," "being trustworthy," "finding trustworthy," "faith," "faith in," "faith that," all usefully overlap and interconnect in ways that hard distinctions fail to register or effectively distort. Granted, he explicitly rejects Wittgenstein's "family relationship" proposal, on the grounds that it fails to allow for "definition"; but that is precisely the aim of Wittgenstein's argument.[41] The latter allows that "boundaries" can be imposed, but they are not given in the language we share.[42] Certainly Schellenberg offers us a "corrected" usage, but gives us no reason for accepting it as "correct," other than that it suits his purposes.[43]

On the other hand, in a trusting relationship there are assertions of trust, trust in, trust that, faith in/that, belief in/that, that could be uttered (and even validated) but are simply inappropriate—a possibility apparently ignored in Schellenberg's *The Wisdom to Doubt*.[44] To express them is to answer a question that does not arise, or to raise a question that already puts the relationship in doubt. If a friend were to say she trusted her husband, believed that he was faithful, trustworthy, I would wonder why she felt I needed the assurance. Were someone to ask me, "Do you trust your wife?" I would be puzzled or affronted. Does my behavior suggest any doubt on my part? But if I decided to overcome my repugnance at the question, or puzzlement at the assurance sought, how would I respond? Suppose a curt "Of course. What an impertinent question," was insufficient to quieten the

40. Argued in detail in Schellenberg, *Prolegomena*; cf. *The Wisdom of Doubt*, 7–8 and 315–16.

41. Schellenberg, *Prolegomena*, 7–12.

42. Compare, for instance, Wittgenstein, *Investigations*, 68, 83-86, 497–99; *Zettel*, 43; Downing, "Ambiguity."

43. Schellenberg, *Prolegomena*,165.

44. Schellenberg, *The Wisdom to Doubt*.

inopportune questioner, and the inquisition persists: "Is your wife in her heart of hearts, faithful to you? Do you know she is? Can you prove it? What evidence do you have?" "Nothing even suggests I should query it." "But perhaps she is a very good actor, while in her heart of hearts, she is unfaithful to you." Does an admission then that I do not "know" in that sense of "cannot prove, cannot provide expermentally tested evidence" invalidate my earlier "Of course"? By this stage "Of course not!" repeated, perhaps louder or slower, is all I am left with. The inappropriateness of "valid-as-experimentally-demonstrable" claims to "know," the irrelevance of "proof" is part of the language game of faith, trust, belief.

That leaves me quite content to say, at length, "I believe, trustingly, in-a-non-evidentially-validatable sense, in God who is real in his/her own right, with, at best, occasional glimpses of assurance, but in a way that I trust will ultimately turn out to be valid. And this (qualified) validating will include many if not all elements of traditional Christian theism, while, I hope, improving on them. So that will at the same time fulfill and expand absorbingly my and others' best intimations of that God's Trinitarian being. All this trust is without my supposing I can justifiably claim to 'know' any of it."

I might still even say, unthinkingly, "I believe that this God exists," when actually I am more used to saying, "We believe in one God . . ." and implying I/we trust her/him as real, trust him/her to be real,[45] as I trust my wife's love to be real without deliberately straining it (trying though I guess I often am).[46]

And integral to others' as to my own trust in God, Father, Son, and Holy Spirit, is the conviction that it is best modeled on ordinary loving human inter-relatedness with a varying balance of openness and reticence. Representing ordinary experience, this most effectively articulates trust in the still un-self-revealed God of traditional Christian theism. Christian theism is much better understood as this sort of trust than the very artificial

45. I have avoided "exist" and discussing "proof of existence" (on which see Evans, "Can God?" 241 and Kenny, *The Unknown God*; on Kierkegaard on proving divine existence see Ellis, "Insatiable, Desire" 265), but it does seem an odd term to use in this context. "Does 'dark matter' exist?" is a surely an ill-formed question. Better is "What do astrophysicists mean by 'dark matter'?" "It is integral to current theories, that 95 percent or so of the universe is unexplained." One can ask, "Is the theory cogent?," but to ask on its own "Does 95 percent of the universe exist?" is very odd. One can ask, "What useable sense, if any, does it make to talk of the God who sustains everything"; but to ask, "And does 'sustaining everything' include existing?" would be very odd.

46. If the monstrous absurdity of "proving" either love or faithfuless is not obvious, I suggest reading Geoffrey Chaucer's *The Clerk's Tale*, and in his *Canterbury Pilgrims* the story "Patient Griselde."

ideal dreamed up some recent Christian theologies of divine self-revelation, the neologism adopted and deployed by Schellenberg.

Having begun with the help of R. S. Thomas, it is worth recalling his persistence and occasional if still enigmatic glimpses of reassurance:

> . . .A bishop
> called for an analysis
>   of the bread and wine. I being
>   no chemist play my recording
>   of his silence over
>   and over to myself only.

with,

> Suddenly after long silence
> he has become voluble.
> He addresses me from a myriad
> directions . . .
>   . . . all
> speaking to me in the vernacular
> of the purposes of One who is.[47]

Schellenberg rightly, to my mind, emphasizes "faith in" as a disposition to act in certain ways (though I could as readily here talk of "belief in" or "trust in," simply for variety's sake), specifically as a way of avoiding a defeasible "belief that"; but I could as readily urge avoiding "faith that" or "trust that" religious—or other—claims that unwarrantably suggest intersubjective demonstrability.[48]

Many Christian theologians these days persist in asserting that the God in whom they and fellow Christians believe/trust/have faith, has already and perhaps still does a lot of revealing including, increasingly in the last century, "self-revealing." This makes just such defeasible and very vulnerable claims.[49] Multiple and vigorous disagreements among them as to the wishes and demands of their God renders any such claim demonstrably untrue in general, and supportable, even initially, only in some minority coherent group.

---

47. Thomas, "Revision," in *Experimenting with an Amen*, 69; and "Suddenly" in *Later Poems*, 201.

48. Schellenberg, *Prolegomena*, 113–24, 165. I allow, besides, that his skeptical atheism is perhaps meant to make space for a Kierkegaardian "pure" faith.

49. See Macdonald, *Ideas*, accepting, as noted earlier, that this is an innovation in Christian theological reflection, though still himself approving it.

That religious diversity significantly and adversely affects claims to divine revelation is thus a conclusion on which I am happy to find myself in agreement with Schellenberg.[50] Yet, in faith, I trust, with many fellow Christians, past and present, that divine self-revelation lies ahead—a divine self-revelation as full as we can be formed and reformed in Christ to engage with. The next chapters seek to suggest ways of exploratively living this kind of "agnostic" trust, inspired, as explained, by 1 Cor 13:12 read in the light of 2 Cor 5:19: "Now we see puzzling reflections in a mirror, then we shall see face-to-face"; for "God in Christ was [and is] uniting the world to himself."

---

50. Schellenberg, *The Wisdom of Doubt*, 88–90, 164–66, 175–83.

166

7

Imaginative Faith While Being Transformed
for Knowing as We are Known[1]

Introduction

Much that is positive should already have emerged in the previous six chapters. Along with the negative, "no, we have no shared (or even plausibly shareable) clarity," there has at least been an exploration of hopes for unity with the God trusted to be present. To explore that positive theme further, it seemed a good idea to begin these final chapters with an exploration of prayer, as talking to God, as engaging trustingly in imaginary conversations with God. This is prayer as being drawn into a deeper imagined and perhaps quite inarticulate, likely amazed, awareness of welcome into the life of God in Trinity. We trust we are drawn closer by God still not demonstrably "known," but imagined as present in reality, and hopefully awaiting a future, much closer acquaintance. We trust we shall be known as ourselves, real, recognizable, but brought into what will be a vast improvement on any already imagined relationship with God in Christian or other traditions.

At least starting with such variegated prayer makes up for there being only two references to praying, and those in passing, in the previous study—and that despite one of these notes stressing prayer's importance. I can't, then, think of a better succinct and traditional appraisal of imaginative prayer than George Herbert's much-admired sonnet, "Prayer (I)," especially as supplemented by his many other prayer poems. Further, Herbert's practice of prayer is set within a faith than is Trinitarian, incarnational, sacramental, churchly, relational, and necessarily open to the poor, as is the faith

---

1. The montage presents a praying figure sharing with God some limited awareness of human life woven into its wider physical setting.

that I affirmed fifty years ago and that here, if in somewhat recast form, I reaffirm.

(a) George Herbert and Puzzling in Prayer

Prayer (I)

Prayer the Church's banquet, Angels' age,
> God's breath in man returning to his birth,
> The soul in paraphrase, heart in pilgrimage,
The Christian plummet sounding heav'n and earth;
Engine against th'Almighty, sinners' tower,
> Reversed thunder, Christ-side-piercing spear,
> The six-days-world transposing in an hour,
A kind of tune, which all things hear and fear;
Softness and peace, and joy, and love, and bliss,
> Exalted Manna, gladness of the best,
> Heaven in ordinary, man well drest,
The milky way, the bird of Paradise,
> Church bells beyond the stars heard, the soul's blood,
> The land of spices; something understood.

I now share reflections on how, if at all, the critical theological, exegetical, and philosophical reflections of chapters 2–6 mesh with those of this very traditional poet-theologian, including Herbert's reflections in the light of the analysis of language in chapter 1.

But first, let this poem from Herbert, and perhaps others, do their work. The reader may have engaged with the sonnet before, relishing its piled-up allusions; or may want to begin by reflecting unaided. For what it may be worth I now offer some suggestions, mostly my own from over the years, a few added more recently, with help from Ann Pasternak Slater and, very recently, John Drury.[2]

A "banquet," Drury tells us, in the seventeenth century denoted preliminaries (drinks with nibbles?), the feast being the Eucharist. "Angels'

---

2. Slater, *George Herbert*, 413–14; and Drury, *Music at Midnight*, 243–44. In "The Church Porch" Herbert advises, "Resort to sermons, but to prayers most: / Praying's the end of preaching" (in Slater, *George Herbert*, 20, 2:408–10.) On the significance of talking to/with God trusted to have encouraged address, Soskice, "The Gift of the Name," 72–75.

age" angels' entire life. "Breath . . . returning (l. 2)," divinely inbreathed life (Gen 2:7; compare l. 13), God's gift, given back; compare the Manna (l. 10). "The soul in paraphrase," (l. 3) picks up Rom 8:26–27, the Spirit prays in us, "translating" what we cannot find words for; compare the final phrase, "something understood" (by God). In prayer our passionate thought travels Godward, in pilgrimage. Then there are further deliberate reversals: our lead-line is thrown up to "sound" (touch, but audibly, l. 4) the heights, not down to depths; we Babel-like sinners (Gen 11:1–9, l. 5) are positively encouraged to attack God's dwelling with a siege-tower, as sure to gain his attention as his thunder gains ours, able to pierce to the very heart of God, emboldened by Christ's death. "A sort of giddy exhilaration results from this topsy-turvydom," as Drury suggests.

Line 7 recalls Gen 1, the whole creation that we can celebrate in prayer (compare "Providence," "Man is the world's high Priest," l:13; "Antiphon 1", "Let all the world"; and "The Elixir," "in all things thee to see"). Our prayer, Herbert trusts, is in turn respected (feared) by all things (l. 8). With line 9 we return to the Holy Spirit, harvesting the heavenly bliss of "love, joy, peace . . . gentleness" (Gal 5:22). "Manna," (l. 10) is noted above; "the best" can only be Jesus, in joy thanking his Father (Lk 10:21–22; cf. Matt 11:25–27): in praying exuberantly we are one with him, our everyday world (l. 11) is already briefly in heaven, for which we are fitted out (by God, Gen 3:21; compare "Employment," l. 25), suitably clothed (Matt 22:11; cf. "Aaron") for the occasion. We are at least on our milky way to heaven (perhaps 1 Pet 2:2), with the Holy Spirit (the only "bird" leading into the Paradise story, Gen 1:2) brooding over us, sure we are heard beyond the visible Milky Way, in heaven, the "land of spices" (from the long traditional reading of the Song of Songs). Prayer, then, is our soul's life-blood, but involves the sensual arousal evoked by this imagery (so, Drury, again). Yet, after all, it is still a "something" that only God fully understands. As for us, we only hope to understand "something, " a "something" that can be evoked by metaphor, but not clearly defined.

For this poet, one can clearly pray to, in imagination, talk with, a God who has not and does not go in for self-revelation. In an incidental and intriguing confirmation of the argument of the previous study, George Herbert does not talk of divine "revelation," let alone "self-revelation," at all. Yet his more purely "humanist" elder brother, Edward, Lord Herbert of Cherbury, does: it is a climactic theme of his carefully thought-out *De Veritate*. A (Stoic) rational providential deity has revealed to humans "common notions" (including the Decalogue), which allow them to know clearly when they've got things right: and this conviction itself, of having indeed got things right, can come as a special revelation. Drury quotes Edward,

"Movements of conscience and prayerful impulses have their beginning and end in revelation. In a word, every original impulse of pity and of joy which springs in our hearts is a revelation." (Nonetheless, as Drury himself comments, this is "not as God's self-revelation in Christ, but as an extraordinary personal experience.")[3] Edward, who shared with George his humanist emphasis on inwardness, is widely taken, however unfairly, as a forerunner of English Enlightenment Deism.[4] Edward's cool Stoic rationalism expects God to grant clarity. George Herbert's passionate and ambivalent person-to-person engagement with a suffering and self-giving God can accept that for now, "we see in a glass darkly." There seems to be much more to God than being a provider of clear answers, an underwriter of Stoic certainties, much more for him to disclose, discover, reveal.[5]

Thus repeatedly in "Home" the younger Herbert pleads,

> O show thyself to me,
> Or take me up to thee!

and in "The Search" he asks,

> Whither, O, wither, art thou fled,
> My Lord, my Love?
> My searches are my daily bread
> Yet never prove.
>
> My knees pierce th'earth, mine eyes the sky,
> And yet the sphere
> And centre both to me deny
> That thou art there.
>
> Lord, dost thou some new fabric mould
> Which favour wins,
> And keeps thee present, leaving th'old
> Unto their sins?
>
> Where is my God? What hidden place
> Conceals thee still?

3. Drury, *Music at Midnight*, 103–104, citing Meyrick H. Carré, ed. and tr., *Edward, Lord Herbert of Cherbury, De Veritate*, 310.

4. Reventlow, *Authority*, 2:2, 185–93. Kennedy, *Introduction*, 59, 127, notes Herbert of Cherbury, *De Veritate*, but quite wrongly has him reject divine revelation to humans and individuals; it is only churchly "special revelation" that is bypassed.

5. Though there are also clear Stoic resonances in George Herbert's "Providence."

What covert dare eclipse thy face?
> Is it thy will?

O let not that of any thing;
> Let rather brass

Or steel, or mountains be thy ring
> And I will pass. . .

O take these bars, these lengths away;
> Turn and restore me.

Be not Almighty, let me say,
> Against, but for me.

As Ann Slater explains, Herbert will often offer a preliminary answer to a question before giving the full response at the end. Why do his prayers seem never to rise (like bread proving) to God? It is in fact our sins that hide God from us; George has to trust, whatever it is that keeps God hidden, it is not his will to stay forever hidden. A barrier of "anything," bar such ill-will, could be surmounted. In fact, what is needed, is this God, deploying his almighty power "for me/us," to "restore" me/us. And even then, as in "Justice (2)" God remains "veiled." Even if no longer puzzlingly "discoloured," or darkened by the "mirror" of sin and error, still God is hidden, but here it is by the sinless glory of Christ, his "pure white veil." But that, as Paul had assured us, is a pure glory meant for sharing; so, though still concealing, it encourages rather than deters.

In this poem (so, Slater invites us to see) Herbert is correlating 1 Cor 13:12 with 2 Cor 3:18, as I did earlier in chapter 3, and, I think, to similar effect.

And then, with the final verse of "The Search":

For as thy absence doth excel
> All distance known,

So doth thy nearness bear the bell
> Making two one.

The paradox of divine nearness and distance sounds Platonic, as does the final emphasis on one-ness. But "My Lord, my love" it is who is present as, it seems, the focus and enabler of unity with God: Christ as the bell-wether, the leading sheep whose bell unites the flock with himself. And so we have "at-one-ment," already, even while we still search, and plead "restore thine image" ("The Sinner"), seeking to be changed, rendered more responsive, fully responsive: "holy, pure, and clear" or at least groaning to be so ("Super-liminare"). So, with different images, we have

> Yet take thy way; for sure, thy way is best:
>> Stretch or contract me, thy poor debtor,
>> This is but tuning of my breast,
>>> To make the music better. ("The Temper (1)")

And in "Windows," "Let thy light to shine within . . . Doctrine and life, colours and light in one."

Unity with God, God in Trinity, appears in more personal terms at the climax of "Trinity Sunday":

> Enrich my heart, mouth, hands in me,
>> With faith, with hope, with charity;
>> That I may run, rise, rest with thee.

Even if the third line is taken as sequential (this life, resurrection, eternal Sabbath), the first, the present "run" is as much "with" God as the third. And much else in Herbert's poetry would at least allow the sense of resting secure already, while still being transformed. I would interpret similarly another poem of Herbert's with the same title.[6] Here "Nature and Grace/With Glory may attain thy Face" I take to refer to Creator, Redeemer, and Spirit (the "glory" of 2 Cor 3:17–18). This poem also ends in the present tense, with the assurance that trusting the one God in Trinity, "He that has one has all."

Being oned, or, perhaps, better, already becoming oned with God involves already conversing, on intimate terms, imaginatively. Even though the poet is often client (e.g., "Redemption"), liege servant (e.g., "The Altar"), child (e.g., "The Collar"), he is also lover and loved (often). And he is on good enough terms to argue (surely, God, you know from your own experience that love is more effective than a rod? "Discipline"), to think that he knows better than his lover ("Dialogue, and Love (3)"), confident enough to complain ("Affliction (1)," and, again, "The Collar").

Herbert does not in his poems reflect on his self's formation in relationships with human friends; but he evinces a vivid sense of his self being re-formed in these dialogues with the divine lover.

This relationship does, however, seem for the most part very individual, celebrated between the divine lover and the poet on his own, separate spokes, if to a single hub for all. The first person plural is rare. Of course, it is implicit in talk of "man," humankind; clearly Herbert had many good friends, and shared his poems with them, shared in common prayer as a

---

6. Slater, *George Herbert*, lvi.

layman and led it as a priest.[7] But awareness of divine love for him seems to drown out any awareness of Christ or the Father's loving awareness of others. Possible exceptions include, for instance, "Love (2)," which has:

Immortal heat, O let thy greater flame
Attract the lesser to it: let those fires
Which shall consume the world, first make it tame;
And kindle in our hearts such true desires
As may consume our lusts, and make thee way.

and, again, in "Giddiness,"

Lord, mend or rather make us: one creation
    Will not suffice our turn:
Except thou make us daily, we shall spurn
    Our own salvation.

(and here, I take it, despite his acceptance of inherited fallenness—e.g., in "Love Unknown"—Herbert reads 2 Cor 5:17 as new creation, not restoration; compare "The Temper (2)," l. 8).

A Christian individual's relationship with neighbor and God together figure in "Constancy," "giving all their due." Trying, if in vain, in gratitude to recompense Christ, might well involve,

If thou dost give me wealth I will restore
    All back unto thee by the poor . . .
I'll build a spittle, or mend common ways,
    But mend my own without delays.
Then I will use the works of thy creation
    As if I used them but for fashion. ("The Thanksgiving")[8]

Then, in "Divinity," he insists, come what may, Christ's own priorities at least are clear, even if our abstract theologizing is puzzling to unpick:

Love God, and love your neighbour. Watch and pray.
    Do as you would be done by.

---

7. In "Misery," though reflecting on "man" he ends with explaining, "My God, I mean myself." But perhaps here it is to admit his own failures, rather than judge others'. "Conscience" bidden "Peace, prattler," is possibly a reprimand to himself for undue self-important wallowing in guilt (compare "Love (3)," "Dialogue," and "A True Hymn").

8. Spittle, of course, hospital; "but for fashion," that is, with detachment (Slater). Compare "The Church Porch," verses 63, 64 (Slater, *George Herbert*, 19, 2:373–84); and even more, in prose, *The Country Parson*, XI and XII.

> O dark instructions; ev'n as dark as day!
>
> Who can these Gordian knots undo?

This wider concern does not for Herbert extend to any critique of social structures, or of hierarchy as such. A magistrate must be "severe," and a father rule his household, if by love more than by fear with his children, still by fear more than love with his servants (barring, perhaps, an ancient loyal retainer).[9] There's no way of telling how Herbert might have responded to the charge of inconsistency, when he tells God,

> Then let wrath remove;
>
> Love will do the deed
>
> > For with love
>
> Stony hearts will bleed,

and then reminds God/Christ of his own divine experience of the change love can work:

> Who can 'scape his bow?
>
> That which wrought on thee
>
> > Brought thee low,
>
> Needs must work on me. ("Discipline")

(and compare "Justice (2)" and "Complaining").

As has been shown, Herbert knows, at least in theory, that we have only puzzling reflections. Yet he does not seem aware of the extent to which his own writing may illustrate such enigmas. For the tension between love and wrath is not the only paradox with which he presents his readers, in trying to piece together coherently the deity he identifies.

Only rarely, it is clear, does Herbert explicitly refer to God as Trinity: just in the two poems already discussed briefly above, and in *Ungratefulness*, where the Trinity's "sparkling light access denies . . . till death blow the dust into our eyes," ("into" referring to the restorative clay of Jn 9:6).

Many among the poems, of course, are vocative, but often it is far from clear whether the address is to the Trinity, or to God as creator, or to God as incarnate Redeemer (I don't think Christ is referred to as agent in creation). God the Holy Spirit is addressed only once, in "Ephes. 4.30. Grieve not the Holy Spirit." (In the third of three verses omitted in the main collection, he

---

9. "The Church Porch" (in Slater, *George Herbert*, 11, 1:85); *The Country Parson*, IX, "The Parson's State of Life," and X, "The Parson in his House." However, a wife's household management is best left with her, unsupervised. There is not sign of awareness of contemporary "feminist" thinking, as in Aemelia Lanyer, 1569–1645: see Clarke, *Women Poets*.

risked feminizing the Holy Spirit, "Show that thy breasts cannot be dry, / But that from them joys purle for ever).[10]

In Col 3:3, "Our life is hid with Christ in God," Christ is clearly referred to, as one

> . . .whose happy birth
> Taught me to live here so, that still one eye
> Should aim and shoot at that which Is on high.

"That which Is on high" might seem to be the one God in Trinity.

"O King of Grief," ("The Thanksgiving"), directly addresses the wounded incarnate Savior, but includes the lines, "That all together may accord in thee, / And prove one God, one harmony." But the Lord invoked in "The Sinner" would seem to be the creator, asked, "Lord restore thine image," as in "Love (1)" and "Love (2)," as is God in "Denial," though God in "Sighs and Groans" is Christ as "Judge and Saviour, feast and rod." The Lord in "Good Friday" is Christ, to whom also "Holy Communion" and "Frailty" are directed. In "Easter Wings (1)" the poet seems to address as Lord the initiating Creator, but then as the risen victor. "H. Baptism (1)" part way through speaks to the redeemer. The Lord spoken to in "H. Baptism (2)," in "Sin (1)," "Mattins," and in "Affliction (1)" and in "Affliction (4)" is not particularized as Father or as Christ or as Trinity, nor is the God (rather than Christ or the Spirit), summoned to indwell his human temple effectively, in "Man." In "Faith" the Lord receiving acknowledgement is other than the Christ referred to; but in "Affliction (2)," "Thou Lord of Life" is the one who died, as in "Affliction (3)." The Lord apostrophied in "Home" had blood "trickling down thy face (l. 8), but at l. 19 is reminded "there lay thy son." The God as Father is rarely referred to, and is invoked in the poems just twice, I think; in "Assurance (v. 3)," and in the final verse of "The Cross" (where Father and divine Son are also distinguished).

The foregoing would seem to support the claim that the strands of theology argued in previous chapters do resonate positively, with Reformed, Catholic, and Orthodox Christian tradition, at least as represented by Anglican George Herbert. How it meshes (or fails to) with more recent theological reflections remains to be argued in the next and concluding chapter. Foremost, then, this Herbert, unlike his elder brother, avoids all talk of revelation or any suggestion at all that we have as yet been given clarity (save being clearly bidden to love God and neighbor). He certainly does not even consider the possibility that God might be thought to stand already "self-revealed." What we do already enjoy is unity with God in love

10. In Slater, *George Herbert*, 331.

while we allow each self, more or less willingly, to be re-formed, as a new creation in the divine image, assured of our forgiveness and even more, of our acceptance: a relationship to be expressed, affirmed, and grown into, in imaginative prayer.

Herbert is bound by the Anglican *Articles of Religion* to insist that no part of Scripture is to be held repugnant to any other.[11] Yet his distinction of the covenants, and even more, his antithesis of "Love and Wrath" come very close to it. And his ambiguity over identifying the persons of the Trinity at least mirrors the ambiguities of the New Testament writings, even if it does not sunder the different traditional identifications as firmly as I in earlier chapters suggested.

Of course, he and I disagree, even diametrically, on a number of other theological positions (but then so do I today with the author of 1964). Herbert accepts, if only occasionally, Adam and Eve and the fall incurring transmitted guilt as involving a price paid (he does not say to whom) by Christ in his going to crucifixion.[12] But then I also note how he can rephrase the outcome, in "Redemption," imagining a tenant wanting the cancellation of a costly lease and its replacement by a manageable one, seeking "the rich Lord"

> In cities, theatres, gardens, parks and courts:
>> At length I heard a ragged noise and mirth
>>> Of thieves and murderers: there I him espied
>>> Who straight, *Your suit is granted*, said, and died.

Herbert trusts divine providence: in general—in Stoic mode—in "Providence," but also in particular, accepting specific pain and loss as divinely directed therapy for himself (the "Affliction" poems), and he feels he has to urge this conclusion with skeptical villagers, in "The Parson Comforting," and even more in "The Parson's Consideration of Providence."[13] (I myself offered a tentative defense of individual divine providence back in 1964, one which I would now still more heavily qualify, with an "as if.")[14]

Yet still much of what he affirms I did and do also: we share a faith that is robustly Trinitarian if imprecise, ready to accord distinct roles to the persons in creation, re-creation, renewal, though even less ready than I was and am to imagine their interpersonal relationships (on which see more in what follows). His faith is thoroughly incarnational, and his divine Son really can

---

11. Articles VII and XX; Herbert in *The Country Parson*, IV.

12. As in "Repentance" and "Love Unknown" (final lines).

13. *The Country Parson*, chs. XV and XXX.

14. Downing, *Has Christianity a Revelation?* 168–69.

share human experience (even if with a concentration on his passion to the exclusion of most else, where I would differ in emphasis). It is sacramental. It is, as already confessed, more prayerful than mine in *Has Christianity?* with prayer that is imaginative, expressive, and at the same time formative. Herbert means his faith to work out in practicalities; though where he is socially conservative, I would reform society, especially in its gross inequalities (which were only dawning on me in 1964). And I may well nonetheless have effected even less than he did.

Obviously, I am claiming that Herbert speaks to me, as he appears to speak to many fellow Christians, and non-believers, despite his and our different ambient cultures. In our defense, it is worth checking Herbert's use of words against the survey of modern appreciations of language in chapter 1, above. One might take a shortcut, and say, all sorts trust that Herbert's contemporary, William Shakespeare, speaks vividly to them. But Shakespeare does not so overtly take to God-talk. So reminders of chapter 1 now follow.

For brevity, if at the cost of elegance, key terms are italicized (so *culture*, above, could have been). On *use* rather than *meaning*, Herbert's richly *imaginative*, visually evocative invention of *metaphors* engages many of us who refuse to pretend that our words "contain" precise senses. To whom or what he is *referring*, what or whom he is *identifying*, we accept we have to reconstruct from clues, in the same or other poems, or elsewhere: we seek what he may have *implied*, not expecting the immediate words on their own to do all the work for us. His language, thus, is inescapably *performative*: in his poems he affirms his questioning faith; *by* what he assembles he seeks to express, arouse and inform others' emotions, and his own, and does that, to stir to action. He does take as *known fact* some assertions that many of us are not able to (e.g., Adam and Eve); but thinking, imagining Godward can be explored in unknowing, its validity undemonstrable. "Prayer (1)" is a brilliant example of *thinking* seeking expression, mind searching its store of words and phrases, relying on others sharing something of the same imaginary, able to make some at least of the same or similar collocations, in a courteous creativity, neither dominated nor dominating; importantly not in thrall to dogmatic metaphysics.

As parson he seems to have been able to communicate by ethos, word, actions with his unschooled parishioners. We have no evidence as to whether he shared any poems with them: he was in no hurry to go into public print, so probably not. Much of his imagery, as Drury vividly illustrates, is aristocratic. He asks for active imagination in readers, hearers—and generously rewards it.

The critical theological reflections enunciated in previous chapters seek to call fellow Christians away from "modernist" aberrations—especially any indefensible claim to clarity, to divine self-revelation already—back to the older tradition represented in the canon and much that followed, tradition as re-presented to us by George Herbert in his poetry.

(b) A Half-Century of Critically Constructive Enrichment

Even a reader who has persevered so far might propose a very different list under this sub-heading than the one that follows. But perhaps there will be at least some overlap.

There has been much more, if still sectional Christian openness to other people's faiths, as mapped and exemplified very recently in *The Presence of Faith*, edited by David Thomas and Douglas Pratt.[15] It must be significant for our attitude to people with non-Christian faiths that we are not able to substantiate any claim that we, and we exclusively, have the demonstrable truth about God. This significance was not brought out in *Has Christianity?*, which was directed towards persuading fellow Christians that we had no basis for telling one another, "We've got God's self-revelation, you've just got mistaken guess-work." The present author, though instinctively universalist-inclusivist, only began to explicitly touch on such issues in print some ten years later. The stance now proposed as congruent with the rest of this book is as follows: if the Christian tradition turns out to be nearest to the truth of God of any, then the only one God there is, and in whom "we live and move and have our being" is a Trinity of persons; one of them is for ever incarnate. This divine Trinity is wide open in love to all who accept the invitation to communion in and with the divine life. But for now we are all (with Muslims, Jews, Hindus, Sikhs, Buddhists, animists, and "humanists" of various sorts) explicit or implicit explorers together. And, even if we Christians at least in our theorizing turn out to have been closer to discerning divine truth, in practice others may well be much closer from their side to that one God, closer than are some, or most, or even all of us Christians. Then, much as we hope and lovingly trust that we are fundamentally on the right lines, we have to accept that we still *could* turn out to be quite fundamentally not nearly as close to the truth of God as is some other (varied or monochrome) set of searchers, both in theory and practice.

A further major change has been the impact of the Second Vatican Council. Building on centuries of discrete adventures in "faith seeking

---

15. Thomas and Pratt, "The Presence of Faith," cover much more than the Anglican Church. Significant for the present writer's development was Victor Gollancz's, *A Year of Grace*, with its quotations from Hasidim, Tagore, Rumi, and very varied Christians; compare especially DiNoia, "What About *Them*?"

understanding," and despite the vigorous affirmation of "revelation" in *Dei Verbum* (briefly discussed earlier), the Council also issued both *Nostra Aetate* and *Lumen Gentium*. The over-all effect has involved a significant increase in openness to outsiders, Christian or other, both in further discussions, Papal pronouncements, and individual theological studies. In practice there is presented much less of an impression of "we know we've got it all right, and settled." This (albeit patchy) opening up appears, unlabeled, in the biblical and patristic discussions of chapters 3, 4, and 5. That no attention to the ecclesiastical allegiance of cited commentators has seemed relevant is itself significant.

Perhaps most important in itself and in its ramifications are the often distinctive, very creative, and warmly welcome increase in the number of published women theologians. Although there were important and influential women theologians in earlier centuries, as well as those contemporary with the drafting of *Has Christianity?*, only one was listed in it, and she, Lotte, in tandem with her husband, Werner Pelz. There will be no attempt here to list comprehensively even those to whom I am most indebted, but I do include, and in what follows, debate with three in particular whose work I have found engaging: Grace Jantzen, Sarah Coakley, and Kathryn Tanner

Grace I got to meet from time to time here in Manchester, England (before her untimely death). Her *Power, Gender and Christian Mysticism* introduced me in particular to Hadewijch of Antwerp, and re-introduced me much more deeply to Julian of Norwich and Hildegard of Bingen, and to their informed, reflective, varied, courageous, and richly imaginative experience.[16]

From Jantzen I take first and foremost her urging that we humans see ourselves as "natals," rather than "mortals," and "embodied mortals," with desire for fulfilment here and now, desire that warrants celebration and fostering, and thus a rejection of the "necrophilia" of much (particularly Western?) Christian reflection.[17] This has helped consolidate my own refusal of much traditional (Western) atonement theory. One regret, however, is that Jantzen did not appear to have taken due account (or much at all) of eastern Orthodoxy. Its traditions might at least seem to have anticipated her, in their emphasis on the at-oneing, "deifying" implications for us humans here and now, of the birth into human life of the God-human, as Jesus of Nazareth. In chapter 4 it was argued with the help of a number of recent studies that in Paul and in the wider New Testament collection, at-oneing was seen as available and urgent in this bodily life: it is now and here that we can and

---

16. Jantzen, *Power, Gender.*
17. Jantzen, *Becoming Divine*, throughout. Cf. Brown, *Grace of Body.*

should be transformed, so as to be able to experience and begin to enjoy our acceptance by the God who loves us.[18] The present resilience of Paul and his colleagues' battered bodies displayed God's life-giving power.[19] (And this theme of deification before death was, of course, taken up again in ch. 5.)

At this point it is appropriate to turn to Sarah Coakley, and her championing of Gregory of Nyssa's conviction that our desire for God can only grow, and never be satisfied, not just in this life, but in life to come.[20] With Coakley I fail to see why life now should not be seen as enriched by such faithful imagining, rather than (so Jantzen) impoverished by hopes of life after death.

Coakley offers a positive, and welcome apologia for "desire," (more persuasive than Jantzen's, both of them arguing against Anders Nygren, *Agape and Eros*).[21] She also offers a sophisticated analysis of Nyssa on gender. This exonerates him from some of the most trenchant standard criticisms of patristic thought, but still without endearing to me the continuing binary stereotypes. In fact Coakley criticizes Jantzen for being apparently still bound by some at least of the binary oppositions that she claims to overcome. Instances are Jantzen's talk of "the male symbolic," and her refusal to allow that in living things, life and death are intertwined, not opposed.[22] However, I would press a case against further binary dichotomies and part company with Coakley. For so much that is traditionally contrasted is much better seen as lying along a spectrum, day merging into night, light into dark, life into death, female into male, perfect into imperfect, good through "shades of grey" into evil; and I would call in support one of Jantzen's villains, the analytical philosopher John L. Austin. Not only, he insists, do truth and falsehood depend on both speaker and diverse hearers, but "by the same token, the familiar contrast of 'normative or evaluative as opposed to the factual' is in need, like so many dichotomies, of elimination."[23]

Another binary opposition, "realist/antirealist," "left open" by Jantzen, was already challenged in the first chapter in the discussion of imagination. Perhaps "imagining God as real" would seem to some still to be on

18. Ch. 4, with reference to Blackwell, *Christosis*; Gorman, *Inhabiting the Cruciform God*; Litwa, *Being Transformed*; Powers, *Salvation through Participation*; Starr, *Sharers in the Divine Nature*. (see footnotes 35–45 in chapter 4.)

19. Heath, *Visual Piety*.

20. Coakley, "Introduction," 6–8, and *God, Sexuality*, 277–78, 281–88. For her critique of Jantzen, "Feminism," 496–505.

21. Coakley, *God, Sexuality*, 30 and 315; Nygren, *Agape*. See also Scruton, *Face*, 101–7.

22. Coakley, "Feminism," 502–3; Jantzen, *Becoming Divine*, e.g., 62–67, 267–70.

23. Austin, *How to Do Things*, 148; cf. also Coakley, *Sacrifice Regained*, lecture 6.

the antirealist side, but the intention was and is to bridge realism and anti-realism, rather as such as Caleb Scharf does, in imagining as real aspects of "black holes": imaginings that cannot now be tested, and may never be testable.[24] But, like Janzten, I see no point in trying to establish "the existence of God." Rather, I would conclude, here with Rowan Williams (in approval of Dostoevsky):

> This does not mean that the reality of God is a matter of indifference . . . or some form of contemporary nonrealism. But the difference between the self-aware believer, the self-aware sinner and the deliberate and self-conscious atheist is not a disagreement over whether or not to add some item to the total of really existent things. It is a conflict about policies and possibilities for human life: between someone who accepts the dependence of everything on divine gratuity and attempts to respond with some image of that gratuity, someone who accepts this dependence but fails to act appropriately in response, and someone who denies the dependence and is consequently faced with the unanswerable question of why one policy for living is preferable to any other.[25]

One binary is nonetheless maintained in these present proposals: that between asserted divine integrity and proposed arbitrary divine interventions in this divinely created-and-sustained universe. Here the choice urged and argued is for trusting divine integrity. God does not indulge in inconsistent interventions. God, as imagined here, maintains creation's systematic independence.[26] Such a conviction leaves plenty of space for many kinds of imagined transformative conversation with God (as in George Herbert), but inevitably conflicts with much practice of petitionary-intercessory prayer.

Such prayer has officially been with the proviso, "Your will be done." It has been addressed "to the Father, in the power of the Spirit, through Christ our Lord": that is, subject to the Spirit's "paraphrase," and in keeping with Christ's character. What God does in response is up to God. Prayer is not telekinesis, moving things at will, at a distance, without discernible electro-mechanical aids. Prayer, in this sense, was itself never supposed to work. It was all taken as resting with God. What I add is prayer seems very clearly

24. Jantzen, *Becoming Divine*, 112, 186–93, 273; cf. Caputo, "The Invention of Revelation"; Scharf, *Gravity's Engines*, 210, 212.

25. Williams, *Dostoevsky*, 227. On "proofs" cf. chapter 6n44; Jantzen, *Becoming Divine*, 18–19. On a "graced" life see the careful discussion in Tanner, *Christ the Key*, chs. 2 and 3, with much more attention to Reformation reflections than I could readily emulate.

26. See, again, Tanner, "Is God in Charge?"

to stay with God, as part of relation-building, transforming conversation. Whether God has some further use for it in some other setting we may want to try imagining, but have no way of knowing.

Here I would take further encouragement from Dietrich Bonhoeffer, in his letter from July 18th, 1944. Far from looking to God as a manipulative loyal "minder," we Christians are invited to stand with and suffer with God in God's powerlessness and grief.[27] The fourth line of the second stanza refers us to Gethsemane, as in the next letter, but as still characterizing the incarnate Lord. But the first three lines seem to echo Matt 25:35–40, "just as much as you did it to one of the least of these . . . you did it to me," interpreted (probably *contra* Matthew) as God present in anyone in need. Reflecting in prayer on others' needs is sharing in God's concern; perhaps we imagine anguished concern. But the real solidarity with the self-limited, self-restrained God is in wisely enacted concern, which is always interpersonal, and so is always also political.

Other binaries, however, I have already suggested, are ill-founded for other reasons: transient/eternal, finite/infinite, immanent/transcendent, time/timeless eternity.[28] I would even include comprehensible/incomprehensible, if the latter is taken as "in principle" rather than "in current experience."[29]

On finite/infinite, for instance, the question presents itself, how could one ever tell whether our universe is finite or infinite? However far one's vision penetrated without a barrier, there might be a stop; but if there were, there might be more of something beyond. As it stands, we seem bounded by the speed of light, so anyway are unable to tell even how far away are stars or other related concentrations of energy/matter. And, as we are transient, we can never find out whether some other more perduring thing or person may be more/other than that. I would argue that at least any imaginable creator-and-sustainer God must maintain an awareness far greater than any human brain could cope with. On that basis, the mind of God is incomprehensible to us. But if we press incomprehensible in principle, how could we explain what we meant? "Incomprehensible" would turn out to be a polysyllabic way of confessing we don't know what we are talking about even well enough to know whether "it itself" is beyond knowing or whether we are just thick, or perverse. (Compare Humpty Dumpty's "impenetrable" as a conversation-stopper.) We may agree; we can imagine no boundary to

---

27. Bonhoeffer, *Letters and Papers*, 198–200; see also 200–202 (21 July 1944).

28. On the latter, Johannes Zachhuber, "Transendenz und Immanenz," carefully analysing the unclarity of this Kantian disjunction.

29. See chapter 1.

God, but to say we know God is boundless, is infinite, is to claim to "know" something we know we cannot know: and that is then an assertion from which no valid conclusion about God can be drawn.

It seems to me worth noting that when the Cappadocian Gregories elaborate on the metaphor of climbing a mountain, they are encouraged by the fact that progress in being formed by God has happened, and is itself allowing glimpses of more to come that spurs them on. It is such repeatedly opening vistas that convince them, not some ps.Dionysian game with inventing new self-contradicting abstractions.[30]

And so with the other dichtomies. Once we posit something beyond our experience, we can say, "God may be unimaginably other." But there is no point in offering a word or phrase for the unimaginable other, and suppose that word itself says anything worthwhile. We can, for instance, say or write that timeless eternity is *totum simul*, "everything instantaneous." But that cannot mean still life, a snapshot, for even registering a snapshot takes time. Further, snapshots say little about the event without some awareness of the temporal sequence and context of their production. A whole pile of superimposed snapshots conveys nothing. It is no help saying timeless eternity means absolute instantaneity when we've no idea what absolute instantaneity betokens.

To be welcomed in Coakley, but also in Scruton, and also in David Brown (in works published earlier than the others', footnoted here), is attention to visual expression and stimulus. And that includes visual imagination, and with this, not just the work of great artists.[31] Far too readily has the biblical prohibition of offering worship to images been taken by Christian theologians to preclude any optical enrichment or enlightenment, even in "interior" imagination (compare the recent critical assessment by Jane Heath).[32]

Also very welcome is the following, again from Sarah Coakley (but compare the piece from Rowan Williams, earlier):

---

30. Ps.Dionysius seems inconsistently sure that he *knows* from his ability to coin self-contradictions that he has not yet arrived. The Cappadocian friends are convinced in trust and in the light of apparent progress so far, that they can discern some more ahead. At least Denys Turner's approving reading of ps.Dionysius persuades me that this contrast is valid (Turner, "Apophaticism," 17–21).

31. Coakley and Scruton as above; Brown, *Tradition and Imagination* and *Discipleship and Imagination*.

32. Heath, *Visual Piety*, 13–37, noting the importance of the visual in the Jewish and wider Hellenistic context of early Christianity, 65–142; on which see also, Downing, *Cynics, Paul*, 128–31, 168–73, 290–91; "God with Everything: Dio," 26–27.

> The task of theology is always, if implicitly, *a recommenda-tion for life.*The vision it sets before one invites ongoing—and sometimes disorientating—response and change, both personal and political, in relation to God. One may rightly call theology from this perspective an ascetical enterprise—one that demands bodily practice and transformation, both individual and social.[33]

Although she later and engagingly devotes a chapter to prayer in "Praying the Trinity: A Neglected Patristic Tradition," there is nothing in the book on possible political ramifications of that or any other praying, and that despite her reflections on what she terms an "incorporative model" of the Trinity, stemming from Rom 8, one which might have seemed to have clearly socio-political ramifications. (Perhaps reflections on prayerful Christian political ascesis will follow in Coakley's planned three remaining volumes.)

For that matter, in the fair number of books on theology and politics on my shelves I have only been able to find one attempt to meet the bill, on praying politics. Perhaps I've not looked hard enough, but the theme has not shouted loud enough to even figure in most indices. Rowan Wiliams has a chapter critical of self-regarding and individualist "spirituality," but it does not touch on sharing our political reflections with God.[34] For an anchor in at all recent reflection, then, I select from one of the earliest of the above, Gustavo Gutierrez, more than forty years ago: "Only [God's] gratuitous love goes to our very roots and elicits true love. Prayer is an experience of gratu-itousness. . . . The gratuitousness of his gift, creating profound needs, frees us from all religious alienation, and, in the last instance, from all alienation."[35] Seen this way, politically aware prayer can constitute an experience already, a foretaste at least, of unity in and with God.

However, if we start with the Eucharist as the theme, then reflections on the political ramifications of shared prayer are these days much easier to find. Gutierrez himself, in his 1971 *A Theology of Liberation,* includes just a couple of pages on the Eucharist as celebrating a communion of humans together with God that implies the abolition of all injustice and exploitation, celebrating the gifts of creation as meant for the building of a better human world.[36] That was followed by a full monograph by Tissa Balasuriya, *The*

33. Coakley, *God, Sexuality*, 18.

34. Such writing from William Temple and Nathaniel Micklem to writing in the period since *Has Christianity a Revelation?* including among others, Gustavo Gutierrez, Duncan Forrester, Jürgen Moltmann, Timothy Gorringe, David Jenkins, and Rowan William; here, Williams, *Public Square*, ch. 7.

35. Gutierrez, *Liberation*, 206.

36. Ibid., 262–63. Gutierrez, or his translator at least, at this date continues to use non-inclusive terminology talking of the Eucharist and human "brotherhood."

Eucharist and Human Liberation (1979); more recently on my shelves there is Andrea Bieler's and Luise Schottroff's jointly authored *The Eucharist: Bodies, Bread, and Resurrection* (2007); and most recently (and very succinctly), Josephine Houghton, "The Priest as 'Defender of the Poor'" (2014).

Bieler and Schottroff engage well with some of the themes of this exploration, with a repeated motif of "eschatological imagination," pointing forward from unity, communion, already being physically enacted and celebrated, to the imagined fulfilment for which we hope but know is not yet realized. And crucially arising from this, not in contrast with it, a better "political" enactment of Eucharistic faith in wider community can always be sought.[37] The Eucharist, one might say, in allusion both to Karl Marx and Charles Kingsley, should be a prayerful, celebratory stimulant to effective political action, not an opiate tranquilizer. We can always try grasping for what we still only dimly perceive in a mirror. "Ah, but a man's reach should exceed his grasp, or what's a heaven for?"[38]

Disappointingly the first four chapters in *The Eucharist* are, for the most part, casually unitarian or possibly binitarian, with no imagination of the triune presence of God.[39] The fifth chapter, "Eschatological Remembrance (Anamnesis)," is, thankfully, much richer: "Anamnesis has a Trinitarian dimension, God's relation to us as creating, redeeming, and sustaining force in the Eucharist is God's remembrance of us." We recall all creation, we recall the anointing Spirit in the life of the present, risen Christ. "Anamnetic empathy" with fellow humans in many situations of pain, despair, frustrated love, and of joy and delight, "stretches the eschatological imagination of worshipping communities."[40] I would add (but the authors do not), this would ideally include imaginative empathy with the shared pain and joy of the three-person God.

To draw these conclusions together somewhat more systematically, I rely mainly on Kathryn Tanner's *Jesus, Humanity, and the Trinity*, augmented by her more recent *Christ the Key*, though with apologies to her

37. Houghton, "Priest," 200; Bieler and Schottroff, *The Eucharist,* 79, with reference to 1 Cor 13:12; but also cf. Tanner, *Jesus, Humanity, Trinity,* 120, quoted below, chapter 8, on liturgy as protest against injustice, 70; Tanner herself cites Eduard Schillebeeckx.

38. Robert Browning, *Andrea del Sarto*; but much earlier, Paul, Phil 3:12, much valued by the Cappadocians.

39. With the arguable exceptions of 122–23, quoting Marjori Suchochki on Eucharistic intercession as "co-creating" with God; and 140–41, expounding 1 Cor 12:12 and other "body of Christ" passages. "Epiclesis," invocation of the Spirit, is noted, but only in passing, 51, 126.

40. Bieler and Schottroff, *The Eucharist,* 166–67.

in advance for possible misreading.[41] I choose her work for its choice of themes, not to claim its general support (though I have already on occasion claimed some such with careful qualification). Her theology (my summary) is firmly Trinitarian, creational, incarnational, sacramental, churchly, politically and socially and gender engaged, with attention (often wider still than mine) to classical roots of Christian reflection, especially among the Cappadocians. She cogently sees God's "at-one-ment" (my hyphenating) of us in Christ in the power of the Spirit as missional, endlessly demanding, endlessly gratuitous ("grace-ful"), endlessly explorative, endlessly hopeful: our at-one-ment as relationally and endlessly (trans)formative, not impersonally transactional nor precociously enlightening.[42]

(c) Disagreements

Having listed shared concerns, I must in advance note important disagreements (with the reader able to judge, so much the worse for these).

(i) Tanner, along with others, of course, has God, especially God as Holy Spirit, at least spiritually active, changing us, enabling us. I have said I cannot coherently imagine a just and compassionate God retaining the freedom to do that, yet with as unjust socio-economic results as we find around us as well as in us. I shall suggest another way of imagining a graced life, but cannot sustain trust in a supposedly compassionate and just interventionist deity. I fail to see how this sort of assertion fits with her careful analysis of God non-interveningly sustaining everything.[43]

(ii) I am happy to concur with Tanner's acceptance of the classical theologians' imaginative (my term) conclusions from their readings of the canonical texts, but I would urge at the same time a more comprehensive assimilation of them in their own terms.[44] In this I am encouraged, anyway, by the Cappadocians' own frequent biblical support for their Platonic or Stoic allegorizing, support drawn from a concurrent more "literal" reading of the more down-to-earth scriptural texts. Note, for example, abstract divine infinity backed by biblical texts on divine creative greatness, and the

41. Tanner, *Jesus, Humanity* and *Christ the Key*.

42. Belatedly I add a recent awareness of Tanner's *Economy of Grace*, and, still more recently, "Is Capitalism a Belief System?" She creatively and critically compares and contrasts secular economies and life in Christ as systems of distribution. For a potentially complementary critical account of economics, from an economist, see Chang, *Economics*.

43. Tanner, "Is God in Charge?"

44. Tanner, *Christ the Key*, ix.

experience of one's growth in Christ as itself (rather than ideas of abstract divine transcendence) pointing to fresh possibilities (see earlier, and chapter 5).

(iii) On the other hand, I would take more encouragement than Tanner or others seem to from the classical theologians' assumption that all our awareness of our world and human activities within it can be theologically relevant. Coakley coins or imports a phrase—*théologie totale*—for assembling a range of topics and integrating them. Without this term I have tried elsewhere to show how comprehensive—even encyclopaedic—the classical theologians, including Paul and Hildegard among others, have been as an encouragment to us to emulate them.

I also accept happily, as noted above, the validation of desire in Tanner and Coakley and others, desire for the triune God as generous, enabling, and liberating love. But for me it has to include the triune God as fascinating creator-and-sustainer of all, human and non-human. All this is here for us to appreciate, even painfully, along with all that we guess we are missing, and all we may imagine lies beyond us, in itself and even more, as in God. I do not find this scientific-cum-aesthetic, inquisitive yearning in these authors, or others. (Perhaps it is there elsewhere ,and I have missed it; perhaps Coakley will range yet more widely in her promised succeeding volumes.)

(iv) However I also have further and very important disagreements both with Tanner, and others again, as well as with our ancient expositors.[45] These days, I would argue, we are simply not justified in taking the Gospels as primarily sources for the man Jesus prior to his death. The Gospels (John especially, but the other three as well) are primarily sources for their writers' post-Easter reflections. Jesus is imagined by them as the one believed now to be raised to divine glory. The oral traditions they received may well have had Jesus convinced of a special prophetic call and sending, with perhaps a sage's sense of divine sonship: but the evangelists read into that conviction an awareness of something more, a more than prophetic empowering, a more than sapiential sonship.[46] Tanner is willing (here, against her classical sources) to see growth in understanding in Jesus. He only gradually becomes aware of his divine sonship. But without John's distinctive account of a Jesus constantly aware in the final months of being of one mind with his divine parent, no one would read the Synoptic source material in terms of that Johannine imagining; and John is too distinctive to carry the day on his own.[47] The Jesus of the Synoptic tradition, as discernible in the first

45. And, encountered most recently, Welker, *God the Revealed*, 1 and 55–103.
46. E.g., Mk 4:41, and parallels, in the light of Pss 65:7; 107:28–29.
47. John 12:27–30, compared with Mk 14:36, and parallels in Matt and Lk. Matthew

three gospels, had no idea of "being divine." That is clear in the matter the evangelists preserve, even while they seem to be moving towards seeing in him "something" more than an empowered prophet, or as son-like to God in his shared attitudes and actions.

I would back this exegetical conclusion with a very simple consideration: quite without importing ideas of abstract divine infinity, the creator God I trustingly imagine and seek to share is caringly and sustainingly aware not just of us and our planet, with its minerals, plantlife, animals, but of the entire universe (whose extent I don't pretend to envisage). That awareness could not be contained in a human brain, marvelous though our brains are. (Whether and how this skepticism might allow me still to talk meaningfully of Jesus as God incarnate follows later.)

Might not a suggestion that God is non-interveningly attentive to everything run counter to the (metaphysical) worry that attention may itself be intrusive? So, it is sometimes asked, how can scientists be sure that the behavior of matter/energy as registered by their instruments may not differ from its behavior totally unobserved? Those philosophical theologians who insist God could be undiscernibly active afford an answer to this question: God's sustaining activity is so total that there is no distinctive sign. But that absence, it is here insisted, is total. There is nothing to discern that is distinctively just, let alone loving.[48]

(v) That God is Trinity is obviously not "revealed" anywhere, but has always been subject to debate (often heated, sometimes violent). On God as Trinity I have since theological college days espoused a "communitarian" model, and that appeared in *Has Christianity?* On any social model, however, we encounter the carefully and vigorously argued objections of Coakley and Tanner and others, though I can still claim support from elsewhere.[49] Those in favor of a relationist, communitarian model of the Trinity are shown, I think conclusively, to have importantly misunderstood what in our formative patristic theologians was a very abstract and thus "impersonal" terminology. So far as it goes that case seems proven. Classical theological talk is of subsistent entities, not of "persons," in a sense common today. It is about grammatical-logical relations (gift implies giver, child implies parent): not interpersonal communion.

11:25–27 with Lk 10:21–22, often seen as "Johannine," is to be read otherwise in each, as argued early in chapter 4.

48. Along with Peacocke, *Theology for a Scientific Age* and *Paths from Science;* and Wiles, *God's Action;* contra, Ward, *Divine Action.*

49. Coakley, *Rethinking Gregory,* and "Introduction" 1–13; Turcescu, "Person;" cf. Tanner, with further argument, *Christ the Key,* 207–46.

However, it seems to have escaped attention that, at least among our Eastern, Greek sources, these abstractions do not constitute the entirety of the reflections shared. Thus, Gregory Nazianzus asks whether on the basis of Scripture the Holy Spirit should be classified among beings who subsist in themselves, or as an aspect of someone else. In support of the former he adduces passages where the Spirit is not the name for someone else's active energy (*energeia*), not even God's. Rather, the Spirit is referred to as one who himself acts, utters words, picks out apostles, can be grieved, and (in Job, LXX) displays anger. In all this he shows self-movement, self-motivation, not someone else's agency. (There is a similar passage in Gregory of Nyssa.)[50] As far as one can tell, this analysis is as near as one could ask for taking the Spirit as a person—at least if one compares it with Aristotle and others, distinguishing a free male citizen from a slave, and discussing the relationships of friends.[51] On the other hand, a quest for a similar account of the Spirit in Augustine, *De Trinitate*, disappointingly drew a blank. One might doubt, then, whether Gregory would have been happy with or easily persuaded to accept the Spirit simply as the *energeia* of love, even though infinite, between Father and Son. Even the role of the Spirit is not universally revealed. One is not obliged to take the Cappadocians as infallible guides; but if they are allowed into the discussion they deserve to be heard in full.

The rejoinder comes: it is only in the respective roles of Father, Son, Spirit that they can be distinguished by the Cappadocians and other classical theologians. And roles are not persons, in our usage. But to make role irrelevant to personhood, "making no difference," seems to me just obtuse.

So I turn in the next chapter to offer the reader an outline affirmation of an imaginative faith that is, as promised: Trinitarian, creational, incarnational, salvific, sacramental, churchly, politically and socially and gender engaged, and expectant.

---

50. Gregory of Nazinazus, *Discourse* 31.6.15; Gregory of Nyssa, *Catechetical Discourse* 3.3. Similar scriptural passages in fact formed the basis for Leonard Hodgson's insistence on the "personhood" of the Spirit, in his *The Doctrine of the Trinity* (which was my introduction, more than fifty years ago, to a "social model" of the triune God), and adduced in support in *Has Christianity a Revelation?*

51. Aristotle, *Politics*, 1253b; *Nichomachean Ethics*, 8–9; *Eudemian Ethics*, 7–8; and cf. Plutarch, *De amic. mult.* (*Moralia* 93A–97B); Cicero, *De amicitia*. For a fuller version of this argument, see Downing, "Friends"; and "(b) Trinity," next chapter.

Isaiah
11: 6-9

8

A Very Brief Agnostic (Unknowing) Systematic Theology for Awaiting God's Self-Revelation [1]

(a) We Believe

Statements of Christian faith do not articulate the kind of "belief that" looks for validating tests. They lack what might warrant it being termed knowledge.[2] This was argued briefly in chapter 1 and more elaborately in chapter 6. Our faithful concern, as argued, has to instead be articulating a relationship of personal trust, as in trust of a parent, sibling, friend, that could only be tested by breaking it. We can only trust, not know, God to be the best we can suppose. The best I can imagine is God as the most wise and creative and sustaining love that our reflections can propose. And this best imagined love is one that evokes in us and others wise and generous love in action. Yet, even if it is in practice richly effective, that is still no proof of God's reality. It could as well be taken to show that auto-suggestion works. For Christian faith, seen in this way, trust as such is primary; "trust that" is derivative commentary.

(b) Trinity

Christians have strong and coherent motives for imagining God in social terms. Granted, none of our classical theologians, reflecting on the Trinity, use models or metaphors such as "family" or "circle of friends." God was not

---

1. The sketch represents many presentations of the Peaceable Kingdom of Isa 11:1–10.

2. The contrary, of course, is claimed; see the discussion in Taliafero, *Philosophy of Religion*, chapter 8, and especially 260–65.

like any three people we might encounter.[3] But when in the early Christian centuries there is talk of human "true" friends, the ideal is for them to be of one mind, equal in virtue, having everything in common, unvarying. "In our friendships' consonance and harmony there must be no element unlike, uneven, unequal, but all must be alike to engender agreement in words, counsels, opinions, and feelings, and it must be as if one soul were apportioned among two or three bodies."[4] Although we never meet this idea realized, it is in such terms that the Cappadocians, at least, talk of the divine "hypostases." I suggest we read what the Cappadocians say about the persons of the Trinity and their unity, in the light of that common ancient understanding of the "personhood" of friends who are "of one mind." Such a reading leaves the Cappadocians' conclusions at least compatible with a social model of the divine Trinity. We may fruitfully compare the reflections of mediaeval Western theologian, Richard of St. Victor. His conclusions are that the persons of the Trinity are to be taken as individual enough for love between them to be not mirrored self-love but genuinely self-giving love.[5] Or, with Paul in Rom 8, we may prefer a family model. But it seems to me that to imagine our God in terms of loving interpersonal relationships is fitting. In such loving and generous relationships we achieve or are granted we may imagine we are being drawn prayerfully into that divine life.[6]

In practice it has mattered that Trinitarian faith has been expressed in terms of two males, of a father-and-son relationship, with a male *Spiritus* (Western) or neuter, *Pneuma*, (Eastern). It would have been good if more attention had been paid to the Cappadocians' insistence that grammatical gender is irrelevant: not only the neuter case of pneuma, but the feminine case of *the(i)otēs*, deity, or of *trias*, Trinity.[7]

---

3. Cf. Gregory of Nyssa, *To Ablabius*. The following discussion is elaborated in Downing, "Friends in God," and the end of the previous chapter.

4. Plutarch, *De amic. mult.*, 8 (*Moralia* 96EF). Paul Fiddes, in his "The Quest for a Place," 51, takes it that "paternity, filiation and spiration" are "relationships of ecstatic, outward-going love, giving and receiving," but without explicit reference. I find nothing of the sort in the actual texts, though I would be very happy to: cf. Gregory of Nazianzus, *Discourse 31* (*Fifth Theological*), 1–10, on relationships; and *Discourse 14*, on unity of will and power.

5. Richard of St. Victor, *The Trinity*, Book 3.

6. Cf. Coakley, *God, Sexuality*, 111–21, despite her rejection of any family model.

7. Syriac, of course, retained feminine *ruah*. On "gender" see further, below. I have lost the precise reference to the discussion on grammatical gender that I found, but I think it was in Gregory Nazianzus. May it, however, then be significant that the irrelevance not only of masculine and feminine terms but also of the (impersonal) neuter case of *pneuma* needs to be stated? God is not to be imagined as abstractly "thing-like."

It is only in such interpersonal relationship terms that I can imagine God as one capable of lovingly bringing into being a universe in which love is a real as well as an engaging possibility.[8] The argument offered in *Has Christianity?* and reaffirmed here is "transcendental/descriptive." It attempts to describe what lies implicit in some of our Christian—commonly urged though rarely if ever fully realized—interpersonal behavior. It does not depend on metaphysical word-play, or biblical or patristic proof-texts (even though support from, or at least acquiescence in the tradition remain welcome). And still, by the thesis argued here, revelatory proof eludes us.[9]

> An insistence, as in the Old Testament, on the oneness of "God" was not motivated by a philosophical delight in mathematical unity. "The Lord your God is one Lord; and you shall love the Lord your God with all your heart and with all your mind and with all your soul." It is an ethical unity, demanding a complete singleness of response. It is opposed to the moral anarchy of a polytheism in which one deity may be played off against another. The unity in love of the "family" which is our God allows no such licence.[10]
>
> It is not a unity patterned on, determined by, human relations; it is a unity which God reproduces, still dimly, in and among us, in love in community; a unity of whose completion we can still speak only formally (i.e., not [yet] experientially). The unity of God is such that each "person" is more fully personal than any human individual; but it is a unity that is more intensely "one" than is that of the most integrated human being. In real love, *agape*, the unity is most real, and yet the lovers are not absorbed by one another, but most truly individuals. It is, we may believe [at least, imagine], to share in such a unity that God is [imagined to be] shaping us. When at last we love like that, we shall be "seeing God"; the "persons" of God will have at last succeeding in "revealing" themselves to us.[11]

However, now I would also add a Nyssan qualification: we may find there is always more in God to be discovered, revealed, yet we should nonetheless have come to know more clearly the direction of our travel, the false tracks

8. On which, see Coakley, *Sacrifice Regained*.

9. Hodgson, *Trinity*, 110–12; he includes a detailed summary of sections of Augustine, *De Trinitate*, while failing to recognize how the terminology is being used; and Downing, *Has Christianity a Revelation?* 188, etc.

10. Additional note, not in my original. On this moral contrast with polytheism, see already Gregory of Nyssa, *Catachetical Discourse* 1.1.

11. Downing, *Has Christianity a Revelation?* 273.

unmistakable, the glimpses more assured, the goal, the prospect still luring us onwards.

(c) Creation

For me, and I guess for not a few others, there are two main competitors. One is to imagine (for there is no proof) a self-instigating, self-exploding, and impersonal universe. Here the only hope seems to be for the wealthy and powerful minority to die fulfilled. Perhaps there is a further hopeless hope: a handful of descendents of some of us escape this planet before it is finally trashed to lifelessness, then to colonize another to wreck in turn. The other dream for some of us is to imagine our universe spun lovingly into independence with, yes, very likely just such a "big bang," and maintained in its existing, by a triunity of divine co-operative persons united in love. This triune God patiently creates and sustains space for that independence, that freedom.[12] This God steadfastly refuses to intervene (as argued earlier in chapter 1, claiming support from Job.)[13] But it is done with the hope that beings at least analogously personal would evolve and be drawable into the love of the divine life. With Sarah Coakley, again, one might well imagine this God envisaging the possibility, and at least the hope that cooperation and altruism, self-giving for the good of others, might be integral to such evolution. The lifestyles indicated by these rival proposals are quite distinctive (see the quotation from Rowan Williams, earlier).[14] There are, of course, many variants of a hope such as this, and other very different preferred alternatives besides (variants of Hinduism and Buddhism, for instance).

The hope the reader is here urged to retain and enrich, or at least, explore and perhaps adopt, is admittedly, a sort of theodicy, an attempt to justify the ways of the God imagined. God is not to be blamed directly for

12. One may compare this "making space" with Isaac Luria's Kabbalistic notion of *zim-zum*, God contracting his otherwise overwhelming might to make room for a relatively independent creation; an idea taken up, for instance, by Jürgen Moltmann, *The Way*, 328–29. Without reference to Luria, but emphasizing God's making space, cf. Arthur Peacocke, *Theology for a Scientific Age*, 121–23. Both the latter have God still "intervening," which is excluded here. On this take on our universe's evolution, Coakley, *Sacrifice Regained*, again.

13. See, again (as in chapter 1, n. 25) Peacocke, *Paths from Science*, 91–115, on God as imagined immanently shaping the direction of the whole system from within it, thus undetectably, with no tests available, and with all the tragedy and injustice allowed for. This is perhaps a good way to imagine God sustaining all there is; but not if so immersed as to preclude our more central trust in his empathetic awareness of each of us in our individual relationships.

14. Above, chapter 7 n. 25.

not preventing each of the world's massive and massively cruel injustices, because, as imagined, God has no such power. As others and I (elsewhere) have argued, traditional theodicies, justifications of the behavior ascribed to an intervening God, can be selfish analgesics in face of the world's pain. Their function is to quieten one's own pained conscience by defensively imagining loving purposes in or behind every torture, massacre, natural disaster. And that is, to my mind, disgusting.[15] The theodicy of sorts offered here is intended, instead, as a spur to renewed active intelligent and effectively loving and likely costly healing concern.

Yet, might one not still blame such a creator? "If you could not contrive a universe in which there would be strong interpersonal dependence and independence, but allowing the most terrible catastrophes, you really should not have bothered." The logic of the issues has been debated without resolution. But if what is argued is that on balance we'd all be better off dead, and possible descendants better unborn, it could be taken seriously only if a proponent was actively engaged in stirring up, say, a nuclear holocaust, or, at least, a rapid increase in life-destroying global warming. Such an "atheodicy" asserted without self-involving political action would itself seem to be posturing hypocrisy.

To move on, we, the evolved persons who have emerged, at least in our tiny corner of this created universe, are to be taken as entirely physical, fleshly stuff with "spiritual" capacities, able to love, imagine, create, hate, but with no spirit-mind "stuff," no "ghost in the machine." The physical is not a hindrance in our response to the God we may imagine. The physical is not even just a necessary catalyst. It is the entirety of each and everyone of us, and makes possible the hate, creativity, imagining, and imaginative love. We cannot demonstrate that we do not just happen. But we may instead trustingly imagine ourselves as created, and created physical, capable of becoming God-like. We take ourselves as capable of being perfected, "graced," in and through the incarnate risen Word and the divine Spirit of life within and among us, into "the image and likeness of God."[16]

We humans have obviously evolved, with many other living things, built for bisexual reproduction, with the ramification, as with a smaller tally of other species, of differing roles in care for our young, and for our relationships with one another as adults. These roles are further and diversely elaborated in different societies, engendering gender stereotypes by partner preference, that are then reflected in heritable psycho-physical structures

15. Surin, *Theology and the Problem*; Downing, *Evils*.

16. Cf. Tanner, *Christ the Key*, 19–20, 25–27, 39–40, picking up and developing this rare vocabulary from Genesis, in the light of later Jewish Wisdom writing, especially in Philo, but more in Paul and ongoing Christian reflection.

and social power. These given roles often work to the signal disadvantage of the potential and actual infant-bearers. We nonetheless take all this as divine creation, producing malleble persons capable of being amended, transformed into the divine likeness.[17]

Paul reminded Christians in Galatia that for them "there is no longer male and female, for you are all one in Christ" (Gal 3:28). Our subsequent Christian traditions have differed in their imagining of the effect of this asserted change. Augustine, meaning to stay with Genesis, would have us forever distinctively male and female. The Eastern Christian theologians were drawn to a different conclusion, influenced by Platonic imagining of an original hermaphrodite (unisex) human, but also by Cynic insistence that *aretē*, excellence—in effect, ideal humanity—was as attainable by ascetic discipline by women as by men.[18]

This latter position seems to me more promising. The version of *askēsis* encouraged among Christians was a training in simplicity. You learned to live, in worldly terms, unpossessively, unacquisitively, enriched and sustained only by "non-positional" goods.[19] You eschewed what might give you status—especially male status—because so few had it, and instead aimed to share a rich intellectual and interpersonal life that was enhanced not diminished by the sharing; and women and artisans, to the disdain of the status seekers, could join in.

As potential heirs to this tradition, we trust that we are accepted by God just as we are and let that faith lead us Godward by a similar discipline. We build on or prune all that we are by learning, from one another, further enriching ways to be human. We do this with no thought of gaining status with God, for that is already given, we are by God's grace already at-oned with God. We seek eagerly but unanxiously to gain from others simply by becoming with them more richly fellow humans together.[20]

And these fellow humans may be explicitly "in Christ" or not, may be of "the other" or of our own genital make-up, and may be (predominantly)

---

17. On sexual evolution, see Coakley, *Sacrifice Regained*, lecture 4.

18. The former influence is widely acknowledged: see Coakley, *Sacrifice Regained*, lecture 4; for the latter, Downing, *Cynics, Paul*, 20–22, and *Cynics and Christian Origins*, 37, 69, 209, 219–20, 222, 237, 245, 263–64, 272, 282, 292–93..

19. On "positional goods," things evaluated by their social ranking and often, there for their scarcity, see Downing, *Threat of Freedom*, 47–49.

20. I trust I am not alone in being enriched by novelists acculturated in western writing but melded with their own very varied cultures of origin. I note recently on my shelves authors from Turkey, India, Pakistan, and Afghanistan; and from north and sub-Saharan Africa; with Leila Abouleia's portrayal in her *Minaret* of a Sudanese woman's Moslem spirituality.

heterosexual, homosexual, or transexual in character.[21] Positively or negatively this is imagining God in Christ in the power of the Spirit reshaping us together into the intensely desirable—erotic, alluring, as Coakley insists—but sexless, genderless, divine image.

We are to be, and hope we are already being, transformed—not just remade from scratch. We could not be built from new and still be ourselves in past and ongoing relationships.[22] Thus in the memory of repentance the shadow of what is pruned, repented of, still remains, as part of our make-up. That is built on and with, along with much that we may value as less qualifiedly good, including our (perhaps malleable) gender identity. It is part of being transformed as we are in relationships accepted faithfully by God to be made one with God (or at least Godward) forever.

Prompted by non-revelatory and diverse traditions of imaginative reflection, one may envisage the initiator, the agent, the enlivener (Source of all being, eternal Word, and Spirit of life, Father, Son, and Spirit) rejoicing in their respective roles and their awareness of each other's as enacted. We may take this to include awareness of each other's appreciation of each other's individuality, sharing a common mind on the creative-transformative end desired, a creative aim that always included our energence as perfectible.

Further, to anticipate prayerful, including sacramental, acceptance of the lure into that imagined creative, sustaining, and transformative divine life must necessarily include the best appreciation of physical reality made available to us. So we attend to and appraise meditatively the whole range of exploratory science—physics, chemistry, biology, sociology, psychology—together with the work of artists/artisans in words, music, shapes, and color, in wood, clay, stone, pigments, concrete and steel. To sum up such praying one might use a version of a classic collect, as expanded, I think, in the Missal:

> Merciful God,
>
> You have prepared for those who love you
>
> such good things as pass human imagining:
>
> pour into our hearts such love towards you
>
> that we, loving you in all things and above all things,
>
> may obtain your promises which exceed all we can desire;
>
> through Jesus Christ our Lord, who with you and the Holy Spirit
>
> live and reign, one God for ever.[23]

21. For recent discussions, papers in *Anglican Theological Review* 93.1 (2011), and *Modern Believing* 55.2 (2014).

22. See DiNoia, "What About *Them?*" 323.

23. I was pleasingly surprised to find not the same but a similar sentiment in the

(d) Divine Attentive Unintervening Presence

What is recalled or offered to the reader's imagination is the creative Trinity sustainingly and lovingly aware of all there is, attentive compassionately to all that occurs, and endlessly patient. The triune God is imagined trusting and hoping that persons able to love freely will evolve, and loving us attentively as we evolve. The relative independence and so freedom we enjoy as emergent persons-in-relationships is enabled by and within the relative independence of the creation as a whole. To such persons-in-relation God in Trinity responds with mixed delight and pain, and, in acceptance of our shared or individual human love, interdependence, loneliness, indifference, hate, happiness, joy, laughter, hope, tedium, sadness, disappointment, grief, pain, despair. This imagined God responds as parent, as sibling, as alter ego, together—resolutely refusing to intervene—actively detached, yet emotionally and mindfully wholly engaged.

Like many other enquiring Christians, I have collected many discussions on science and religion, concerned with how to show the Creator as undetectably active in her/his world.[24] On the criteria sketched in this book, I cannot claim to know that God does not intervene, undetected, not even in response to (some of) our prayers. But I continue to maintain that I do know that there are no signs of just and loving and consistent divine intervention. Job and Qoheleth and some of the Hebrew psalmists were right.

There is, as insisted, no revelation of any of this, save, perhaps, the clear possibility of its imagining, together with the complete and assured ("revealed") absence from the scene of a freedom threatening, intervenient, powerful deity, even if just and caring. It at least in some measure resembles the relationship of some modern, Western parents with their progeny and other, younger friends, as fellow adults. There is still a significant difference: that divine awareness of us is complete, uncensored by us, only imaginable in general, not in detail; compare Psalm 139.

As Dietrich Bonhoeffer (as also recalled in *Has Christianity?* and here in the previous chapter) argued, humankind has come of age. We have no

---

mediaeval anonymous work, *The Cloud of Unknowing*; "Good though it may be to think of God's acts of kindness, and to love and praise him for them, it is far better to think of his naked being and praise him for himself" (27). I would demur, however, on "naked being," pure existence: I have argued rather, and here repeat, that God's "self" includes the entire Trinitarian "economy," engaged creative, sustaining, and transforming activity.

24. See, chapter 1, n. 25, and above, nn. 12, 13, and e.g., Deane-Drummond, *Christ and Evolution* and *Creation through Wisdom*; van Huyssteen, *Duet or Duet?*; Peacocke, *Theology for a Scientific Age*; Polkinghorne, *Exploring Reality* and *Science and the Trinity*; Ward, *God, Chance, and Necessity*.

justification for relying for our physical or spiritual wellbeing on a tutelary deity, an omniscient and omnipotent divine "minder."[25] But we may still imagine that three-person God lovingly present and empathetically aware of each and everyone of us.

It is in these terms that a petitionary and intercessory prayer, but perhaps rephrased, remains not just appropriate but pressing. We surrender any expectation that God may possibly, sometimes but arbitrarily, arrange things to suit us, including to suit others we care about. Yet we still talk over our hopes, concerns, worries, horrors, joys, and delights with this caring parent-friend. Perhaps, "I offer you my thoughtful attempts to help . . . and share with you my concern for those for whom I accept I can do nothing more than sympathize, empathize." While we maintain solidarity with less agnostic fellow Christians in common prayer we may find we can still echo the traditional formularies, imaginatively. We may be invited together to ask for "blessings on," to offer "prayers for," or to "remember before God" Julie and Fred and Syrian refugees, and we may ask to "hear us," "graciously hear us." But all this, and more, is within the traditionl brackets of "your will" and "through Christ" and with the Spirit as our interpreter. (In some years of hearing intercessions led by members of a congregation, I can affirm with gratitude, that I have suffered none asking for a change in the weather or for spare parking places for those visiting the sick.) At best we respond in growing faith and deepening love to the Giver of all, without reference to (let alone hope for) special gifts for us or anyone here and now.

We pray to the Source of all being through the creative Word. In this we respond to the Life-giver's trustingly imagined insight into us and desire for us to live and grow in the relationship (Rom 8:26–27). We do this simply as integral to living our response to the engaged Trinitarian concern that we are invited to imagine.[26] For sure, in thinking Godwards, we may also find ourselves renewing our commitment to live our faith. But our prayer is firmly addressed to God, not undertaken as soliloquy, self-address.

Although one meets with prayer thought of as having power in itself, classical Christian prayer has always, as recalled earlier, been further filtered by "in the name of Christ" (through Christ, in Christ's character) to God the Father, thus for God to deal with as God deems fit; even though it may

---

25. Bonhoeffer, *Letters and Papers*, 193–97; though Bonhoeffer continued to talk of God's guidance (e.g., 213 [letter 14 August 1944]).

26. I take current encouragement from a chance reading at the time of typing, this assurance from Edgar Ruddock, in *Pray with Us*, 1: "Prayer is one way of letting God come alongside us, in all our fragility, giving us space to say how it really is with us, knowing we will be listened to, profoundly"(though I would say, the only appropriatate way, and have "trustingly imagine" rather than "know").

be with the Spirit ignored or taken for granted. If I am right, and God in Trinity has decided against intervening, then our prayers, I take it, are heard and likely registered, but not otherwise here and now acted on. Rather they become integrally part of each person-in-relationships whom God is to be trusted to raise to continually transformative new life within the divine life. (Perhaps God may use them still further in ultimately healing, renewing, enlightening, at-one-ing in the divine life those for whom we prayed?)

(e) Incarnation: A Truly Human and Truly Divine Birth, Life, Death, Resurrection

This sketch might seem to have deprived me of any possibility of belief in Jesus as God incarnate. How could Jesus in any way be seen as the God-man without God intervening in the lives of Mary and Joseph and their baby, at least? And how could Jesus "be God" without knowing it (as insisted in the previous chapter) without Jesus (impossibly) sharing the whole mind of God?

In *A Man for Us and a God for Us*, a few years after *Has Christianity?*, I attempted an answer. I include now an adapted version of what I wrote then, but in the light of my still later *Jesus and the Threat of Freedom* and other pieces published since. The nub of my christological argument was and is that we are invited to imagine the divine Son/Word identifying with the entire psycho-physical human life of Jesus, from conception to grave and beyond, without a hint of a divine takeover of that life.

It might seem easier to imagine this self-identification being affected after Jesus had completed his good life, when it had turned out good enough to be a model for encouraging explorations in divine self-giving generosity. But I prefer to imagine the Word taking the risk from the start, even if with some positive appreciation in advance of the likely effect on their child's personality of Mary and Joseph and their Galilaean neighbors.

I now sketch that life as I read the ongoing scholarship, reflections with which I have myself continued to engage and to which I have in a small way, I trust, contributed. I take it that Jesus was the result of sexual union between Joseph and Mary, with ongoing psycho-physical nurturing by both and by other villagers in his formative years. (Paul sees him as of David's physical "seed," not Davidic by adoption. Matthew's and Luke's virginal conception tales are later imagining that threatens to undermine trust in Jesus' full humanity.)[27]

---

27. As argued in Downing, "Women and Men," 181–89.

I urge that we accept as coherently imaginable, as plausibly but by no means provenly factual, elements of the Synoptic tradition in its portrayal of Jesus.[28] He saw himself as led by the Spirit, called by God, enlightened, empowered to heal, sent to try to share his understanding of God's will for him and those of his people around him. As a would-be reforming prophet he made his own selection of his Jewish people's diverse traditions as currently understood, with an emphasis on unpossessive, unforced sharing of simple necessities: health, food, clothing, friendship, in dependence (yes) on a deity trusted to be generally and perhaps individually providential. This Father was one whose rule he urgently pressed people to accept, in the limited time during which he expected the choice to remain open. In that, as in much else, he was a man, a male, of his day and local society. He was open to women and children, himself engaging in "feminine" compassion and vulnerbility, refusing "virile" masterfulness; yet he deployed only male emissaries. He objected strongly to concentrations of wealth and power, yet seems to have accepted legalized slavery, at least in his appeal to hearers' imaginations. Much of his practice and teaching also resonates with variants of contemporary Cynicism in its puritan form. (I have argued at length that these similarities in the narration are so extensive as to suggest the presence of Cynic practice and ethos in the Galilaean society from which the synoptic tradition stemmed.[29] But that need not distract the reader here.) In all, then, his was only a small and brief and ultimately very bitter taste of possible human experience.

Nonetheless, despite his grounding in his people's traditions, his lifestyle, teaching, and following all attracted hostility from the Sadducean aristocracy. He also seems to have alienated other would-be reformers of Judaism, importantly among them Pharisees, despite or even bcause of significant common aims. His intransigence, his determined "invasion" of the heart of privilege in Jerusalem led to his arrest and his cruel and shaming crucifixion in connivance with the Roman ruler of Judea. He shrank from but refused to escape the death he foresaw, though in a last meal with a dozen or so of his male friends he symbolically drew them into identifying with him in it. Only the women on the edge of his following are said to have remained loyal throughout.

Some identification with him and at least something of his cause continued. His followers rallied to his memory, teaching, practice. It seems to

28. On "compossible" sketches of Jesus, see Downing, *Church and Jesus*, 178–92; and "Dissident Jesus," esp. 294–97.

29. See Downing, *Cynics and Christian Origins*, and (with a fresh assessment of Paul and early tradition) *Cynics, Paul and the Pauline Churches*; and, again, most recently, "Dissident Jesus."

have appeared to some of them and others as though he was alive, again, and available to them. They could imagine him, and effectively envision him, still influential, with God, in God's good heaven, raised to divine glory (with a burial place assumed empty [1 Cor 15:42–44] without needing to be looked for, let alone discovered). Such followers found themselves with a renewed determination to live the kind of life he lived and taught. Even before conception, some came to imagine, he had been a celestial being, of the human-like kind various other fellow Jews imagined.[30] People, many people, Paul included, had visions of him, alive and celestial. Stories of an empty tomb, and then of physical contact, even of eating together with some followers, grew up later. These last, however, seemed untold and unknown to Paul even twenty years on: 1 Cor 15:1–8, 42–50. Paul trusted in a distinctively post-physical, spirit-bodied Jesus, neither tangible nor expected to eat physical food.

I am aware that many Christians, sophisticated theologians among them, would argue that the empty tomb and physical seeing came first, necessary to stimulate his disciples' renewed identification with Jesus as the Christ. But others and I argue that without the ongoing effective identification, significant if imperfect, the vacant tomb and encounters, even if considered, would have been a passing curiosity. It is their shared willingness and ability to live something of his message that persuaded those earlier followers and their successors of his living and effective presence among them, and that of the divine Spirit-breath. It is on this ground that the validity of such visions were claimed. For Paul, the hallmark of Christian experience is existence in the Spirit of those who have received the Spirit, that is, the power and presence of God, not on evidence of appearances or empty tomb.[31] The experience validates and demands the stories, not the other way round. And we may ourselves imagine as much.

But the Word's identification with this Jesus? To quote my 1968 suggestion with a few additions:

> The Son, I must believe, was accepting as his own every experience, every action and sensation, of that physical organism, Jesus; and not as an observer, but as a subject (a co-subject) of all that was done by or happened to that fully personal Jesus. . . . This was God, accepting the dreaming innocence of the womb, the anguish of birth, the pain of separation [from Mary], the coming to self-consciousness. God the Son was accepting

---

30. Cf. Hurtado, *Lord Jesus Christ*, and scholarship discussed there.

31. On which, e.g., Evans, *Resurrection*, 159. See especially, Catchpole, *Resurrection People*; McDonald, *Resurrection*; Perkins, *Resurrection*; Wedderburn, *Resurrection*; more "conservative" and very thorough, Wright, *Resurrection*.

ignorance and hunger and the flavour of bread baked on the hearth, the excitement of wine at village parties. He was [formed and] battered by social conditioning, by the urge to pride and hatred, to cruelty, callousness, self-righteousness, narrow sectarianisms. This was God, taking all that came the way of the human organism Jesus, with no pretence, no protection. The love was the love of an ordinary sensual man, the pain was the pain of ordinary nerves and brain.

This was God. Jesus was God, without knowing it, because God was Jesus by deliberate choice, commitment, acceptance. God bled, God let his mind be torn to shreds by pain, to reconcile his world to him [with Father and Spirit], to be part of the pain [and joy] that his love had seen good to let his world suffer. God accepted the pain [and joy] of a man who loved as well, it seems, as any ordinary man [or woman] has loved.[32]

I would now add in support the analogy (again, partial analogy) of identifying with a character in a play, film, opera, novel, or with anyone close to you, in ways that for us can be fully physiological (we sweat, salivate, tense up) and even an identification deliberately prolonged. And, I would further suggest, the Word continues to identify with the risen human Jesus as that Galilaean Jewish reformer continues to allow himself to be adapted, along with the rest of us, further into the Trinitarian life of God.

In terms of the classical christological dogmatic imagining, does this not end up with the discarded "Antiochene" two sons? Well, it refuses the Antiochene separation of the two, the human and the divine, held to be separate lest the changeless infinity of the divine appear compromised. In what I invite the reader to imagine, the involvement of the divine Word in the human experience is total. It is not a matter of the divine Son performing miracles, the human Son feeling pleasure and pain. Nor are we called to imagine now praying to two Jesuses. When we address prayer to the Word by the name Jesus, it is (should be) to the Word in his continuing self-identification with Jesus. Thus, it will not be prayer to Jesus son of Joseph and Mary, the fellow human who is now transformed or being transformed to understand (and, incidentally, to have revealed to him his unwitting part in the loving and saving incarnation of God).[33]

Others may, justifiably, feel they have better ways of coping with the paradoxical but alluring images of variegated Christian believing. This is one I have tested in my own praying, living, and reflecting and sharing

32. Downing, A Man for Us, 67–68.

33. On the continuity of the Galiaean, resurrected, heavenly-and-returning Christ, I welcome the insistence of Welker, God the Revealed, 4 and 209–50.

for more than half a century, as well as in books. I have still to find a rival account that to my mind does better in theory, even if others succeed in stimulating better practice. It is only glimpses of something of the latter, more effective Christian living among those with interventionist beliefs, that can risk unsettling my imaginative conclusions. Just other imaginings on their own fail to convince.

But the validity or mistakenness of anyone's imagining, however informed by biblical or later tradition, cannot warrant claims to be in any way given or "revealed" by God. And, of course, our imagining must always remain open to revision. Indeed, at least for me, openness to revison is central to my trust, the hope of ultimate salvation.

(f) "For Us and for Our Salvation"

It is worth noting that *sōteria,* "salvation," in ordinary usage, was a very general term for wellbeing: Caesar could be acclaimed as bringer of civic and economic wellbeing, Epicurus as having provided instructions on attaining individual wellbeing. The kind of wellbeing, salvation, has to be made clear by the context.

The saving may quite likely be more positive than negative, betokening what we are saved for rather than saved from. When in the Synoptic tradition Jesus tells a sufferer, "Your faith has given you well-being," the negative, the illness, is implied but the emphasis is on the wellbeing, the health, gained. The evangelists may, admittedly, have thought more implied: perhaps endless wellbeing after death as well as now. But that is not said; still less is there any indication here of salvation from unpayable debt or from condemnation to endless torment.

The account offered here is to see God's involvement in the whole life of Jesus as the Word's responsive self-giving to the Father in, through and with us, in the power of the Spirit: the supreme instance of such self-giving.[34] This is the Son's pressing and enabling invitation to us to allow ourselves to be drawn further and further into the Trinitarian life of God, as the summit of wellbeing, only but vitally saving us "from" nothing other than the absence of such advance. Formally what I want to say is well summarized by Tanner (not ignoring my disagreement with her the social Trinity):

---

34. The self-giving to which aspects of evolution may seem to point, as argued by Coakley in *Sacrifice Regained,* esp. lecture 4. I admire, but am unpersuaded by her quixotic attempt to rescue the word "sacrifice" from a common English sense of sheer destruction. I feel "responsive self-giving" (Heb 10) less distracting.

An incarnational model of atonement insists upon the relationship between the cross and the rest of Jesus'life, since the mechanism of salvation on the cross is at work throughout Jesus' life.
And the effects of this salvific mechanism—its point—are, indeed, much clearer away from the cross than on it—for example,
in Jesus' healing ministry to the sick and the outcast, the advent
of the new community of God, and Jesus' resurrected life.[35]

And I feel here able at last to call on Johannine theology, if in implicit
and only partial support: "We know that we have passed from death to life
because we love one another" (1 Jn 3:14; cf. Jn 5:24, and more). Clearer still
are the summaries we find from Athanasius onwards: "The Word became
human so we might become divine"; "He became one with us physically
so we might become one with him spiritually"; "He came to share our life
so we might share his." His life, lived to the full, is the essential start; our
appropriation of it is the end.[36]

But I add a note, in line with what I quoted in the previous section
from my own earlier writing and picking up a hint in chapter 2. If there is
any price paid, any salvific "atoning for," the incarnate life of the Word may
be seen as the penalty the Trinity accepted for creating and sustaining an
imperfect universe as the only basis for persons freely accepting transformation towards divine fullness.[37] This is the triune, creative God's saving
solidarity with us, to make us one with him.

This insistence on the Son's very physical sharing in a full human life
links closely with the majority early Christian insistence that he is and was
Son of the same creator God spoken of in Jewish Scriptures but also an agent
in creation (all this against varieties of Gnosticism).[38] The saving, at-one-ing
life of the creative Word involves the whole universe, not just humankind
torn out of context (Rom 8:19–23; cf. the later expansion in Col 1:15–20).

---

35. Tanner, *Christ the Key*, 262. On salvation "from" and "for" cf. McIntyre, *The
Shape of Soteriology*, 33–34.

36. See the discussion in Downing, "God . . . Patristic Method," 236, 242, and e.g.,
Athanasius, *De incarnatione*, 54–55; Hilary, *De trinitate*, 2:24; Augustine, *De trinitate*,
4:2 [2:4].

37. Cf. folksong writer and singer Sidney Carter's "Friday Morning": "It was God
who made the Devil / And the Woman and the Man / And there wouldn't be an apple
/ If it wasn't in the Plan. / It's God they ought to crucify / Instead of you and me, / I
said to the carpenter / A-hanging on the tree." God in Christ accepted the logic of this
argument.

38. In effect, emphasizing common strands in Paul, John, Synoptics and more, thus
in some measure in balance against the diversity among these on other issues, as emphasized by Tuckett, "New Testament Study."

(g) The Holy Spirit

Our salvation is, of course, Trinitarian. The Father, the Source of being, accepting the Son's identification with us sinners, and in doing that accepts us: all is set right from his side, he has united, at-oned us to himself, and freely. There has been no call for the Word, the Son, to mollify him, appease him, twist his arm or soften his heart. The Spirit, we may imagine, wills and longs for and awaits our appropriation in trust of the Father's acceptance of us, our enjoyment of at-one-ment, of being right with God. The Life-giver interprets our faltering responses, ready to pick up and restore to life and integrate into the divine community each whole relational human person on death.

The Spirit has tended to be the divine person most readily and conveniently ignored.[39] The tendency, especially in the West, has been to imagine the Spirit domesticated and tamed within the organizational church, or as having pre-scripted himself [sic] in Scriptures as interpreted by the magisterium, or as affording individual or in-group experiential enhancement. The thought of the Spirit as freely blowing those reborn wherever he will (Jn 3:8, however interpreted) can be unacceptably disturbing. In defense of this Western Christian reserve however, I could allow that these restrictions on the Spirit's freedom of movement might themselves be held to anticipate a non-interventionist theology such as that outlined here. The Spirit has never really been expected or actually "allowed," to "do" anything. Can I—with my God imagined, engaged with us but non-intervening—offer anything better?

It is possible to imagine, at least from time to time, the Spirit disturbing us out of our set ways into a life more Christianly fruitful but still sustainable, and then to imagine sharing—not imposing—just such a vision with family and friends. Perhaps then we might share visions of creative disruption with a wider Christian congregation. Such radical disturbance does happen, even among members of mainstream churches. But, I confess, my own imagination soon fails me, even if refreshed by stories of others who have done better, sometimes much better. I will not weary the reader with an account of my own very unremarkable (shared) efforts, in terms of hospitality, direct community engagement, and financial and other comfortably affordable support for good causes.[40]

---

39. See Cockin, *Holy Spirit*; Comblin, *Holy Spirit and Liberation*; Congar, *Holy Spirit*; Green, *Holy Spirit*; Jenkins, *Holy Spirit*; Taylor, *Go-Between*.

40. E.g., Pears, "My father . . . my hero," reminiscences of a priest, father of an open, cooperative family, a deserted husband able to console his ex-wife's deserted lover.

Such social disturbance imagined is, of course, political. It includes a concern with our environment and its conservation, reduction in armed and other conflicts, with a much more equitable—egalitarian and genuinely sustainable—sharing of the planet's resources of water, energy, food. That sharing would benefit others here and now but also endanger future generations. Such ideals seem to me both to inform and to flow from the Trinitarian theology here outlined. They do not specify the practicalities of persuading others to accept them, let alone make them work. Current democratic party politics worldwide inspire little hope.

Perhaps if Christians were themselves prepared to live their ideals more effectively, the example might attract others, even if it might as readily alienate. Elsewhere I have argued that the significant degree of egalitarianism among early Christians will have constituted an important factor in attracting and retaining converts, in the light of the intensely "agonistic," competitive society of the day.[41] (The costs of inequality, costs to all, not just the poorest, in our global village are effectively assembled in studies by Richard Wilkinson and Kate Pickett.)[42]

(h) One Holy, Catholic, and Apostolic Church

We will probably agree with Augustine in admitting that no valid instantiation of an ideal church anywhere visibly exists. That it nonetheless does exist is instantiated, but invisibly and in individuals. But, more impressed by Gregory of Nyssa than by Augustine, I can only imagine it as a hope for a life in God to be grown into after our physical death. Meanwhile it remains an ideal to be aimed towards, aimed at least towards allowing it to happen, trusting we echo the Spirit's eager hope for us.

Taking it that our unity is already given, God has in Christ already at-oned us to himself; we work at learning to enjoy growing into his acceptance of us, in practice, together. Paul told his Corinthian friends, "You are the body of Christ, and individually members [limbs/organs] of it" (1 Cor 12:27; cf. Rom 12:5).[43] I am among many (including many less agnostic than I am), who have been challenged and encouraged by words popularly ascribed to Teresa of Avila:

---

41. Downing, "Fairly Simple."

42. Wilkinson, *Cost of Inequality*; Wilkinson with Pickett, *Spirit Level.*

43. The Paul of the authentic letters remains patriarchal in many ways, but his "body" talk is explicitly egalitarian, whereas his followers, in Col 1:18 and Eph 1:22, are much more hierarchic: Christ there is head, not whole.

Christ has no body now but yours,
no hands, no feet on earth but yours.
Yours are the eyes through which he looks
with compassion on this world,
yours are the feet with which he walks to do good,
yours are the hands, with which he blesses all the world.
Yours are the hands, yours are the feet, yours are the eyes:
you are his body.
Christ has no body now but yours,
No hands, no feet on earth but yours.[44]

Teresa herself seems, in what I have read, was sure that God intervenes in her mind/spirit/soul, talking with her. But practically, as indicated in the foregoing, this God does not act in the wider world independently of us. Rather we imagine we may be serving him in serving one another. So we learn to live into and so share the unity that we trust God has already granted us with himself. This, much more than just sharing words, is to be apostolic and evangelical.[45]

It is in such loving and generous service and acceptance of others' service, that we affirm to ourselves (and just possibly to onlookers) that we are, at least at times and together, distinctively his: that is, holy. Although I am drawn to Karl Rahner's generous-sounding idea of "anonymous Christians," I am reluctant to make imperialistic claims to every kind, generous, compassionate fellow human as "really ours," whether or not they would welcome the gesture.[46] Thus, for me, God's church is not catholic, universal, until all have allowed themselves to be drawn irreversibly and fully aware into the divine life (on which, see further, shortly). Those of us who would want to "be church" are in reality "apostolic" when we do what we are sent, "apostled": live as Christ's body, serving generously, and drawing others in, or joining with them while they stay outside.[47] "You will know them by their fruits" (Matt 7:16–20; cf. Lk 6:43–44, some texts).

---

44. Teresa of Avila, as included in a number of websites, without textual reference; sometimes in broken lines, as here, but they are clearly not from a poem of hers. I found no lead to them in Alison Peer's edition of Teresa, *Complete Works*.

45. See, e.g., recently, Kreider, "*Resourcement* and Mission."

46. See, yet again, the brief but careful discussion in DiNoia, "What About *Them*?"

47. Apostolic order, with tactile succession of bishops, is historically very dubious. Numerically, episcopal order became dominant. Whether for individuals or for congregation it is the most effective order (as enabling Christ's hands, feet, voice) I would like to know, but do not. As a cradle Anglican I'd be pleased if it were, but remain very doubtful; especially when independent, loosely federated Pentecostalist congregations are admirably taking on a wide civic responsibility.

(i) Baptism and Other Sacraments

Sacramental practice and prayer mesh integrally with every clause of the creed outlined (in obvious continuity with ongoing Christian tradition). Baptism, immersion in or sprinkling with ordinary water, is "In the name of the Father and of the Son and of the Holy Spirit," perhaps best interpreted as being our initiation into "the living character" of God in Trinity. In churches that practice the baptizing of infants, it is taken as the very physical enactment of divine gratuitous acceptance, at-oneing, inviting lived appropriation (see Gal 3:26–28 and much more). And a helpful metaphor, to my mind, is it's the gift of life membership of a fitness club: unless you use it, for getting ever fitter (for receiving God's self-revealing), it is useless, though still yours. In churches that prioritize the individual response of the candidate, it is a sacrament of human appropriation of a sense of prior divine acceptance or call, at-one-ment, acceptance of free membership, with intent, as least, to use it. So, at least in part, is confirmation (with hands or oil or both, and ordination, similarly) in most communions: a gracious reminder, with no recrimination, to use the membership given. Adult baptism, confirmation, and ordination are all clearly meant to focus both grace and response together. We are, or should be, drawn to imagine these as more than the symbolic acts they appear to be, but rather divine creative use of divinely created matter-in-action.

In Episcopalian churches where the bishop is taken as the sacramental focus of unity among individuals and individual congregations, the oil he or she has blessed is a sacrament of unity in the body of Christ at baptism, confirmation, ordination, and in healing.[48]

The thanksgiving and intercessory and adorational prayers of the Eucharist are addressed to the Father through the Son, inviting the living presence of the Spirit. (This is only now explicit, in Western liturgies, while having been so from earliest days in those of the East.) In the Eucharistic action as a whole we are enabled and encouraged to imagine the creative Word, the Son identified with Jesus, identifying us with him in his lifelong self-giving to the Father in the power of the Spirit, and identifying himself with us in our eager or sluggish formation to enjoy sharing his divine life. And in so doing, he is renewing our appropriation of the Father's baptismal acceptance of us, to our divine parent's delight. (Among much else, we here may recall 1 Cor 10:16, 11:23, and 12:4–6, 12–13.) For myself, I would see the Eucharist as therefore the primary "sacrament of reconciliation," of

---

48. Save when, as in my present Church of England, the oil must currently have been blessed by a chosen bishop among choosey male priests. On the Christian effectiveness of such a focus of unity, see the doubts expressed in the previous note.

at-one-ment, rather than restricting that terminology to confession and absolution, whether corporate or individual. And that at-one-ing should be seen as condemning the vicious divisive inequalities our world, and as urging communicants' pressing opposition to them (see chapter 7).

It would make good sense to me, as it does to others, to allow an open invitation to share the bread and the wine, the body and the blood of the Lord, with those who have not yet been made members of the club. They are invited to "taste and see that the Lord is good" (1 Pet 2:5), just as they may be doing already, unawares.[49]

But the creative Word is surely also to be acknowledged in the Eucharist as the priest of all his creation: the entire creation, with us included, offered in love to its Source. Human community within the entire created commonwealth should ideally be richly in our minds and words and symbols, in our thanks, confession, and intercession (and not just incidentally). Nor is this an innovative add-on. As Gorringe and others have pointed out, creation has figured from early on (probably with firm roots in Jewish practice) within eucharistic prayers.[50]

Gorringe ties this creational-incarnational celebration of divine valuation of the physical in with the other sacraments included in many Christians' practice. Confirmation and ordination (with unction) have already been noted. Marriage is the most obviously and inextricably expressive of our trust that God affirms our sensuous/sensual human personhood. God in Trinity did so in Jesus—the fruit of a sensuous union of Mary and Joseph.[51] Admitted, Jesus himself missed marriage and progeny, along with much else. He only lived one and that probably quite short life, affording the divine Word only a selection of human sensual experience. But it is a great pity that so many fellow Christians (and others) suppose that a few scriptural authors' rejection of any but heterosexual and at least potentially procreative union must be their God's finally announced view on the matter. Clearly such a conclusion is traditional; but taking an ancient desire to sustain male rights of inheritance as revealing God's eternal will on human sexuality seems particularly implausible. And this is especially so when so many ancient views on our human psycho-physical make-up have since clearly turned out to be mistaken. Any caring and generous physical deep and mutual self-giving can surely best be imagined as a very positive gift

49. See just above, on "anonymous Christians," and also Tatarrnic, "Whoever Comes."

50. Gorringe, "Sacraments," 165–66.

51. Accepting Paul's and others' insistence on Jesus's lineal descent, rather than Luke or Matthew; see, above, and, again, Downing, "Women and Men," 181–89.

from the divine giver of its possibility and potential, and best celebrated and recognized as "marriage."

(j) The Resurrection of the Dead and the Life of the World to Come

Resurrection of the flesh seems to many of us picturable (as in Stanley Spenser's Cookham series of paintings). On further reflection, however, even Paul with his unexplained "spiritual body" rejects it: "flesh and blood cannot inherit the kingdom of God" (1 Cor 15:44, 50). But if, as seems the case, we have to accept that we are entirely physical organisms—embodied minds with no function for a non-physical "ghost in the machine"—then we are at any one time constituted by a finite set of atoms with their electro-chemical interlinkages. The set is changing in its constituent cells and their inter-relationships all the while, but with massive continuities. It is specifiable and, I urge as before, that we trust God knowingly to sustain each and every changing complex. Our embodied mind-selves, I am persuaded, are "analog" not "digital"; but they are still finite and, in theory, thus both specifiable and reproducible.[52] God may be intelligibly imagined as after our death reconstituting each with the free flexibility of analog awareness and multiple analog communication skills. We may imagine ourselves being reconstituted as finite, bounded, persons-in-resumed-relations, recognisable to others and ourselves. And all of this because we are already at-oned with God by God, in a relationship that God in love will remain true to, continuously enhance, and never relinquish.

As outlined above (c), we hope we may continue to mature, by learning from one another, human males from many different human (and non-human?) females and males; human females from many different human (and non-human?) males and females. Among the humans, again, we may surely continue to include people of other faith complexes, as our Judaeo-Christian traditions historically always have, if untrumpeted. In this we also have to look forward to gaining from those ahead of us, our forebears, God's saints already brought into, or being brought deeper into the divine life.

And, yet again, we may trust, imaginatively, that the creative Word continues to self-identify with the risen Jesus. Incarnation is always his, not a passing episode.

---

52. On physical (and modular) minds, see Carruthers, *Language and Thought*; Carruthers, "Thinking in Language" and *Architecture of the Mind*; on "analogue," in the latter, chapter 5, "Creative Cognition in Modular Mind," 277–334, and 284–304 in particular.

However, looking to post-mortem, after death, fulfillment might seem to risk distracting us from this world and the plight of our contemporaries. "Our" planet, "our" universe might risk being seen only as our transient staging post. Many of us are persuaded, as Tanner notes, that the sun will in fact ultimately burn or freeze its planets on the way to its own extinction; and the universe itself will finally descend into entropic chaos: "the world . . . ultimately has no future."[53] We could suppose the science is mistaken, and/or expect a divine reversal to suit our own particular slant on biblical authority. But rather than these escapes, Tanner cogently urges us to take seriously the quality of life we trust God has already opened up to us and is, we trust, drawing us further into. That life with and in God in Trinity can only be lived now in present sharing. That life, with its trusted promise, exerts the imperative to help enhance the life to which many contemporaries and others yet unborn are subject and condemned:

> One is led to see the way the world currently runs as an insufferable, unacceptable affront, not by the disparity between the present and God's coming future, but by the utter disjunction between patterns of injustice, exclusion, and impoverishment, which make up the realm of death, and the paradigm of existence empowered by life in God as a force working in the present. In short, complacency is ruled out, not by a transcendent future but by a transcendent present—by present life in God as the source of goods that the world one lives in fails to match. If liturgy is the place where our life in God becomes present to us, it exists as a protest against the world as it is, fuelling an opposition to the world of sin, like Jesus' [opposition to it].[54]

Despite this cogent insistence on the physical here and now, my reading of Tanner suggests a de-temporalizing and de-spatializing of us in relation to God, which I find it hard to imagine.[55] Her insistence that God's relationship with God's world/universe can be confidently left to God seems eminently acceptable. But our imagining cannot be that we could "be us" while shorn of anything clearly analogous to time, space, and touch. Touch, space, and time are integral to us as persons-in-relation. No "thought experiment along such lines seems to make coherent sense (see binaries in

---

53. Tanner, *Jesus, Humanity*, , 98. Tanner does not, to my regret, explicitly expand chapter 4 in the further reflections of her more recent *Christ the Key*.

54. Tanner, *Jesus, Humanity*, 120 (citing Eduard Schillebeeckx). On this, see also, above, chapter 7.

55. Tanner, *Jesus, Humanity*, 111.

chapter 7). Well, certainly not to me.[56] It smacks too much of some philosophers' "brain in a vat" theorizing; or the proposal that a computer could be programmed to "think" like a human without any creative, sensuous interaction with other sensuous bodies, or its own, or its environment. With not even an analogy to spatial, sensuous and temporal distinctiveness, continuity with who we were would be lost. And yet further, as I have proposed on divine sustaining creativity, our present physical, spatial, temporal selves should be taken as existing "in" God: for God these constitute aspects of the reality constantly held in being by God's awareness of them.[57] Life to come for us is to be imagined on this cosmic scale, assured by the character of the God we trust.[58] To come to know God more fully must at least involve and include our growing awareness of God forever taking these human realities lovingly, seriously, delightedly—for us to come to share the delight and the love. We may in such trust look forward to being brought, perhaps endlessly being brought, towards the self-revelation of our loving creator, sustainer, redeemer.

Dear God,
Thank you for your love and wisdom,
Creator, Redeemer, Spirit of life.
We thank you for creating us, sustaining us, renewing us.
You are with us, you let us be.
You share our life that we may come to share yours.
Blessed are you for ever.
Amen.

---

56. On this, see e.g., Carruthers, again, *Architecture*, 289–304.

57. The reader might possibly suppose I am here by contrast siding with Wright, *Resurrection*, 347–56, on bodily spiritualization. I do appreciate Wright's emphasis on bodiliness, but do not concur with his insistence that we should suppose a transmogrification of the physical (to fit in with legends of Jesus' empty tomb).

58. Cf. the Church of England's Doctrine Commission, *Mystery of Salvation*, 180–200. Its unexamined use of "revelation" is balanced by a much better meditation on 1 Cor 13:12 from the Sri Lankan Anglican, Laksam Wikremesinghe, 183.

Bibliography

Aitchison, Jean. *The Articulate Mammal: An Introduction to Psycholinguistics*. 5th ed. London: Routledge, 2011.

Anderson, Arthur A. *The Book of Psalms*. NCB. 2 vols. London: Oliphants, 1972.

Anderson, Gary A. *Sin: A History*. New Haven, CT: Yale University Press, 2009.

Anon. *The Cloud of Unknowing and Other Works*. Edited and translated by Anthony C. Spearing. New York: Penguin, 2001.

Arberry, A. J. *Sufism: An Account of the Mystics of Islam*. Boston: Allen and Unwin, 1950. Reprinted 1979.

Arendt, Hannah. *The Human Condition*. Chicago: University of Chicago Press, 1958.

Asurmendi, Jésus. *Du non-sense: L'Ecclésiaste*. Paris: Cerf, 2012.

Atherton, John. *Public Theology for Changing Times*. London: SPCK, 2000.

Atria, Fernando. "Reconciliation and Reconstitution." In *Law and the Politics of Reconciliation*, edited by Scott Veitch, 33–47. Burlington, VT: Ashgate, 2006.

Audi, Robert. *Epistemology: A Contemporary Introduction to the Theory of Knowledge*. 3rd ed. London: Routledge, 2011.

Austin, John L. *How to Do Things with Words*. Edited by J. O. Urmson. Oxford: Clarendon, 1962.

———. "Unfair to Facts." In *Philosophical Papers*, edited by J. O. Urmson, 102–22. Oxford: Clarendon, 1961.

Baillie, John. *The Idea of Revelation in Recent Thought*. Oxford: Oxford University Press, 1956.

Balasuriya, Tissa. *The Eucharist and Human Liberation*. Maryknoll, NY: Orbis, 1979.

Bankowski, Zenon. "The Cost of Reconciliation." In *Law and the Politics of Reconciliation*, edited by Scott Veitch, 49–67. Burlington, VT: Ashgate, 2006.

Bannet, Eve Tavor. *Structuralism and the Logic of Dissent: Barthes, Derrida, Foucault, Lacan*. London: MacMillan, 1989.

Barr, James. *The Concept of Biblical Theology: An Old Testament Perspective*. London: SCM, 1999.

———. "Revelation." *Harper's Bible Dictionary*, 2nd ed. Edinburgh: T. & T. Clark, 1963.

Barth, Karl. *Church Dogmatics*. 4 vols. Translated by Geoffrey W. Bromily and T. F. Torrance. Edinburgh: T. & T. Clark, 1936–77.

Barton, John, and John Muddiman, eds. *The Oxford Bible Commentary*. New York: Oxford University Press, 2001.

Bauckham, Richard, and Carl Mosser, eds. *The Gospel of John and Christian Theology*. Grand Rapids: Eerdmans, 2008.

BCC (British Council of Churches). *The Forgotten Trinity: The Report of the BCC Study Commission on Trinitarian Doctrine Today*. London: British Council of Churches, 1989.

Beare, Francis W. *The Epistle to the Philippians*. BNTC. London: Black, 1959.

Beeley, Christopher A. *Gregory Nazianzus on the Trinity and the Knowledge of God: In Your Light Shall We See Light*. New York: Oxford University Press, 2008.

Beeman, Josiah H., and Robert Mahoney. "Churches and the Process of Reconciliation In Northern Ireland: Recent Progress in Presbyterian-Roman Catholic Relations." In *Northern Ireland and the Politics of Reconciliation*, edited by Dermot Keogh and Michael H. Haltzel, 150–59. Cambridge: Cambridge University Press, 1993.

Begbie, Jeremy S., and Stephen R. Guthrie, eds. *Resonant Witness: Conversations between Music and Theology*. Grand Rapids: Eerdmans, 2011.

Benhabib, Seyla. *Situating the Self: Gender, Community and Postmodernism in Contemporary Ethics*. Cambridge: Polity, 1992.

Berleujung, Angelika. "Divine Presence for Everybody: Presence Theology in Everyday Life." In *Divine Presence and Absence in Exilic and Post-Exilic Judaism: Studies of the Sofja Kolalevskaja Research Group on Early Jewish Monotheism*, edited by Nathan MacDonald and Izaak J. de Hulster, 67–93. FAT 2.61. Tübingen: Mohr Siebeck, 2013.

Bernecker, Walther L. "Vergangenheitsaufarbeitung in Spanien: Zwischen Amnesie und kollectiver Erinnerung." In *Versöhnung, Strafe and Gerechtigkeit: Das schwere Erbe von Unrechts-Staaten*, edited by Michael Bongardt and Ralf K. Würstenberg, 149–67. Kontexte. Neue Beiträge zur historischen unde systematischen Theologie 40. Göttingen: Ruprecht, 2010.

Bernstein, Basil. *Class, Codes and Control*. 4 vols. London: Routledge, 1971–76.

Bhandar, Brenna. "'Spatialising History' and Opening Time: Resisting the Reproduction of the Proper Subject." In *Law and the Politics of Reconciliation*, edited by Scott Veitch, 93–110. Burlington, VT: Ashgate, 2006.

Bieler, Andrea, and Luisa Schottroff. *The Eucharist: Bodies, Bread, and Resurrection*. Minneapolis: Fortress, 2007.

Bieringer, Raimund. "Dying and Being Raised For: Shifts in the Meaning of ὑπέρ." In *Theologizing in the Corinthian Conflict: Studies in the Exegesis and Theology of 2 Corinthians*, edited by Raimund Bieringer et al., 163–74. BiTS 16. Leuven: Peeters, 2013.

———, et al., eds. *Theologizing in the Corinthian Conflict: Studies in the Exegesis and Theology of 2 Corinthians*. BiTS 16. Leuven: Peeters, 2013.

Blackwell, Ben. C. *Christosis: Pauline Christology in Light of Deification in Irenaeus and Cyril of Alexandria*. WUNT 2.314. Tübingen: Mohr Siebeck, 2011.

Blenkinsopp, Joseph. *David Remembered: Kingship and National Identity in Ancient Israel*. Grand Rapids: Eerdmans, 2013.

———. *Isaiah: A New Translation with Introduction and Commentary*. AB, 3 vols. New York: Doubleday, 2000–2003.

Blythe, Ronald. *Talking about John Clare*. Nottingham: Trent, 1999.

Boesel, Chris, and Catherine Keller, eds. *Apophatic Bodies: Negative Theology, Incarnation, and Relationality*. New York: Fordham University Press, 2010.

Bongardt, Michael. "Endstation Strafe? Auf der Suche nack ein Kultur der Vergebung." In *Versöhnung, Strafe and Gerechtigkeit: Das schwere Erbe von Unrechts-Staaten*. edited by Michael Bongardt and Ralf K. Wüstenberg, 149–67. Kontexte. Neue Beiträge zur historischen unde systematischen Theologie 40. Göttingen: Ruprecht, 2010.

————., and Ralf K. Würstenberg, eds. *Versöhnung, Strafe and Gerechtigkeit: Das schwere Erbe von Unrechts-Staaten*. Kontexte. Neue Beiträge zur historischen unde systematischen Theologie 40. Göttingen: Ruprecht, 2010.

Bonhoeffer, Dietrich: *Letters and Papers from Prison*. Edited by Eberhard Bethge. Translated by Reginald Fuller and revised by Frank Clarke et al. London: SCM, 1964.

Bonnard, Pierre. *L'Épitre de Saint Paul aux Philippiens*. CNT X. Paris: Delachaux et Niestlé, 1950.

Bovon, François. *Das Evangelium nach Lukas*. EKKNT, 4 vols. Zürich: Benziger and Neukirchener, 1991.

Bowlby, John. *Child Care and the Growth of Love*. Edited and abridged by Margaret Fry. 2nd ed. Harmondsworth: Penguin, 1965.

Bridge, Anthony. *The Image of God and the Death of Symbols*. London: Hodder and Stoughton, 1960.

Brooke, George J. "Memory, Cultural Memory, and Rewritten Scripture." In *Reading the Dead Sea Scrolls: Essays in Method*, edited by George J. Brooke, 51–65. Atlanta: SBL, 2013. Due to appear also in *"Rewritten Bible" after Fifty Years*. Edited by Jóseph Zsengellér. Leiden: Brill, forthcoming.

————. *Reading the Dead Sea Scrolls: Essays in Method*. Atlanta: SBL, 2013.

Brown, David. *Discipleship and Imagination: Christian Radition and Truth*. New York: Oxford University Press, 2000.

————. *God and Enchantment of Place: Reclaiming Christian Experience*. New York: Oxford University Press, 2004.

————. *God and Grace of Body: Sacrament in Ordinary*. New York: Oxford University Press, 2007.

————. *God and Mystery in Words: Experience through Metaphor and Drama*. New York: Oxford University Press, 2008.

————. *Tradition and Imagination: Revelation and Change*. New York: Oxford University Press: 1999.

Brown, Raymond E. *The Gospel According to John*. AB, 2 vols. New York: Doubleday, 1966 and 1970.

Brümmer, Vincent. *The Model of Love*. Cambridge: Cambridge University Press, 1993.

Buber, Martin. *I and Thou*. Translated by Ronald G. Smith: Edinburgh: T. & T. Clark, 1937.

Bultmann, Rudolf. *The Gospel of John: A Commentary*. Translated by George R. Beasley-Murray. Oxford: Blackwell, 1971.

————. *Theology of the New Testament*. 2 vols. Translated by Kendrick Grobel. London: SCM, 1952 and 1955.

Butler, John. *Rock of Ages? The Changing Faces of the Christian God*. Cambridge: Lutterworth, 2013.

Byrne, Peter. "Book Notes." *RS* 29 (1993) 569–71.

Campbell, Douglas A. "Reconciliation in Paul: The Gospel of Negation and Transcendence in Galatians 3.28." In *The Theology of Reconciliation*, edited by Colin Gunton, 39–65. New York: T. & T. Clark, 2003.

Caputo, John D. "The Invention of Revelation: A Hybrid Hegelian Approach with a Dash of Deconstruction." In *Revelation: Claremont Studies in the Philosophy of Religion Conference 2012*, edited by Ingolf U. Dalferth and Michael Rodgers, 73–91. RPT 74. Tübingen: Mohr Siebeck, 2014.

Carroll, Lewis (Charles L. Dodgson). *Through the Looking Glass.* In *The Annotated Alice,* edited by Martin Gardner. Harmondsworth: Penguin, 1963.

Carruthers, Peter, ed. *The Architecture of the Mind: Massive Modularity and the Flexibility of Thought.* New York: Oxford University Press, 2006.

———. "Conscious Thinking." In *Consciousness: Essays from a Higher Order Perspective,* edited by Peter Carruthers, 115–33. New York: Clarendon, 2005.

———. *Consciousness: Essays from a Higher Order Perspective.* New York: Clarendon, 2005.

———. "Thinking in Language? Evolution and a Modularist Possibility." In *Language and Thought: Interdisciplinary Themes,* edited by Peter Carruthers and Jill Boucher, 94–119. New York: Cambridge University Press, 1998.

———, and Jill Boucher, eds. *Language and Thought: Interdisciplinary Themes.* New York: Cambridge University Press, 1998.

Carston, Robyn. *Thoughts and Utterances: The Pragmatics of Explicit Communication.* Malden, MA: Blackwell, 2002.

Cavanagh, Lorraine. *By One Spirit: Reconciliation and Renewal in Anglican Life.* Bern: Peter Lang, 2009.

———. "Hearing the Truth in Love: A Response to 'Splitting Up.'" *Modern Believing* 49.2 (2008) 25–32.

Chang, Ja-Joon. *Economics: The User's Guide.* A Pelican Introduction. New York: Penguin, 2014.

Charlesworth, James H., ed. *The Old Testament Pseudepigrapha.* 2 vols. London: Darton, Longman and Todd, 1983.

Cherbury, Edward, Lord Herbert of. *De Veritate.* Translated with an introduction by Meyrick H. Carré. Bristol: University of Bristol Press, 1937.

Chester, Tim. *Unreached: Growing Churches in Working Class and Deprived Areas.* Nottingham: InterVarsity, 2012.

Chittick, William C. *The Self-Revelation of God: Principles of Ibn Al-'Arabi.* New York: State University of New York Press, 1998.

Church of England Doctrine Commission. *The Mystery of Salvation: The Story of God's Gift.* London: Church House, 1995.

Christensen, Duene L. *Deuteronomy 21:10–34:12.* WBC 3. Nashville: Thomas Nelson, 2002.

Ciampa, Roy E., and Brian S. Rosner. *1 Corinthians.* Pillar Commentaries. Grand Rapids: Eerdmans, 2010.

Clarke, Danielle, ed. *Isabella Whitney, Mary Sidney, and Aemelia Lanyer: Renaissance Women Poets.* New York: Penguin, 2000.

Clarke, W. K. Lowther, ed. and trans. *The First Epistle of Clement to the Corinthians.* London: SPCK, 1935.

Clarkson, Carrol. "The Time of Address." In *Law and the Politics of Reconciliation,* edited by Scott Veitch, 229–40. Burlington, VT: Ashgate, 2006.

Clines, David J. A. *Job 1–20.* WBC 17. Dallas: Word, 1989.

Coakley, Sarah. "Feminism and Analytical Philosophy of Religion." In *The Oxford Handbook of Philosophy of Religion,* edited by William J. Wainwright, 494–525. New York: Oxford University Press, 2005.

———. *God, Sexuality, and the Self.* New York: Cambridge University Press, 2013.

————. "Introduction—Gender, Trinitarian Analogies, and the Pedagogy of the Song." In *Rethinking Gregory of Nyssa*, edited by Sarah Coakley, 1–14. Oxford: Blackwell, 2003.

————, ed. *Rethinking Gregory of Nyssa*. Oxford: Blackwell, 2003.

————. "Sacrifice Regained: Evolution, Cooperation and God." The Gifford Lectures, 2012. Available online at http://www.abdn.ac.uk/gifford/documents/Gifford Lectures.

Cochrane, Kira. "Pregnancy: The Ultimate Drag Act." *The Guardian*, April 12, 2014, page 3.

Cockin, F. Arthur. *God in Action: A Study in the Holy Spirit*. Harmondsworth: Penguin, 1961.

Collins, Raymond F. *First Corinthians*. Sacra Pagina 7. Collegeville, MN: Liturgical, 1999.

Comblin, José. *The Holy Spirit and Liberation*. Translated by Paul Burns. Maryknoll, NY: Orbis, 1989.

Congar, Yves M. J. *I Believe in the Holy Spirit*. Translated by David Smith. 3 vols. New York: Chapman and Seabury, 1983.

Conzelmann. Hans. *1 Corinthians*. Translated by James W. Leitch. Hermeneia. Philadelphia: Fortress, 1979.

Cook, Stephen L. "God's Real Absence and Real Presence in Deuteronomy and Deuteronomism." In *Divine Presence and Absence in Exilic and Post-Exilic Judaism: Studies of the Sofja Kolalevskaja Research Group on Early Jewish Monotheism*, edited by Nathan MacDonald and Izaak J. de Hulster. FAT 2.61. Tübingen: Mohr Siebeck, 2013.

Cordrey, Benjamin S. "Divine Hiddenness and Belief *de re*." *RS* 45 (2009) 1–19.

Coulson, John. *Religion and Imagination: "In Aid of a Grammar of Assent."* New York: Clarendon, 1981.

Crabbe, M. James C., ed. *From Soul to Self*. New York: Routledge, 1999.

Crystal, David. *How Language Works*. London: Penguin, 2005.

Culpepper, R. Alan. *Anatomy of the Fourth Gospel: A Study in Literary Design*. Philadelphia: Fortress, 1983.

Cupitt, Don. *Christ and the Hiddenness of God*. 2nd ed. London: SCM, 1985.

Curtis, Adrian. *Psalms*. Epworth Commentaries. Peterborough: Epworth, 2004.

Czarnota, Adam. "Sacrum, Profanum and Special Time: Quasi-theological Reflections on Time and Reconciliation." In *Law and the Politics of Reconciliation*, edited by Scott Veitch, 147–62. Burlington, VT: Ashgate, 2006.

Dainton, Barry. "The Self and the Phenomenal." In *The Self?*, edited by Galen Strawson, 1–25. Oxford: Blackwell, 2005.

Dalferth, Ingolf U. "Introduction: Understanding Revelation" In *Revelation: Claremont Studies in the Philosophy of Religion Conference 2012*, edited by Michael Rodgers, 1–25. RPT 74. Tübingen: Mohr Siebeck, 2014.

————, and Michael Rodgers, eds. *Revelation: Claremont Studies in the Philosophy of Religion Conference 2012*. RPT 74. Tübingen: Mohr Siebeck, 2014.

Daly, Erin, and Jeremy Sarkin. *Reconciliation in Divided Societies. Finding Common Ground*. Philadelphia: University of Pennsylvania Press, 2007.

Dancy, Jonathan. *Introduction to Contemporary Epistemology*. Oxford: Blackwell, 1985.

Danielou, Jean. S. J. *Grégoire de Nysse: La Vie de Moïse*. SC 1. Paris: Cerf, 1955.

Davies, Oliver, and Denys Turner, eds. *Silence and the Word: Negative Theology and Incarnation*. Cambridge: Cambridge University Press, 2002.

Deane-Drummond, Celia. *Christ and Evolution: Wonder and Wisdom*. Minneapolis: Fortress, 2009.

———. *Creation through Wisdom: Theology and the New Biology*. Edinburgh: T. & T. Clark, 2000.

Derrida, Jacques. *Of Grammatology*. Translated by Gayarti Chakravorty Spivak. Baltimore: John Hopkins University, 1974.

———. *L'écriture et la différence*. Paris: Éditions du Seuil, 1967.

Dickinson, T. Wilson. "Emptying Apophasis of Deception: Considering a Duplicitous Kierkegaardian Declaration." In *Apophatic Bodies: Negative Theology, Incarnation, and Relationality*, edited by Chris Boesel and Catherine Keller, 251–72. New York: Fordham University Press, 2010.

Dietrich, R. *Psycholinguistik. 2. actualisierte und erweiterte Auflage*. Sammlung Metzler 342. Weimar: Metzler, 2007.

Dillistone, Frederick W. *The Christian Understanding of Atonement*. London: SCM, 1968.

DiNoia, J. A. "What About *Them*? Christians and Non-Christians." In *Essentials of Christian Theology*, edited by William C. Placher, 318–28. Louisville: Westminster John Knox, 2003.

Dorival, Gilles. "La formation du canon biblique de l'Ancien Testament: Position actuelle et problèmes." In *Recueils normatifs et canons dans l'Antiquité: Actes du colloque organisé dans le cadre du programme plurifacultaire. La Bible à la croisées des savoirs de l'Université de Genève 11-12 avril 2002*, edited by Enrico Norelli, 83–112. Lausanne: Éditions du Zèbre, 2004.

Downing, F. Gerald. "Ambiguity, Ancient Semantics, and Faith." *NTS* 56:1 (2009) 139–62. Reprinted in *Order and (Dis)order in the First Christian Century: A General Survey of Attitudes*. NovTSup 151. Leiden: Brill, 2013.

———. *The Church and Jesus: A Study in History, Philosophy and Theology*. SBT 2.10. London: SCM, 1968.

———. *Cynics, Paul and the Pauline Churches*. New York: Routledge: 1998.

———. "Dissident Jesus." In *Order and (Dis)order in the First Christian Century: A General Survey of Attitudes*, 283–311. NovTSup 151. Leiden: Brill, 2013.

———. *Doing Theology Thoughtfully is Very like Doing All Sorts of Other Things: The Theologian's Craft*. Lancashire: Downing, 1974.

———. *Doing Things with Words in the First Christian Century*. JSNTS 200. Sheffield: Sheffield Academic, 2000.

———. "Fairly Simple: The Impact of Life-Style." In *God with Everything: The Divine in the Discourse of the First Christian Century*, 64–90. SWBA 2.2. Sheffield: Sheffield Phoenix, 2008.

———. "Forgivingness? Or Forgiveness? Or the Remission of Offences?" In *Making Sense in (and of) the First Christian Century*, 62–77. JSNTS 197. Sheffield: Sheffield Academic, 2000.

———. "Friends in God: A Foundational Motif in Classical Reflections on the Divine Economy." *ATR* (2015) forthcoming.

———. "God and the Problems of Evils." In *Sophia* 7.1 (1968) 12–21.

———. *God with Everything: The Divine in the Discourse of the First Christian Century*. SWBA 2.2. Sheffield: Sheffield Phoenix, 2008.

———. "God with Everything: Dio Chrysostom." In *God with Everything: The Divine in the Discourse of the First Christian Century*, 20–42. SWBA 2.2. Sheffield: Sheffield Phoenix, 2008.

———. "God with Everything: Paul." In *God with Everything: The Divine in the Discourse of the First Christian Century*, 43–63. SWBA 2.2. Sheffield: Sheffield Phoenix, 2008.

———. "God with Everything: The Wide Compass of Patristic Theological Method." In *God with Everything: The Divine in the Discourse of the First Christian Century*, 228–64. SWBA 2.2. Sheffield: Sheffield Phoenix, 2008.

———. *Has Christianity a Revelation?* LPT. London: SCM, 1964.

———. *Jesus and the Threat of Freedom.* London: SCM, 1987.

———. "Justification: A Critical Examination of Judicial Verdicts in Paul's Literary and Actual Contexts." *CBQ* 74.2 (2012) 298–318. Reprinted in *Order and (Dis)order in the First Christian Century: A General Survey of Attitudes*, 231–54. NovTSup 151. Leiden: Brill, 2013.

———. "'Let Everything be Done Decently and in Order (EUSXHMENON KAI KATA TACIN)' (1 Cor 14.40): Unity, Order and Problems of Diversity. A. Greeks, Romans, Jews." In *Order and (Dis)order in the First Christian Century: A General Survey of Attitudes*, 9–48. NovTSup 151. Leiden: Brill, 2013.

———. "Magic and Scepticism in and around the First Christian Century" (2000/2003). In *Making Sense in (and of) the First Christian Century*, 208–22. JSNTS 197. Sheffield: Sheffield Academic, 2000. Also in T. Klutz, ed. *Magic in the Biblical World: From the Rod of Aaron to the Seal of Solomon*, 86–99. JSNTS 245. London: T. & T. Clark, 2003.

———. *Making Sense in (and of) the First Christian Century.* JSNTS 197. Sheffield: Sheffield Academic, 2000.

———. *A Man for Us and a God for Us.* London: Epworth, 1968.

———. "On Doubting Dichotomies: A Response to Don Cupitt." *Theology* 8.1 (2015) forthcoming.

———. "Our Access to Other Cultures, Past and Present." *The Modern Churchman* 21.1 (1977) 28–42.

———. "Ontological Asymmetry in Philo and Christological Realism in Paul, Hebrews and John. *JTS* NS 41 (1990) 423–40. Reprinted in *Making Sense in (and of) the First Christian Century*, 188–207. JSNTS 197. Sheffield: Sheffield Academic, 2000.

———. *Order and (Dis)order in the First Christian Century: A General Survey of Attitudes.* NovTSup 151. Boston: Brill, 2013.

———. "Order Within: Passions, Divine and Human. A. In the Wider Graeco-Roman World." In *Order and (Dis)order in the First Christian Century: A General Survey of Attitudes*, 83–101. NovTSup 151. Boston: Brill, 2013.

———. "Order Within: Passions, Divine and Human. B. Among Second Temple Jews and the First Christians." In *Order and (Dis)order in the First Christian Century: A General Survey of Attitudes*, 103–20. NovTSup 151. Boston: Brill, 2013.

———. "Persons in Relation." In *Making Sense in (and of) the First Christian Century*, 43–61. JSNTS 197. Sheffield: Sheffield Academic, 2000.

———. "Reconciliation, Theology and Politics." *Modern Theology*, forthcoming.

———. "Revelation, Disagreement and Obscurity." *RS* 21.3 (1986) 219–30.

————. *Strangely Familiar: An Introductory Reader to the First Century, to the Life and Loves, the Hopes and Fears, the Doubts and Certainties, of Pagans, Jews and Christians.* Manchester: Downing, 1985.

————. "Theological Breadth, Interconnection, and Gender: Hildegard, Hadewijch, and Julian Today." *ATR* 86 (2004) 423–50.

————. "Ways of Deriving 'Ought' from 'Is.'" *PQ* 22.4 (1972) 234–47.

————. "Women and Men, Mary, and Woman-Talk." In *God with Everything: The Divine in the Discourse of the First Christian Century*, 174–94. SWBA 2.2. Sheffield: Sheffield Phoenix, 2008.

————."Words and Meanings." In *Doing Things with Words in the First Christian Century*, 57–74. JSNTS 200. Sheffield: Sheffield Academic, 2000.

Drury, John. *Music at Midnight: The Life and Poetry of George Herbert.* New York: Allen Lane, 2013.

Dulles, Avery. *Models of Revelation.* New York: Doubleday, 1983.

Dumsday, Travis. "Divine Hiddenness and the Responsibility Argument: Assessing Schellenberg's Argument against Theism." *Philosopia Christi* 12 (2010) 357–71.

————. "Divine Hiddenness as Divine Mercy." *RS* 48 (2012) 183–98.

————. "Divine Hiddenness, Free-will, and the Victims of Wrongdoing." *Faith and Philosophy* 27 (2010) 423–38.

Dunn, James D. G. *Romans 1–8.* WBC 38a. Dallas: Word, 1988.

Durham, John I. *Exodus.* WBC 3. Nashville: Nelson 1987.

Eaton, John. *The Psalms: An Historical and Spiritual Commentary with an Introduction and New Translation.* London: T. & T. Clark, 2003.

Edwards, Ruth. *Discovering John.* London: SPCK, 2003.

Elliott, J. K. "Extra-Canonical Early Christian Literature." In *The Oxford Bible Commentary*, edited by John Barton and John Muddiman, 1306–30. New York: Oxford University Press, 2001.

Ellis, Fiona. "Insatiable Desire." *Philosophy* 88.344 (2013) 243–66.

Erskine, Noel Leo. "How Do We Know What to Believe? Revelation and Authority." In *Essentials of Christian Theology*, edited by William C. Placher, 33–49. Louisville: Westminster John Knox, 2003.

Esler, Philip F. *Conflict and Identity in Romans: The Social Setting of Paul's Letter.* Minneapolis: Fortress, 2003.

————. *Galatians.* New York: Routledge, 1998.

Evans, C. Stephen. "Can God be Hidden and Evident at the Same Time? Some Kierkgaardian Reflections." *Faith and Philosophy* 23 (2006) 241–53.

Evans, Christopher F. *Resurrection and the New Testament.* SBT 2.12. London: SCM, 1970.

————. *Saint Luke.* TPINTC. Philadelphia: Trinity, 1990.

Evans, Donald D. *The Logic of Self-Involvement: A Philosophical Study of Everyday Language with Special Reference to the Christian Use of Language about God as Creator.* LPT. London: SCM, 1963.

Faber, Roland. "Bodies of the Void: Polyphilia and Theoplicity." In *Apophatic Bodies: Negative Theology, Incarnation, and Relationality*, edited by Chris Boesel and Catherine Keller, 200–23. New York: Fordham University Press, 2010.

Fallbush, Erwin et al., eds. *The Encyclopedia of Christianity.* Grand Rapids: Eerdmans, 2005.

Farrer, Austin. "Revelation." In *Faith and Logic: Oxford Essays in Philosophical Theology,* edited by Basil Mitchell, 84–107. London: Allen & Unwin, 1957.

Farrow, Douglas. "Ascension and Atonement." In *The Theology of Reconciliation,* edited by Colin Gunton, 67–92. New York: T. & T. Clark, 2003.

Feldt, Laura. "Wild and Wondrous Men: Elijah and Elisha in the Hebrew Bible." In *Credible, Incredible: The Miraculous in the Ancient Mediterranean,* edited by Tobias Nicklas and Janet E. Spittler. WUNT 321. Tübingen: Mohr Siebeck, 2013.

Fiddes, Paul S. "The Quest for a Place Which is 'Not-a-Place': The Hiddenness of God and the Presence of God." In *Silence and the Word: Negative Theology and Incarnation,* edited by Oliver Davies and Denys Turner, 35–60. Cambridge: Cambridge University Press, 2002.

———. "Salvation." In *The Oxford Handbook of Systematic Theology,* edited by John Webster et al., 176–96. Oxford: Oxford University Press, 2007.

Finlan, Stephen, and Vladimir Kharlamov, eds. *Theosis: Deification in Christian Theology.* 2 vols. Eugene, OR: Pickwick, 2006.

Flew, Antony, and Alasdair MacIntyre, eds. *New Essays in Philosophical Theology.* LPT. London: SCM, 1955.

———. "Theology and Falsification." In *New Essays in Philosophical Theology,* edited by Antony Flew and Alasdair MacIntyre, 96–99 and 106–8. LPT. London: SCM, 1955.

Forster, E. M. *A Passage to India.* New York: Penguin, 1936.

Foster, Roy. "Anglo-Irish Relations and Northern Ireland: Historical Perspectives." In *Northern Ireland and the Politics of Reconciliation,* edited by Dermot Keogh and Michael H. Haltzel, 13–32. Cambridge: Cambridge University Press, 1993.

Fowl, Stephen E. *Philippians.* Two Horizons New Testament Commentary. Grand Rapids: Eerdmans, 2005.

Fraassen, Bass C. van. "Transcendence of the Ego (The Non-Existent Knight)." In *The Self?,* edited by Galen Strawson, 87–110. Oxford: Blackwell, 2005.

Frend, William H. C. *The Early Church.* London: Hodder & Stoughton, 1965.

Friedland, Jonathan. "Whatever Gerry Adams' Past, Peace Trumps Justice." *The Guardian* (May 4, 2014) 35.

García Martinez, Florentino, and Eibert J. C. Tigchelar. *The Dead Sea Scrolls in English: Study Edition.* 2 vols. Grand Rapids: Eerdmans, 1997–1998.

Gauck, Joachim. "Gerechtigkeit, Versöhnung und Strafe als gesellschaftliche und politische Herausforderung." In *Versöhnung, Strafe and Gerechtigkeit: Das schwere Erbe von Unrechts-Staaten,* edited by Michael Bongardt and Ralf K. Würstenberg, 17–28. Kontexte. Neue Beiträge zur historischen unde systematischen Theologie 40. Göttingen: Ruprecht, 2010.

Gerdes, Kirsten. "Materiality of Metaphor: The Risk of Revelation." In *Revelation: Claremont Studies in the Philosophy of Religion Conference 2012,* edited by Ingolf U. Dalferth and Michael Rodgers, 185–200. RPT 74. Tübingen: Mohr Siebeck, 2014.

Gill, Robin. *Society Shaped by Theology.* Sociological Theology 3. Burlington, VT: Ashgate, 2013.

Gilligan, Carol. *In a Different Voice: Psychological Theory and Women's Development.* Cambridge, MA: Harvard University Press, 1982.

Gorman, Michael J. *Inhabiting the Cruciform God: Kenosis, Justification, and Theosis in Paul's Narrative Soteriology.* Grand Rapids: Eerdmans, 2009.

Gorringe, Timothy J. *Discerning Spirit: A Theology of Revelation*. London: SCM, 1990.
———. *God's Just Vengeance: Crime, Violence, and the Rhetoric of Salvation*. CSIR 9. Cambridge: Cambridge University Press, 1996.
———. "Sacraments." In *The Religion of the Incarnation: Anglican Essays in Commemoration of Lux Mundi*, edited by Robert Morgan, 158–71. Bristol: Bristol Classical, 1989.
———. "The Theological Roots of Judicial Punishment." In *Restorative Justice: Ideas, Values, Debates*, edited by Gerry Johnstone, 160–62. 2nd ed. New York: Routledge, 2011.
Grabbe, Lester L. "Leviticus." In *The Oxford Bible Commentary*, edited by John Barton and John Muddiman, 91–110. New York: Oxford University Press, 2001.
Grant, Robert M. *Greek Apologists of the Second Century*. London: SCM, 1988.
Green, Garrett. *Imagining God: Theology and the Religious Imagination*. New York: Harper & Row, 1989.
Green, Michael. *I Believe in the Holy Spirit*. Revised ed. London: Hodder & Stoughton, 1985.
Grégoire de Nazianze. *Discours 20–23*. Edited and Translated by Justin Mossay. SC 270. Paris: Cerf, 1980.
———. *Discours 27–31*. Edited and Translated by Paul Gallay. SC 250. Paris: Cerf, 1978.
———. *Discours 32–37*. Edited and Translated by Paul Gallay. SC 318. Paris: Cerf, 1985.
———. *Discours 38–41*. Edited by Claudio Moreschini. Translated by Paul Gallay. SC 358. Paris: Cerf, 1990.
Grégoire de Nysse. *Discours Catéchétique*. Edited and Translated by Raymond Winling. SC 453. Paris: Cerf, 2000.
———. *Homilies on the Song of Songs*. Edited and Translated by Richard A. Norris Jr. Atlanta: SBL, 2012.
———. *La Vie de Moïse*. Edited and Translated by Jean Danielou. SC 1b. Paris: Cerf, 1955.
Grenz, Stanley J. "How Do We Know What to Believe? Revelation and Authority." In *Essentials of Christian Theology*, edited by William C. Placher, 11–33. Louisville: Westminster John Knox, 2003.
Grice, H. Paul. *Studies in the Way of Words*. Cambridge, MA: Harvard University Press, 1989.
Griffiths, A. Phillips, ed. *Knowledge and Belief*. Oxford: Oxford University Press, 1967.
Grogan, Geoffrey W. *Psalms*. Two Horizons Old Testament Commentary. Grand Rapids: Eerdmans, 2008.
Gunton, Colin. *A Brief Theology of Revelation*. Edinburgh: T. & T. Clark, 1995.
———, ed. *Cambridge Companion to Christian Doctrine*. Cambridge: Cambridge University Press, 1997.
———. "Introduction." In *The Theology of Reconciliation*, edited by Colin Gunton, 1–11. New York: T. & T. Clark, 2003.
———, ed. *The Theology of Reconciliation*. New York: T. & T. Clark, 2003.
———. "Towards a Theology of Reconciliation." In *The Theology of Reconciliation*, edited by Colin Gunton, 167–74. New York: T. & T. Clark, 2003.
Guttierez, Gustavo. *A Theology of Liberation: History, Politics, and Liberation*. Translated by Caridad Inda and John Eagleson. Maryknoll, NY: Orbis, 1973.
Hägg, Henny Fiskå. *Clement of Alexandria and the Beginnings of Christian Apophaticism*. New York: Oxford University Press, 2006.

Hamlyn, David W. *The Theory of Knowledge*. New York: Macmillan, 1970.

Harris, Murray J. *The Second Epistle to the Corinthians: A Commentary on the Greek Text*. NICGT. Grand Rapids: Eerdmans, 2005.

Haught, John F. *Mystery and Promise: A Theology of Revelation*. Collegeville, MN: Michael Glazier, 1993.

Hawthorne, Gerald F. *Philippians*. WBC 43. Dallas: Word, 1983.

Hazlett, Ian, ed. *Early Christianity: Origins and Evolution. In Honour of W. H. C. Frend*. London: SCM, 1991.

Heath, Jane. M. F. *Paul's Visual Piety: The Metamorphosis of the Beholder*. Oxford: Oxford University Press, 2013.

Helm, Paul. *The Divine Revelation*. London: Marshall, Morgan and Scott, 1982.

Henry, Douglas V. "Reasonable Doubt and Reasonable Nonbelief." *Faith and Philosophy* 25 (2008) 276–89.

Herbert, George. For poems, see Slater, Ann Pasternack.

Héring, Jean. *La Première Épitre de Saint Paul aux Corinthiens*. 2nd ed. CNT 7. Paris: Delachaux et Niestlé, 1959.

———. *La Seconde Épitre de Saint Paul aux Corinthiens*. CNT 8. Paris: Delachaux et Niestlé, 1958.

Heschel, Abraham J. *Man Is Not Alone: A Philosophy of Religion*. New York: Farrar, Straus and Giroux, 1979.

———. *The Prophets*. New York: Harper and Row, 1962.

Higton, Mike. *Christian Doctrine*. London: SCM, 2008.

Hodgson, Leonard. *The Doctrine of the Trinity*. London: Nisbet, 1943.

Holloday, William L. *Jeremiah 2*. Hermeneia. Minneapolis: Fortress, 1998.

Hoppe, Thomas. "Erinnerung, Gerechtigkeit und Versöhnung: Zur Aufgabe eines angemessenen Umgangs mit belasteter Vergangenheiteine sozialethische Perspektiv." In *Versöhnung, Strafe and Gerechtigkeit: Das schwere Erbe von Unrechts-Staaten*, edited by Michael Bongardt and Ralf K. Würstenberg, 29–53. Kontexte. Neue Beiträge zur historischen unde systematischen Theologie 40. Göttingen: Ruprecht, 2010.

Horowitz, Donald L. "Conflict and Incentives to Political Accommodation." In *Northern Ireland and the Politics of Reconciliation*, edited by Dermot Keogh and Michael H. Haltzel, 173–88. Cambridge: Cambridge University Press, 1993.

Hossenfelder, Malte. *Die Philosophie der Antike, 3: Stoa, Epicureismus und Skepsis*. 2nd ed. Munich: Beck, 1995.

Houghton, Josephine. "The Priest as 'Defender of the Poor.'" *Theology* 117.3 (2014) 198–202.

Huang, Yan. *Pragmatics*. Oxford: Oxford University Press, 2007.

Hudson, Richard A. *Sociolinguistics*. 2nd ed. Cambridge: Cambridge University Press, 2001.

Hughes, Murray J. *The Second Epistle to the Corinthians: A Commentary on the Greek Text*. NIGTC. Grand Rapids: Eerdmans, 2005.

Hurtado, Larry W. *Lord Jesus Christ: Devotion to Jesus in Earliest Christianity*. Grand Rapids: Eerdmans, 2003.

Huyssteen, J. Wentzel van. *Duel or Duet? Theology and Science in a Postmodern World*. London: SCM, 1998.

Hyatt, J. Philip. *Commentary on Exodus*. NCB. London: Oliphants, 1971.

Jackson, Bernard S. *Studies in the Semiotics of Biblical Law*. JSOTS 314. Sheffield: Sheffield Academic, 2000.

Jaeger, Werner et al. *Gregorii Nyssenii Opera*. 13 vols. Leiden: Brill, 1960.

Jantzen, Grace M. *Becoming Divine: Towards a Feminist Philosophy of Religion*. Manchester: Manchester University Press, 1998.

———. *Power, Gender and Christian Mysticism*. Cambridge: Cambridge University Press, 1995.

Jenkins, David E. *God, Jesus and Life in the Spirit*. London: SCM, 1985.

Jenson, Robert W. "Reconciliation in God." In *The Theology of Reconciliation*, edited by Colin Gunton, 159–74. New York: T. & T. Clark, 2003.

Jeon, Jaeyoung. "Scribal Rivalry between Zadokites and Levites in the Persian Period: The Story of Korach and 1 & 2 Chronicles." Unpublished paper, Seminar on Social Sciences in Biblical Studies, Manchester-Sheffield-Lausanne, April 2014.

Jewett, Robert. *Romans*. Hermeneia. Minneapolis: Fortress, 2007.

Johnstone, Gerry. *Restorative Justice: Ideas, Values, Debates*. 2nd ed. New York: Routledge, 2011.

Kadri, Sadakat. *Heaven on Earth: A Journey through Sharia Law*. London: Vintage, 2013.

Kalas, J. Ellsworth. *The Parables of Paul: The Master of the Metaphor*. Nashville: Abingdon, 2015.

Kang-Kul Cho, Paul. "The Integrity of Job 1 and 42:11–17." *CBQ* 76.2 (2014) 230–51.

Kee, Howard C. "The Testaments of the Twelve Patriarchs." In *The Old Testament Pseudepigrapha*, edited by James H. Charlesworth, 755–828. 2 vols. London: Darton, Longman and Todd, 1983.

Keener, Craig S. *1–2 Corinthians*. NCB. Cambridge: Cambridge University Press, 2005.

———. *The Gospel of John: A Commentary*. 2 vols. Peabody, MA: Hendrickson, 2003.

Keller, Catherine. "The Cloud of the Impossible: Embodiment and Apophasis." In *Apophatic Bodies: Negative Theology, Incarnation, and Relationality*, edited by Chris Boesel and Catherine Keller, 25–44. New York: Fordham University Press, 2010.

Kennedy, Philip. *A Modern Introduction to Theology: New Questions for Old Beliefs*. New York: Tauris, 2006.

Kenny, Anthony. *The Unknown God: Agnostic Essays*. New York: Continuum, 2004.

Keogh, Dermot, and Michael H. Haltzel, eds. *Northern Ireland and the Politics of Reconciliation*. Cambridge: Cambridge University Press, 1993.

Kitamori, Kazu. *Theology of the Pain of God*. Translated by M. E. Bratcher. London: SCM, 1966.

Knox, John. *The Death of Christ: The Cross in New Testament History and Faith*. London: Collins, 1959.

Koehler, Ludwig. *Old Testament Theology*. Translated by A. S. Todd. London: Lutterworth, 1957.

Kohl, Katrin. *Metapher*. Sammlung Metzler Bd. 352. Stuttgart: Metzler, 2007.

Kramer, Werner. *Christ, Lord, Son of God*. Translated by Brian Hardy. SBT 50. London: SCM, 1966.

Kreider, Alan. "*Ressourcement* and Mission." *ATR* 96.2 (2014) 239–62.

Kurek-Chomycz, Dominica A. "The Scent of (Mediated) Revelation? Some Remarks on Fanero/w with a Particular Focus on 2 Corinthians." In *Theologizing in the Corinthian Conflict: Studies in the Exegesis and Theology of 2 Corinthians*, edited by Raimund Bieringer et al., 69–107. BiTS 16. Leuven: Peeters, 2013.

LaCugna, Catherine M. *God for Us: The Trinity and Christian Life*. New York: HarperCollins, 1991.

Lakoff, George, and Mark Johnson. *Metaphors We Live By*. Chicago: University of Chicago Press, 1980.

Lambrecht, Jan. *Second Corinthians*. Sacra Pagina 8. Collegeville: Liturgical, 1999.

Levelt, Willem J. M. et al. "A Theory of Lexical Access in Speech Production." *Behavioural and Brain Sciences* 22 (1991) 1–75.

Lewis, C. S. *A Grief Observed*. London: Faber, 1961.

———. *Till We have Faces: A Myth Retold*. London: Bles, 1956.

Liddell, Henry George, and Robert Scott, eds. *A Greek-English Lexicon*. Oxford: Clarendon, 1940.

Lieu, Judith M. *I, II & III John: A Commentary*. Louisville: Westminster John Knox, 2008.

Limburg, James. *Psalms*. Westminster Bible Companion. Louisville: Westminster John Knox, 2000.

Lincoln, Andrew T. *The Gospel according to St. John*. BNTC. Peabody, MA: 2005.

Litwa, M. David. *We Are Being Transformed: Deification in Paul's Soteriology*. BZNW 187. Berlin: de Gruyter, 2012.

Luibhead, Colm, ed. Translated by Paul Rorem. *Pseudo-Dionysius: The Complete Works*. CWS. New York: Paulist, 1987.

Luz, Ulrich. *Matthew 8–20: A Commentary*. Edited by Helmut Koester. Translated by James E. Crouch. Hermeneia. Minneapolis, 2001.

Lycan, William C. *Philosophy of Language: A Contemporary Introduction*. New York: Routledge, 2000.

MacDonald, Nathan, and Izaak J. de Hulster, eds. *Divine Presence and Absence in Exilic and Post-Exilic Judaism: Studies of the Sofja Kolalevskaja Research Group on Early Jewish Monotheism*. FAT 2.61. Tübingen: Mohr Siebeck, 2013.

———. "The Spirit of YHWH: An Overlooked Conceptualization of Divine Presence in the Persian Period." In *Divine Presence and Absence in Exilic and Post-Exilic Judaism: Studies of the Sofja Kolalevskaja Research Group on Early Jewish Monotheism*, edited by Nathan MacDonald and Izaak J. de Hulster, 95–119. FAT 2.61. Tübingen: Mohr Siebeck, 2013.

MacDonald, William, et al. *The New Catholic Encyclopaedia*. 14 vols. New York: McGraw-Hill, 1967.

Macmurray, John. *Persons in Relation: The Form of the Personal*. London: Faber, 1957.

———. *The Self as Agent: The Form of the Personal*. London: Faber, 1957.

Macquarrie, John. *Principles of Christian Theology*. London: SCM, 1966.

Martin, Ralph P. *2 Corinthians*. WBC 40. Dallas: Word, 1986.

Mays, A. D. H. *Deuteronomy*. NCB. Grand Rapids: Eerdmans, 1981.

McBrayer, Justin P., and Philip Swenson. "Scepticism about the Argument from Divine Hiddenness." *RS* 48 (2012) 129–50.

McConville, J. Gordon. "Forgiveness as Private and Public Act: A Reading of the Biblical Joseph Narrative." *CBQ* 75.4 (2013) 635–48.

McCreary, Mark L. "Schellenberg on Divine Hiddenness and Religious Scepticism." *RS* 46 (2010) 207–55.

McDonald, H. D. *Ideas of Revelation*. London: MacMillan, 1959.

———. *Theories of Revelation*. London: Allen & Unwin, 1963.

McDonald, James I. H. *The Resurrection: Narrative and Belief*. London: SPCK, 1989.

McEwan, Ian. *Atonement*. London: Cape, 2001.

McFall, Michael T. "Can We have a Friend in Jesus? An Aristotelian Analysis." *Philosophia Christi* 14 (2012) 315–34.

McGinn, Bernard. "The Hidden God in Luther and Some Mystics." In *Silence and the Word: Negative Theology and Incarnation*, edited by Oliver Davies and Denys Turner, 94–114. Cambridge: Cambridge University Press, 2002.

McGrath, Alister. *Christian Theology: An Introduction*. 5th ed. Chichester: Wiley-Blackwell, 2011.

McGregor, Lorna. "Reconciliation: Where is the Law?" In *Law and the Politics of Reconciliation*, edited by Scott Veitch, 94–128. Burlington, VT: Ashgate, 2006.

MacGregor, Neil, and Erika Langmuir. *Seeing Salvation: Images of Christ in Art*. London: BBC Worldwide, 2000.

MacIntyre, Alasdair. "God and the Theologians." *Encounter* 120 (Sept. 1963) 3–10.

McIntyre, John. "Frontiers of Meaning." *SJT* 10.2 (1957) 122–39.

———. *The Christian Doctrine of History*. Edinburgh: Oliver and Boyd, 1957.

———. *The Death of Christ*. London: Collins, 1959.

———. *The Shape of Soteriology*. Edinburgh: T. & T. Clark, 1981.

McKelvey, R. Jack. *Pioneer and Priest: Jesus Christ in the Epistle to the Hebrews*. Eugene, OR: Pickwick, 2013.

Mbabazi, Isaac K. *The Significance of Interpersonal Forgiveness in the Gospel of Matthew*. Eugene, OR: Wipf and Stock, 2013.

Micklem, Nathaniel. *A Religion for Agnostics*. London: SCM, 1965.

Middlemas, Jill. "Divine Presence in Absence: Aniconism and Multiple Imaging in the Prophets." In *Divine Presence and Absence in Exilic and Post-Exilic Judaism: Studies of the Sofja Kolalevskaja Research Group on Early Jewish Monotheism*, edited by Nathan MacDonald and Izaak J. de Hulster, 183–211. FAT 2.61. Tübingen: Mohr Siebeck, 2013.

Millbank, John. *The Word Made Strange: Theology, Language, Culture*. Oxford: Blackwell, 1997.

Miller, Kerby A. "Revising Revisionism: Comments and Reflections." In *Northern Ireland and the Politics of Reconciliation*, edited by Dermot Keogh and Michael H. Haltzel, 52–61. Cambridge: Cambridge University Press, 1993.

Mitchell, Basil, ed. *Faith and Logic: Oxford Essays in Philosophical Theology*. London: Allen & Unwin, 1957.

Mitchell, Margaret M. *Paul and the Politics of Reconciliation: An Exegetical Investigation of the Language and Composition of 1 Corinthians*. Tübingen: Mohr Siebeck, 1991.

Mkenda, Festo. "Language, Politics, and Religious Dialogue." In *Reconciliation, Justice and Peace: The Second African Synod*, edited by Agbonkhianmeghe E. Orobator, 37–47. Maryknoll, NY: Orbis, 2011.

Moloney, Francis J. *The Gospel of John*. Sacra Pagina. Collegeville, MN: Liturgical, 1999.

Moltmann, Jürgen. *The Way of Jesus Christ: Christology in Messianic Dimensions*. Translated by Margaret Kohl. London: SCM, 1990.

Montenbruck, Axel. "Versöhnung, Strafe und Gerechtigkeit in juristischer Perspektiv." In *Versöhnung, Strafe and Gerechtigkeit: Das schwere Erbe von Unrechts-Staaten*, edited by Michael Bongardt and Ralf K. Würstenberg, 99–126. Kontexte. Neue Beiträge zur historischen unde systematischen Theologie 40. Göttingen: Ruprecht, 2010.

Moon, Clare. "Reconciliation as Therapy and Compensation: A Critical Analysis." In *Law and the Politics of Reconciliation*, edited by Scott Veitch, 163–83. Burlington, VT: Ashgate, 2006.

Morgan, Robert, ed. *The Religion of the Incarnation: Anglican Essays in Commemoration of Lux Mundi.* Bristol: Bristol Classical, 1989.

Moseley, Daniel J. R. S. "'Parables' and 'Polyphony': The Resonance of Music as Witness in the Theology of Karl Barth and Dietrich Bonhoeffer." In *Resonant Witness: Conversations between Music and Theology*, edited by Jeremy S. Begbie and Stephen R. Guthrie, 240–70. Grand Rapids: Eerdmans, 2011.

Motha, Stewart. "Reconciliation as Domination." In *Law and the Politics of Reconciliation*, edited by Scott Veitch, 69–91. Burlington, VT: Ashgate, 2006.

Murariu, Cosmin-Constantin. "Impermissibility or Impossibility? A Re-Examination of 2 Cor 12:4." In *Theologizing in the Corinthian Conflict: Studies in the Exegesis and Theology of 2 Corinthians*, edited by Raimund Bieringer et al., 379–98. BiTS 16. Leuven: Peeters, 2013.

Murphy, Roland E. *Proverbs.* WBC 22. Nashville: Thomas Nelson, 1998.

Nasr, Seyyed Hussain. *Ideals and Realities of Islam.* London: Allen and Unwin, 1966.

Newman, John Henry. *An Essay in Aid of a Grammar of Assent.* New York: Doubleday, 1955.

Nicholls, William. *Revelation in Christ.* London: SCM, 1958.

Nicholson, Reynold A. *The Mystics of Islam.* London: Bell, 1915.

Niebuhr, H. Richard. *The Meaning of Revelation.* New York: Macmillan, 1941.

Norelli, Enrico, ed. *Recueils normatifs et canons dans l'Antiquité: Actes du colloque organisé dans le cadre du programme plurifacultaire.* La Bible à la croisées des savoirs *de l'Université de Genève 11-12 avril 2002.* Lausanne: Éditions du Zèbre, 2004.

North, Wendy E. S. "'Lord, If You had Been Here . . .' (John 11.21): The Absence of Jesus and Strategies of Consolation in the Fourth Gospel." *JSNT* 36.1 (2013) 17–38.

Nygren, Anders. *Agape and Eros.* Translated by A. G. Herbert. London: SPCK, 1953.

Oakes, Peter. *Reading Romans in Pompeii: Paul's Letter at Ground Level.* Minneapolis: Fortress, 2009.

O'Collins, Gerald. *Foundations of Theology.* Chicago: Loyola University Press, 1971.

Okure, Teresa. "Church-Family of God: The Place of God's Reconciliation, Justice, and Peace." In *Reconciliation, Justice and Peace: The Second African Synod*, edited by Agbonkhianmeghe E. Orobator, 13–24. Maryknoll, NY: Orbis, 2011.

Orobator, Agbonkhianmeghe E., ed. *Reconciliation, Justice and Peace: The Second African Synod.* Maryknoll, NY: Orbis, 2011.

Osborne, Eric F. *The Beginnings of Christian Philosophy.* Cambridge: Cambridge University Press, 1981.

———. *The Philosophy of Clement of Alexandria.* Cambridge: Cambridge University Press, 1957.

Painter, John. *1, 2, and 3 John.* Sacra Pagina. Collegeville, MN: Liturgical, 2008.

Patterson, Sue. "Between Women and Men." In *The Theology of Reconciliation*, edited by Colin Gunton, 125–40. New York: T. & T. Clark, 2003.

Pattison, George. *Art, Modernity and Faith.* London: SCM, 1991.

Peacocke, Arthur. *Paths from Science towards God: The End of All Our Exploring.* New York: One World, 2001.

————. *Theology for a Scientific Age: Being and Becoming—Natural, Divine and Human.* 2nd ed. London: SCM, 1993.

Pears, Tim. "Why My Father Will Always be My Hero." *The Guardian*, April 12, 2014, page 5.

Perkins, Pheme. *First Corinthians.* Paideia. Grand Rapids: Baker Academic, 2012.

————. *Resurrection: New Testament Witness and Contemporary Reflection.* New York: Doubleday, 1984.

Perrson, Ingmar. "Self-Doubt: Why We are Not Identical to Things of Any Kind." In *The Self?*, edited by Galen Strawson, 26–44. Oxford: Blackwell, 2005.

Philpott, Daniel. *Just and Unjust Peace: An Ethic of Political Reconciliation.* Oxford: Oxford University Press, 2012.

Pinker, Steven. *The Blank Slate: The Modern Denial of Human Nature.* New York: Penguin, 2002.

Pinnock, Charles H. *Most Moved Mover: A Theology of God's Openness.* Grand Rapids: Baker, 2001.

Placher, William C. *Essentials of Christian Theology.* Louisville: Westminster John Knox, 2003.

Plummer, Alfred. *A Critical and Exegetical Commentary on the First Epistle of St. Paul to the Corinthians.* ICC. Edinburgh: T. & T. Clark, 1911.

Polkinghorne, John. *Exploring Reality: The Intertwining of Science and Religion.* London: SPCK, 1989.

————. *Science and the Trinity: The Christian Encounter with Reality.* London: SPCK, 2004.

Porter, Stanley E., ed. *Handbook of Classical Rhetoric in the Hellenistic Period 330 BC–AD 400.* Leiden: Brill, 1979.

————, and D. A. Carson, eds. *Discourse Analysis.* JSNTS 160. Sheffield Academic, 1995.

————. and Thomas H. Olbricht, eds. *The Rhetorical Analysis of Scripture: Essays from the 1995 London Conference.* JSNTS 166. Sheffield: Sheffield Academic, 1997.

Poston, Ted, and Trent Dougherty. "Divine Hiddenness and the Nature of Belief." *RS* 43 (2007) 138–98.

Powers, Daniel G. *Salvation through Participation: An Examination of the Notion of the Believer's Corporate Unity with Christ in Early Christian Soteriology.* Leuven: Peeters, 2001.

Quash, Ben. "Revelation." In *The Oxford Handbook of Systematic Theology*, edited by John Webster et al., 325–44. Oxford: Oxford University Press, 2007.

Quine, William V. O. *From a Logical Point of View.* Cambridge, MA: Harvard University Press, 1953.

————. *Word and Object.* Cambridge, MA: MIT Press, 1960.

Rae, Murray. "A Remanant People: The Ecclesia as Sign of Reconciliation." In *The Theology of Reconciliation*, edited by Colin Gunton, 93–108. New York: T. & T. Clark, 2003.

Ramsey, Ian T. *Religious Language.* London: SCM, 1957.

Reventlow, Henning Graf. *The Authority of the Bible and the Rise of the Modern World.* Translated by John Bowden. London: SCM, 1984.

Richard of St. Victor. *Twelve Patriarchs: Mystical Ark. Book 3 of the Trinity.* Edited and translated by Grover A. Zinn. New York: Paulist, 1979.

Rinke, Stefan. "Die Gegenheit der Vergangenheit: Chile in den 1990er-Jahren." In *Versöhnung, Strafe and Gerechtigkeit: Das schwere Erbe von Unrechts-Staaten*, edited by Michael Bongardt and Ralf K. Würstenberg, 149–67. Kontexte. Neue Beiträge zur historischen unde systematischen Theologie 40. Göttingen: Ruprecht, 2010.

Ritschl, Albrecht. *The Christian Doctrine of Justification and Reconciliation*. Edited and translated by H. R. Macintosh and A. B. Macauley. Reprint. Clifton, NJ: Reference, 1988.

Rodd, C. S. "Psalms." In *The Oxford Bible Commentary*, edited by John Barton and John Muddiman, 355–404. New York: Oxford University Press, 2001.

Rodgers, Michael. "Finding Meaning in God's Actions: A Response to William J. Abraham." In *Revelation: Claremont Studies in the Philosophy of Religion Conference 2012*, edited by Ingolf U. Dalferth and Michael Rodgers, 47–50. RPT 74. Tübingen: Mohr Siebeck, 2014.

Roetzel, Calvin J. *2 Corinthians*. ANTC. Nashville: Abingdon, 2007.

Rogers, Eugene F. "Same-Sex Marriage as an Ascetic Practice in the Light of Romans 1 and Ephesians 5." *Modern Believing* 55.2 (2014) 115–25.

Rosen, Harold. *Language and Class: A Critical Look at the Theories of Basil Bernstein*. 3rd ed. Bristol: Falling Wall, 1974.

Rowland, Christopher. *The Open Heaven: A Study of Apocalyptic in Judaism and Early Christianity*. London: SPCK, 1982.

Ruddock, Edgar, ed. *Pray with Us*. London: Us (erstwhile USPG). 13th April–16th August) 2014.

Ryle, Gilbert. *The Concept of Mind*. London: Hutchinson, 1949. Repr. Harmondsworth: Penguin, 1963.

Sanders, Ed P. et al., eds. *Jewish and Christian Self-Definition*. 3 volumes. Philadelphia: Fortress, 1980–1982.

Sarot, Marcel. *God, Passibility and Corporeality*. Kampen: Kok Pharos, 1992.

Sauter, Gerhard. "Reconciliation." In *The Encyclopedia of Christianity*, edited by Erwin Fallbush et al., 504–5. Grand Rapids: Eerdmans, 2005.

Schaap, Andrew. "The Time of Reconciliation and the Space of Politics." In *Law and the Politics of Reconciliation*, edited by Scott Veitch, 9–31. Burlington, VT: Ashgate, 2006.

Schäfer, Peter. *The Origins of Jewish Mysticism*. Tübingen: Mohr Siebeck, 2009.

Scharf, Caleb. *Gravity's Engines: The Other Side of Black Holes*. New York: Penguin, 2013.

Schechtman, Marya. "Self-Expression and Self-Control." In *The Self?*, edited by Galen Strawson, 45–62. Oxford: Blackwell, 2005.

Schellenberg, John L. *Divine Hiddenness and Human Reason*. Ithaca, NY: Cornell University Press, 1993.

———. "The Hiddenness Argument Revisited. I." *RS* 41 (2005) 201–15.

———. "The Hiddenness Argument Revisited. II." *RS* 41 (2005) 287–303.

———. "The Hiddenness Problem and the Problem of Evil." *Faith and Philosophy* 27 (2010) 46–50.

———. "How to be an Atheist and a Sceptic, Too: Response to McCreary." *RS* 46 (2010) 227–32.

———. "On Reasonable Nonbelief and Perfect Love: Replies to Henry and Lehe." *Faith and Philosophy* 22 (2005) 330–42.

————. *Prolegomena to a Philosophy of Religion.* Ithaca, NY: Cornell University Press, 2005.

————. "Religious Experience and Religious Diversity: A Reply to Alston." *RS* 30 (1994) 151–59.

————. "Response to Tucker on Hiddenness." *RS* 44 (2008) 289–93.

————. "On Unnecessarily Darkening the Glass: A Reply to Poston and Dougherty." *RS* 43 (2007) 199–204.

————. "What the Hiddenness of God Reveals: A Collaborative Discussion." In *Divine Hiddenness and Human Reason,* edited by John L. Schellenberg, 33–61. Ithaca, NY: Cornell University Press, 1993.

————. *The Wisdom to Doubt: A Justification for Religious Scepticism.* Ithaca, NY: Cornell University Press, 2007.

Schenker, Adrian. *Versöhnung und Widerstand: Bibeltheologische Untersuchung zum Strafen Gottes und der Menschen, besonders im Lichte von Exodus 21–22.* SBS 139. Stuttgart: Katolisches Bibelwerk, 1990.

Schoedel, William R. *Ignatius of Antioch.* Hermeneia. Philadelphia: Fortress, 1985.

Schrage, Wolfgang. *Der erst Brief an die Korinther.* 4 vols. EKK. Zürich and NeukirchenerVluyn: Benziger and Neukirchener, 1999–.

Schreiter, Robert J. *The Ministry of Reconciliation: Spirituality and Strategies.* Maryknoll, NY: Orbis, 1998.

Schwöbel, Christoph, and Colin Gunton, eds. *Persons Divine and Human: Kings College Essays in Theological Anthropology.* Edinburgh: T. & T. Clark, 1991.

————."Reconciliation: From Biblical Observations to Dogmatic Reconstruction." In *The Theology of Reconciliation,* edited by Colin Gunton, 13–38. New York: T. & T. Clark, 2003.

Scruton, Roger. *The Face of God.* New York: Continuum, 2012.

Scutton, Anastasia. "'The Truth Will Set You Free': Salvation as Revelation." In *The Gospel of John and Christian Theology,* edited by Richard Bauckham and Carl Mosser, 359–68. Grand Rapids: Eerdmans, 2008.

Second Vatican Council. *Dei Verbum. Dogmatic Constitution on Divine Revelation* (Promulgated 1965). http://www.vatican.va/archive/hist_councils/ii_vatican_council/documents/vat-ii_const_19651118_dei-verbum_en.html.

Shepherd, Nan. *The Living Mountain: A Celebration of the Cairngorm Mountains of Scotland.* New York: Canongate, 2008.

Silva, Moisés. *Philippians.* 2nd ed. Grand Rapids: Baker, 2005.

Slater, Ann Pasternak, ed. *George Herbert: The Complete English Works.* Everyman's Library 204. London: Random House, 1995.

Smalley, Stephen S. *1, 2, 3 John.* WBC. Waco, TX: Word, 1984.

Snyder, Daniel H., and Paul K. Moser, eds. *Divine Hiddenness: New Essays.* Cambridge: Cambridge University Press, 2002.

Soards, Marion. *1 Corinthians.* NIBC. Peabody, MA: Henrickson, 1999.

Sorabji, Richard. "Soul and Self in Ancient Philosophy." In *From Soul to Self,* edited by M. James C. Crabbe, 8–32. New York: Routledge, 1999.

Soskice, Janet Martin. "The Gift of the Name: Moses and the Burning Bush." In *Silence and the Word: Negative Theology and Incarnation,* edited by Oliver Davies and Denys Turner, 61–75. Cambridge: Cambridge University Press, 2002.

————. *Metaphor and Religious Language.* Oxford: Clarendon, 1985.

Starr, James M. *Sharers in the Divine Nature: 2 Peter 1:4 in its Hellenistic Context.* CB.NTS 33. Stockholm: Almqvist & Wiksell, 2000.

Sterling, Gregory E. *Historiography and Self-Definition: Josephos, Luke–Acts & Apologetic Historiography.* Leiden: Brill, 1992.

Stewart, R. L. "Reconciliation." In *The New Catholic Encyclopaedia,* edited by William MacDonald et al., 129–30. 14 vols. New York: McGraw-Hill, 1967.

Still, Todd D. "Christos as Pistos: The Faithfulness of Jesus in the Epistle to the Hebrews." *CBQ* 69 (2007) 746–55.

Strawson, Galen. "Against Narrativity." In *The Self?,* edited by Galen Strawson, 63–86. Oxford: Blackwell, 2005.

———. *The Self?* Oxford: Blackwell, 2005.

Strawson, Peter F. *Individuals: An Essay in Descriptive Metaphysics.* London: Methuen, 1959.

Sumney, Jerry L. *Philippians: A Greek Student's Intermediate Reader.* Peabody, MA: Hendrickson, 2007.

Surin, Kenneth. *Theology and the Problem of Evil.* Oxford: Blackwell, 1986.

Taliaferro, Charles. *Contemporary Philosophy of Religion.* Oxford: Blackwell, 1988.

Tanner, Kathryn. *Christ the Key.* Cambridge: Cambridge University Press, 2010.

———. *Economy of Grace.* Minneapolis: Fortress, 2005.

———. "Is Capitalism a Belief System?" *ATR* 92.4 (2010) 617–35.

———. "Is God in Charge? Creation and Providence." In *Essentials of Christian Theology,* edited by William C. Placher, 116–31. Louisville: Westminster John Knox, 2003.

———. "Jesus Christ." In *Cambridge Companion to Christian Doctrine,* edited by Colin Gunton, 245–72. Cambridge: Cambridge University Press, 1997.

———. *Jesus, Humanity, and the Trinity: A Brief Systematic Theology.* Minneapolis: Fortress, 2001.

———. *Theories of Culture: A New Agenda for Theology.* Minneapolis: Fortress, 1997.

Tatarnic, Martha Smith. "Whoever Comes to Me: Open Table, Missional Church." *ATR* 96:2 (2014) 287–304.

Taylor, Charles. *Sources of the Self: The Making of Modern Identity.* Cambridge: Cambridge University Press, 1989.

Taylor, John V. *The Go-Between God: The Holy Spirit and the Christian Mission.* London: SCM, 1972.

Teresa of Avila, Saint. *Complete Works of St. Theresa of Jesus.* Edited and translated by E. Allison Peers. London: Sheed and Ward, 1946.

Terrien, Samuel. *The Elusive Presence: Towards a New Biblical Theology.* Eugene, OR: Wipf and Stock, 2000.

———. *The Psalms. Strophic Structure and Theological Commentary.* Grand Rapids: Eerdmans, 2003.

Thatcher, Adrian. *Truly a Person, Truly God: A Post-Mythical View of Jesus.* London: SPCK, 1990.

Thomas, David, and Douglas Pratt. "The Presence of Faith: A Century of Anglican Engagement with World Religions." *ATR* 96 (Winter 2014).

Thomas, R. S. *Counterpoint.* Newcastle-upon-Tyne: Bloodaxe, 1990. Now in *Collected Later Poems 1988–2000.* Newcastle-upon-Tyne: Bloodaxe, 2004.

———. *Experimenting with an Amen.* London: Macmillan, 1986.

———. *Later Poems, 1972–1982.* London: Macmillan, 1983.

Thompson, Francis. "The Kingdom of God: 'In No Strange Land.'" In *The Oxford Book of Christian Verse*, edited by Lord David Cecil, 516. Oxford: Clarendon, 1940.

Thrall, Margaret E. *A Critical and Exegetical Commentary on the Second Epistle to the Corinthians*. Volume 1 of *Introduction and Commentary on II Corinthians I-VII*. ICC. London: T. & T. Clark, 1994.

Tillich, Paul. *Systematic Theology*. 3 Vols. Chicago: Chicago University Press, 1951–63.

Toit, H. Louise den. "Feminism and the Ethics of Reconciliation." In *Law and the Politics of Reconciliation*, edited by Scott Veitch, 185–213. Burlington, VT: Ashgate, 2006.

Topping, Richard R. *Revelation, Scripture, and Church*. Aldershot: Ashgate, 2007.

Torrance, Alan J. *Persons in Communion: Trinitarian Description and Human Participation*. Edinburgh: T. & T. Clark, 1996.

Towey, Anthony. *An Introduction to Christian Theology: Biblical, Classical, Contemporary*. New York: Bloomsbury, 2013.

Tracy, David. *The Analogical Imagination: Christian Theology and the Culture of Pluralism*. New York: Crossroad, 1981.

Traxler, Matthew J. *Introduction to Psycholinguistics: Understanding Language Science*. Oxford: Blackwell, 2012.

Trigg, Joseph Wilson. *Origen: The Bible and Philosophy in the Third Century*. Atlanta: John Knox, 1983.

Tucker, Chris. "Divine Hiddenness and the Value of Divine-Creature Relationships." *RS* 44 (2008) 269–87.

Tuckett, Christopher M. "'What is New Testament Study?' The New Testament and Early Christianity." *NTS* 60.2 (2014) 157–84.

Tudge, Colin. *Genes are Not Selfish and People are Nice: A Challenge to the Dangerous Ideas that Dominate Our Lives*. Edinburgh: Floris, 2013.

Turcescu, Lucian. "'Person' versus 'Individual,' and Other Modern Misreadings of Gregory of Nyssa." In *Rethinking Gregory of Nyssa*, edited by Sarah Coakley, 97–131. Oxford: Blackwell, 2003.

Turner, Denys. "Apophaticism, Idolatry and the Claims of Reason." In *Silence and the Word: Negative Theology and Incarnation*, edited by Oliver Davies and Denys Turner, 11–34. Cambridge: Cambridge University Press, 2002.

Tutu, Desmond. *No Future Without Forgiveness*. London: Rider, 1999.

van Inwagen, Peter. "The Self: The Increduous Stare Articulated." In *The Self?*, edited by Galen Strawson, 111–24. Oxford: Blackwell, 2005.

van Kooten, George H. *Cosmic Christology in Paul and in the Pauline School: Colossians and Ephesians in the Context of Graeco-Roman Cosmology*. WUNT 2.171. Tübingen: Mohr Siebeck, 2003.

———. *Paul's Anthropology in Context: The Image of God, Assimilation to God, and Tripartite Man in Ancient Judaism, Ancient Philosophy and Early Christianity*. WUNT 232. Tübingen: Mohr Siebeck, 2008.

van Marle, Karin. "Constitution as Archive." In *Law and the Politics of Reconciliation*, edited by Scott Veitch, 215–28. Burlington, VT: Ashgate, 2006.

van Tilborg, Sjef. *Imaginative Love in John*. BIS 2. Leiden: Brill, 1993.

Veitch, Scott, ed. *Law and the Politics of Reconciliation*. Burlington, VT: Ashgate, 2006.

Wahlde, Urban C. *The Gospel and Letters of John*. 3 vols. Grand Rapids: Eerdmans, 2010.

Wainwright, William J., ed. *The Oxford Handbook of Philosophy of Religion*. New York: Oxford University Press, 2005.

Walterstoff, Nicholas. *Divine Discourse: Philosophical Reflections on the Claim that God Speaks.* Cambridge: Cambridge University Press, 1995.

Ward, Graham. *Christ and Culture.* Oxford: Blackwell, 2005.

Ward, Keith. *Divine Action.* London: Collins, 1990.

———. *God, Chance, and Necessity.* Oxford: One World, 1996.

Warnock, Mary. *Imagination.* Boston: Faber and Faber, 1976.

Webster, John. "The Ethics of Reconciliation." In *The Theology of Reconciliation,* edited by Colin Gunton, 109–24. London: T. & T. Clark, 2003.

———, et al., eds. *The Oxford Handbook of Systematic Theology.* Oxford: Oxford University Press, 2007.

Wedderburn, Alexander J. M. *Beyond Resurrection.* London: SCM, 1999.

Welker, Michael. *God the Revealed: Christology.* Translated by Douglas W. Scott. Grand Rapids: Eerdmans, 2014.

Welz, Claudia. "Resonating and Reflecting the Divine: The Notion of Revelation in Jewish Theology, Philosophy, and Poetry." In *Revelation: Claremont Studies in the Philosophy of Religion Conference 2012,* edited by Ingolf U. Dalferth and Michael Rodgers, 141–83. RPT 74. Tübingen: Mohr Siebeck, 2014.

Werle, Gerhard. "Das Völkerstrafrecht im Jahrhundert der Weltkriege." In *Versöhnung, Strafe and Gerechtigkeit: Das schwere Erbe von Unrechts-Staaten,* edited by Michael Bongardt and Ralf K. Würstenberg, 129–47. Kontexte. Neue Beiträge zur historischen unde systematischen Theologie 40. Göttingen: Ruprecht, 2010.

Westphal, Merold. "The Importance of Mystery for the Life of Faith." *Faith and Philosophy* 22 (2007) 367–84.

Whitely, Denis E. H. *The Theology of St. Paul.* 2nd ed. Oxford: Blackwell, 1974.

Wiles, Maurice. *God's Action in the World: The Bampton Lectures for 1986.* London: SCM, 1986.

Wilkinson, Richard G. *The Impact of Inequality: How to Make Sick Societies Healthier.* New York: Routledge, 2005.

———, with Kate Pickett. *The Spirit Level: Why More Equal Societies Almost Always Do Better.* New York: Penguin, 2009.

Williams, Rowan. *On Christian Theology.* London: Blackwell, 1999.

———. *Dostoevsky: Language, Faith and Fiction.* Waco, TX: Baylor University Press, 2008.

———. *The Edge of Words: God and the Habits of Language.* New York: Bloomsbury, 2014.

———. *Faith in the Public Square.* New York: Bloomsbury, 2012.

———. *The Wound of Knowledge: Christian Spirituality from the New Testament to St. John of the Cross.* London: Darton, Longman and Todd, 1979.

Williams, Stephen W. *Revelation and Reconciliation: A Window on Modernity.* Cambridge: Cambridge University Press, 1995.

Winnicott, David W. *The Child, the Family, and the Outside World.* Harmondsworth: Penguin, 1964.

Witherington, Ben, III. *Paul's Letter to the Romans: A Socio-Rhetorical Commentary.* Grand Rapids: Eerdmans, 2004.

———. *Philippians: A Socio-Rhetorical Commentary.* Grand Rapids: Eerdmans, 2001.

Wittgenstein, Ludwig. *Lectures and Conversations on Aesthetics, Psychology and Religious Belief.* Edited by C. Barrett. Oxford: Oxford University Press, 1966.

———. *Philosophical Investigations*. Translated by G. Elizabeth M. Anscombe. 2nd ed. Oxford: Blackwell, 1958.

———. *Zettel*. Edited and translated by G. Elizabeth M. Anscombe. Oxford: Blackwell, 1967.

Wright, Nicholas Thomas. *The Resurrection of the Son of God: Christian Origins and the Question of God* 3. London: SPCK, 2003.

Wüstenberg, Ralf Karolus. "Gibt es eine Politik der Versöhnung? Theologisches Anmerkungen auf der Auferbeitungsanstrengunen in Sudafrika und Deutschland." In *Versöhnung, Strafe and Gerechtigkeit: Das schwere Erbe von Unrechts-Staaten*, edited by Michael Bongardt and Ralf K. Würstenberg, 99–126. Kontexte. Neue Beiträge zur historischen unde systematischen Theologie 40. Göttingen: Ruprecht, 2010.

Zachhuber, Johannes. "Transendenz und Immanenz als Interpretationskategorien antiken Denkens im 19. und 20. Jahrhundert." In *Divine Presence and Absence in Exilic and Post-Exilic Judaism: Studies of the Sofja Kolalevskaja Research Group on Early Jewish Monotheism*, edited by Nathan MacDonald and Izaak J. de Hulster, 23–53. FAT 2.61. Tübingen: Mohr Siebeck, 2013.

Zahn, Molly M. *Rethinking Rewritten Scripture: Composition and Exegesis in the 4QReworked Pentateuch Manuscripts*. Leiden: Brill, 2011.

Zumbansen, Peer. "Transnational Law and Societal Memory." In *Law and the Politics of Reconciliation*, edited by Scott Veitch, 129–46. Burlington, VT: Ashgate, 2006.

Ancient Document Index

DEAD SEA SCROLLS

JEWISH HELLENISTIC LITERATURE

GRAECO-ROMAN WRITINGS

NICENE AND POST-NICENE CHRISTIAN WRITINGS

Recent Author Index

Subject Index

A

Abrahamic (faith), xx
abstract, abstraction, 19
—and see metaphysics
acknowledge, 95
—and see know
Adam and Eve and "the Fall," 36, 42,
    81, 111–12, 141, 176
affection—see freeze, love
agnosticism, xx
agreement, 12–14, 41, 44–45, 65–66
—and see difference
allegory, 131
—and see use (of words)
alone with God, 143–44, 172–73
—and see loneliness
ambiguity, 23
—and see flexibility
analogy—see metaphor
Analysis, Analytical Philosophy,
    xviii
anthropomorphism, 54
Antioch, Antiochene, 203
Aristotle, Aristotelian, 13, 158
—and see Ancient Document
    Index
artists, arts, 1, 19, 102, 180, 183, 197
—and see senses
askesis, training, 96, 196
—and see Ethos, Transformation
atheism, xix–xx, 148–62
atonement, at-one-ment, xvi, xviii,
    20, 35–46, 110–18, 171–72,
    186, 193, 205, 209–10
—as objective, atoning for,
    "theories of," 41–46, 81,
    112–13, 139, 142–43, 176,
    179, 205
—as process, 39
—and see (re)conciliation

B

baptism, 209
being (and see ontology), 131
belief—see faith
benevolence of God—see Gift, Love
Bible, xv
—and see Scriptures, Jewish
    Canon, New Testament;
    Ancient Document Index
binary oppositions, 28, 180–83
—and see dichotomies
body, body-and-soul, -and-mind,
    195–96, 210–12
—and see brain
    body language, see language
    body of Christ – see in Christ;
    solidarity
brain
    in-a-vat, 158, 211
    modular, 48, 211, 213

C

canon, Jewish, xix, 69–87
—and see Ancient Document
    Index, Bible
Cappadocians, 134–39, 183, 186,
    189, 192
—and see Ancient Document
    Index (Nicene and Post-

Lightning Source UK Ltd.
Milton Keynes UK
UKOW04f0033220515

252094UK00002B/56/P